Care of the Skin

Care of the Skin

AUDREY GITHA GOLDBERG
M.C.S.P., S.R.P.
Senior Lecturer
Abraham Moss College of Further Education

Drawings: **JEAN PERRY**, *A.I.M.B.I.*

HEINEMANN : LONDON

William Heinemann Ltd
10 Upper Grosvenor Street, London W1X 9PA

LONDON   MELBOURNE   TORONTO
JOHANNESBURG   AUCKLAND

ISBN 0 434 90673 5

Filmset and printed by BAS Printers Limited,
Over Wallop, Hampshire

Preface

Beauty is such an abstract quality that no two persons see it alike. The idea of the 'beautiful woman' has undergone many changes over the centuries. Yet despite the archetypal beauty which emerges from time to time every woman has her own private image of how she looks or would like to look. The complete concept of beauty, subjective as it is, does not remain only at skin level and for the beholder can include so much more than the physical form.

Although beauty treatments are as old as the hills, it has until now been mainly women who have benefited. Today, however, with more products available to enhance the outward appearance than ever Cleopatra could have dreamed of, men also are showing enormous interest. Facial treatments for the male, including masks and packs, are sought after together with advice from the beauty therapist about slimming and keeping fit. In their quest for health, relaxation, and rejuvenation, men are now able to share and reap the beneficial effects hitherto enjoyed by women alone.

Such treatments and cosmetics are not sought after purely out of vanity. Nor out of necessity or fashion. They are popular simply because they are wanted and always

have been. Fashion, however, is a method of shaking the old ideas around in a bag and pulling one out from time to time revived and updated. The fashion scene in make-up changes slowly and revolves mainly round a 'look' or a colour. Original fashions are often very bizarre and it is not until they are eventually modified, producing saner results, that the average woman can use them. This may involve anything from a foundation cream to sequined false eyelashes.

Basically the make-up and skin care chosen for the client is determined by her bone structure, fleshiness, size of the eyes, shape of the nose and lips, oil and moisture content of the skin, as well as other individual features which all have to be studied critically and expertly. Whatever the fashion of the day, the treatment must fulfil a purpose and the make-up must suit the wearer and her skin type.

This book has attempted to provide all the essentials for achieving perfect skin care. It has been written for students and teachers of beauty therapy, and also as a handy reference book for those already practising as beauticians. However, all women who are interested in looking after their skin and appearance should find this book useful.

The City and Guilds syllabus for the

Beauty Therapist's Certificate, the Higher Diploma in Beauty Therapy, the Society of Cosmetology and Beauty Therapy (CIDESCO), the Society of International Health and Beauty Therapists (NHBC) and other relevant examining bodies have been borne in mind whilst writing this book.

The text includes chapters on the physiology of the skin, skin types, techniques of facial treatments and the application of make-up, as well as details of the cosmetic materials applied. Special attention has been given to the eye area, and popular treatments to be found in beauty salons, such as leg waxing, are dealt with in the section on hair removal. Some of the more general body treatments have been described in the final chapter. These refer mainly to ultraviolet radiation, electronic muscle stimulation, and electrical massage treatments, as well as heat treatments.

I would like to thank all those concerned in helping me with this book, especially Mrs. Wendy Parr, J.P., M.A.Bth.; J. R. Moore, M.P.S.; Janet Simms, F.S.Bth.; Janine Nadin, beauty therapist; the Pamela Holt Model Agency; Mrs. Pauline Wheatley, Head of the Hairdressing and Beauty Therapy Department at the Abraham Moss Centre, Cheetham Crumpsall Complex, Manchester; my colleagues in the beauty therapy department, and my clients.

I am also most grateful to the following organizations for supplying and allowing me to make use of their excellent photographs:

Helena Rubinstein (*frontispiece*)
Orlane (Plates 1A, 2B, 6A, 7L, and 9H)
The Christine Shaw Company (Plates 9A-F)
The Christine Shaw Company and Nemectron Ltd. (Plates 7C; 7I-K; 9E; 9G-K)

A.G.G.

Preface to the second Edition 1983

It was with some mixed emotions that I was asked to revise this book, not the least of which was an uncertainty as to whether we would be able to bring the necessary expertise to bear.

Fortunately, I have had the full and willing collaboration of Karen Wilkins, an ex-student of the Abraham Moss College in Manchester who has been a tower of strength in the technical aspects of the art which have changed significantly since the book was first written.

I am sure that Audrey would have been delighted to have one of her students help revise the book and it is a tribute to her memory that it was possible.

My very sincere thanks are due to Karen for her understanding and incisive work on the revisions.

There are certain other changes which have occurred since the last edition, not the least of which is the retirement of Mrs Pauline Wheatley from the Beauty Therapy Department at the Abraham Moss College, Manchester to whom goes my sincere thanks for her constant help and encouragement which have been as unstinting to me as they were to Audrey.

Two areas of interest, relatively new to the profession, have been included in this edition. Both UVA sunbeds and laser therapy have grown at a great rate in the last few years and we have endeavoured to bring these subjects to the notice of students.

Ivan J Goldberg
CHEADLE

Contents

I. *The Skin*

One of the aims of the beauty therapist, or beautician, is to improve the appearance and preserve the youthfulness of the skin for as long as possible. This is an exacting and difficult feat, and requires the deepest possible understanding of this delicate and sensitive tissue. A thorough knowledge of its structure and function is necessary if the programme of planned beauty treatments is to be based on a solid scientific foundation. The pure study of the skin is called 'dermatology' and of the tissues of the body 'histology'. There are many excellent books written on these subjects in all their aspects which would enable the reader to obtain a more complete background picture of understanding so helping to perfect her skill.

Description

During the early embryonic stage of the baby different cells group together to form their own identity, as four basic kinds of tissue. These are the epithelial, muscle, connective, and nervous tissues. Each tissue has its own individual characteristics but together and in varying combinations and ways, they build up the different organs of the body. The skin is said to be the largest organ in the body, being thinnest in the face, eyelids, and lips, and thickest on the palms and soles.

Essentially the skin can be described as a tough protective outer covering of the body, enveloping the whole of its surface and dipping into its orifices in continuation with the mucous membranes. From the skin, various structures such as nails, hair, sweat, and sebaceous glands develop, enabling it to carry out its many important functions efficiently.

Principally, it consists of three regions (*See* Figure 1). The dermis or corium, which is very rich in blood vessels is sandwiched between the epidermis above and by the subcutaneous region below. The dermis contains specialized organs such as hair follicles, sweat and sebaceous glands. Many peripheral sensory nerve endings are found in the skin and it plays an important role in heat regulation of body temperatures, as well as possessing excretory and absorbing powers.

The Epidermis

The superficial region of this layer is composed of a hard durable protein, keratin, and

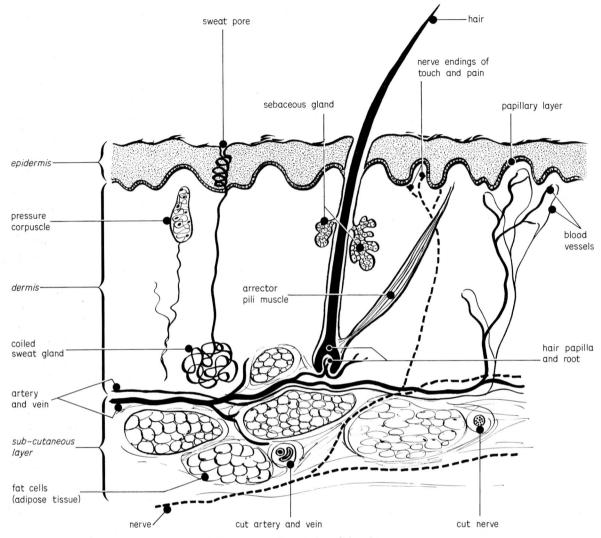

sweat pore

sebaceous gland

hair

nerve endings of
touch and pain

papillary layer

epidermis

pressure
corpuscle

dermis

coiled
sweat gland

artery
and vein

sub-cutaneous
layer

fat cells
(adipose tissue)

arrector
pili muscle

blood
vessels

hair papilla
and root

nerve

cut artery and vein

cut nerve

FIGURE I   Structure of the skin

its under surface covers and adheres to the dermis, moulding to its undulating irregular surface most faithfully. Consisting of stratified epithelial tissue (layered cells) this region has no blood vessels. Its thickness varies, for instance the epidermis of the soles of the feet and palms of the hand is very much thicker and more horny on the surface than elsewhere on the body. The face has a thin epidermis and that of the eyelid is finer still. The epidermis has two distinct zones. The uppermost is referred to as the horny zone and the lower one is cellular, and contains the germinative layer in the lower section. Fine lines can be seen on the surface of the skin crossing and intersecting each other to form a variety of patterns. Joint movements and 'loose skin' emphasize these lines and over the years they become more distinct on the face as creases and wrinkles, reflecting constant pathways of expressions of everyday life.

The epidermis is free from pain nerve endings but rich to the sensation of touch.

LOWER REGION

This consists of:

1. Basal Layer
   or   : layer of reproduction
   Stratum Germinativum

2. Prickle layer
   or   : cellular layer
   Stratum Spinosum
   or
   Mucosum

UPPER REGION

This consists of:

3. Granular layer
   or
   Stratum Granulosum

4. Transparent layer
   or   : palms and soles
   Stratum Lucidum

5. Horny layer
   or   : most superficial
   Stratum Corneum   region

LOWER REGION

This is the deepest area of the epidermis. It is in this zone that the cells are constantly dividing and reproducing. The regrowth of cells can be affected by several factors and can be increased or decreased accordingly. Apart from being affected by age, state of health, diet, exposure to heat, cold, light, and X-rays, certain drugs and chemicals, cellular regeneration remains a constant factor throughout the whole life span although it slows up with age. A blooming youthful skin reflects on the healthy activity of this zone. The average normal life cycle of each new cell from reproduction in the basal layer to discardation in the horny layer is gauged at about six weeks.

Basal layer cells are columnar and arranged perpendicularly to the skin surface, and their lower surface is attached to the underlying dermis. This layer of columnar, nucleated epithelium gradually ascends towards the surface, making way for new replacement cells. In so doing, it gradually changes shape becoming more cuboidal but is still capable of cell division in special circumstances.

Prickle layer (mucosum) consists of those cells above the basal layer. They become progressively elongated the more superficial they become. Here each cell connects with its colleague by means of fine threads filled with tissue fluid (protoplasm), although they are not as closely joined together as their underlying neighbours. Because of these fine interlinking projections, they acquire a spiky, or prickly appearance, and hence their name. Between the cells there are minute channels through which nutrients reach the epidermal cells. Towards the upper layer of this region the nuclei begin to disintegrate and chemical changes take place as they are transformed into the hard durable keratin on the outermost part of the skin surface.

UPPER REGION

This consists of keratinized cells and is the outermost zone of the epidermis. Pressure and friction due to occupation or sport can cause thickening of this zone. Rough wear and tear or exposure to winds will have a desiccating effect on this region. It is interesting to note that some scientific experiments over the past years on allergic asthma and hay fever have found that the majority of bedroom dust contains dead, dry skin from this horny zone.

Granular layer consists of several layers of flattened spindle shaped cells which have lost their nuclei but contain a number of granules. This layer is a transitional region between the living cells of the prickle layer,

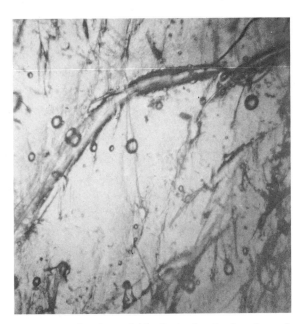

PLATE 1A   Section of skin from the cheek enlarged
on the screen 85 times

and the dead horny one. The granules contain a substance known as eleidin, or keratohyaline. The granules are believed to be the precursors of the keratin that covers the skin surface, and it is in this area that the process of keratinization or cornification takes place. Keratinization is termed an active process because of the respiratory enzymes that have been found in this layer. One proposal is that these enzymes are put into the granular layer from the projections of the melanocytes but this is still being researched. The keratin is laid down in the outer part of the cell, and the nucleus and cell contents are digested by phagocytic cells until a space is left in the middle of the cell. This forms a very pliable keratin in thickened skin areas such as the soles and palms where most of the cell is keratinized. Abnormal keratinization can result in such skin conditions as psoriasis.

Traces of disintegrated nuclei may occasionally be found in this layer. Water and fats are present in this zone.

Horny layer in turn consists of several layers of keratinized epithelial cells tightly packed together. Because they contain the protein keratin they are very tough and horny and there is no nucleus whatsoever at this level. If over-exposed to heat, or sunlight without careful application of protective oils and lotions it can be dried out completely leaving a dry flaky mass of scales. At the bottom of this layer however a fatty substance resembling bees-wax has been found. This helps to prevent normal evaporation of water whilst at the same time acting as an added protection of water proofing the skin from over-absorption. It may also have a slightly antiseptic effect on the skin against bacteria. The outermost layers of cells in the horny layer are the dead scales which become loosened when completely desiccated and finally shed. Usually they are rubbed off in the normal wear and tear of the skin, but if not shed will leave a powdery film. It is this outer layer which can form a barrier on the skin trapping and harbouring grime, dirt, and grease, so becoming the main objective and focus of attention for the many cleansing beauty treatments available. Through this layer cosmetic nutrients, which try to restore the elasticity, water, and fat content of the skin, are applied.

The Dermis

Sometimes called the corium or true skin, it is tough, highly elastic, and flexible. In the palms of the hands and soles of the feet it is thick, but like the epidermis thinner and delicate in areas such as the eyelids. It is a highly sensitive vascular layer of fibrous tissue, containing innumerable blood channels, nerve endings, sebaceous glands, papillary muscles, hair follicles, and sweat glands, all of which are reinforced by a fine meshwork of interlaced elastic fibres. The dermis contains a higher water content than any other region of the skin. Drastic water loss from the skin due to various causes such as dieting or exposure to abnormally high temperatures may cause premature ageing effects, the appearance of which, with all the finest beauty care in the world may be difficult to improve or remedy. It consists of a superficial and a deep layer.

STRUCTURE OF DERMIS

SUPERFICIAL LAYER

This is irregular in shape with many conical eminences and protrusions into the epidermis which are called papillae. The undulations and ridges produce corresponding impressions on the under surface of the epidermis so that the two are interlocked. The finger prints which are found in the pads of the thumbs and finger tips are an extension of these ridges and form curved parallel whorls on the surface of the skin. The function of the whorls and ridges on the digits is to supply a surface of greater friction than can be found in smooth skin, so enabling a firmer grip to be made when walking and grasping. Many nerve endings of touch are found in this part of the dermis. These end in rounded bodies, while those of pain, cold, and heat terminate in delicate branched nerve endings. Fine capillary loops and veins are found here, bringing nourishment and oxygen to the skin, and carrying away waste products. They lie in very close proximity to the under surface of the epidermis which is otherwise bloodless. Together with the germinal zone, the papillary edge provides the skin with a most active and vital area.

DEEP LAYER

This is sometimes called the recticular layer and consists of strong fibrous tissue reinforced with a finer network of elastic fibres. Both the fibrous and elastic tissues in this region, and in the dermis as a whole, are responsible for the elasticity of the skin. With age the elastic qualities disappear and when it is stretched it remains stretched, and so the tone of the skin diminishes. Fatty globules fill in the spaces left by the bundled fibres and this area also gives rise to many sweat and sebaceous glands. Nerves of touch, deep pressure, pain, cold, and heat can be found in this layer. The meshwork of fine veins and arteries passing through this layer link up with those of the papillary capillaries. Attached to each hair root and sebaceous gland in this strata lies an unstriated (involuntary) muscle extending from the upper edge. When it contracts it causes the hair to stand upright. Shivering is a reflex action which operates when the body temperature begins to drop. It is a spasmodic contraction of the muscles, actually producing heat which helps to raise the body temperature again. These involuntary muscles are called the 'arrector pili' muscles. Birds fluff out their feathers by this contraction of the arrector pili muscles, trapping a layer of air round the skin, and improving their insulation and so reducing heat loss. In the human being, similar contractions merely produce 'goose pimples' causing the hairs to stand on end.

The Subcutaneous Region

This is a layer of loose areolar tissue which is referred to as the superficial fascia. It separates the dermis from the subjacent muscles and the deep fascia so allowing the skin to move freely in most parts of the body over the underlying structures. Almost like an extension of the dermis an abundance of yellow elastic fibres and white fibrous tissue, makes the subcutaneous region, or hypo-

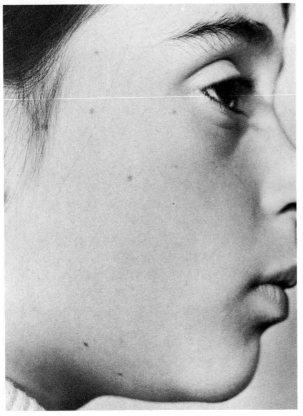

PLATE 1B   Eight years' old skin

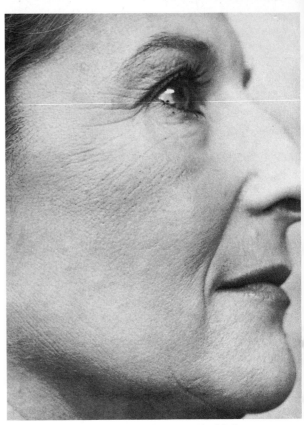

PLATE 1D   Forty-five years' old skin

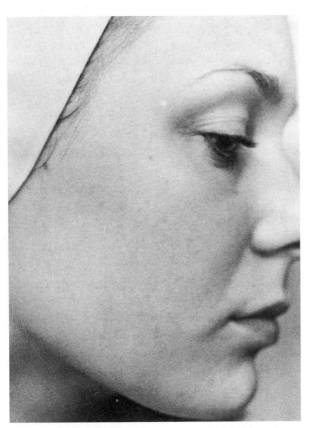

PLATE 1C   Twenty-two years' old skin

dermis, highly elastic and flexible. Containing mostly fatty tissue it is regarded as a fat storage depot and is thicker in women than men, thus giving a softer, more rounded appearance to their contours. The fat cells cushion and protect the mass of blood vessels and nerve endings in this region. Fat being a poor conductor of heat, helps to reduce loss of heat through the skin and so keeps the body warm.

BLOOD SUPPLY

The blood supply to the skin is from a network of vessels from the arteries in the subcutaneous region which sends out branches directly to the sweat glands, hair follicles, and fat. Other branches unite into central depots, or plexus, directly beneath the dermis, which in turn send up capillaries into the vascular papillary layer. So the skin and its appendages receive food, nourishment and oxygen. A fine meshwork of veins carry away the waste products in much the same manner as the arteriole system, except that the flow is directed back towards the heart for purification. No capillaries enter the epidermis, the cells in this layer obtaining their nourishment from the lymphatic system.

The lymph supply to the skin is by a superficial and deep network which mainly follows the venous system. The lymph fluid is formed from the tissue fluids and supplements the veins in the return of these fluids to the blood, helping to carry away the waste products. They also carry the tissue fluids and broken down tissue debris towards the lymph glands where they are absorbed and dealt with by the products of the lymph stream.

NERVE SUPPLY

Motor nerve fibres supply the papillary muscles and sebaceous glands. They also send off slips to the muscular coat of the veins and arteries constricting or relaxing them reflexly or according to the messages received in the brain. Motor nerves also supply the muscles of the face, which can be contracted at will. Sensory sensations such as touch, deep pressure, and stretch end in round bodied corpuscles whilst those of pain, heat, and cold are registered by branched nerve end receptors in the dermis. They are the means by which all types of sensations are relayed to the brain where they are felt and interpreted, so making the human being aware of his surroundings in every possible way. It can be seen that massage and the application of cosmetics to the skin must affect the nerve endings and certain nerves

to produce specific effects. Therefore, by the correct use of these factors the skin should ultimately benefit.

The Appendages of the Skin

These include sebaceous glands, sweat glands, hairs, and nails.

SEBACEOUS GLANDS

These are small sac like organs found in the dermis. They usually open into the hair follicles but are found in moist regions of the body where they open directly onto the skin as minute orifices. The sebaceous glands are particularly abundant in the scalp and face especially round the nose, cheeks, chin, and forehead. It is in these regions where they may become exceptionally enlarged, due to an excessive and over-accumulation of secretions. Sebum is the name given to the oily secretion of this gland. Too much secretion can create a greasy look to the skin and leaves the hair limp and oily. It can also attract and trap dirt, picking up dust and germs which must be constantly removed from the skin. Otherwise it can block up the pores of the sweat glands, causing blackheads, spots, and other conditions such as acne, although it is thought to have some toxic effect on bacteria acting as an antiseptic. However, too little sebum can cause dry patches of skin and create irritations which may in turn become infected through scratching, also causing dry, dull, brittle hair. Those sebaceous glands which open into the hair follicle give the hair water repellent properties, keeping the epidermis supple and reducing the tendency for it to become dry. Many factors are responsible for the productivity of sebum. These include the influence of male sex hormones, for example, Testerone which causes the glands to enlarge and the female hormone, Oestrogen which decreases the size of the glands. The age of the client and the weather also affect the production of sebum. The amount of sebum produced in any one area plays an enormous role and is a decisive factor in the choice of cosmetic preparations when applying beauty treatments to the face and skin.

SWEAT GLANDS

Sweat glands are found in every part of the skin, being situated in the subcutaneous fatty region of the skin as small coiled tubes. They lie in pits under the surface of the dermis and below the level of the sebaceous glands. One end of these tubular ducts, the lowest portion, coils deeply into a ball or the body of the gland, whilst the duct ascends through the dermis to reach the epidermis to open up as a pore or funnel shaped duct on the external surface of the skin. Where the epidermis is thick, such as in the palms of the hands, that part of the duct is found to be twisted and spirally coiled. The shape and structure of these ducts helps to prevent them from being blocked by foreign bodies. In the areas where perspiration is greatest the glands are most numerous and large. Some of these areas in particular are the palms of the hands, soles of the feet, axilla, groin, forehead, and across the chin. These secretory cells absorb fluid by a process called 'osmosis', from the surrounding tissues, capillaries and lymph passing it into the tube through which it tunnels till it reaches the surface of the skin. Water is mainly contained in the fluid but there are some calcium and potassium salts, sodium chloride, and small quantities of urea and lactic acid. Sometimes the sweat gland may open into a hair follicle which in turn surfaces by its own exit. Because the hair emerges vertically from the skin, these pores are more susceptible to infection and

dirt accumulation particularly during puberty and adolescence when they are in a process of over-activity and hyperdevelopment. The sweat glands which are connected to the hair follicle are sometimes referred to as the 'apocrine' glands. It is from these glands that the varying odours which emanate from the skin when the body perspires particularly from the axilla. The apocrine glands contain fatty substances which react with the air and are responsible for the stronger smell. Surface bacteria also produce a chemical reaction with these secretions. Their main function is to help regulate the body temperature and they are not of much importance as excretory organs. Body heat is used up when the fluid reaches the surface of the skin for evaporation purposes; it is this evaporation which cools the body down.

Although the body loses water vapour through the skin constantly under normal temperatures, the millions of sweat glands do not really come in to full action until the body temperature is raised 2 or 3 degrees Centigrade above normal. This happens in fevers, common colds, influenza, perhaps in fear, and in beauty therapy with application of heat baths. This heat can be dry as in a sauna bath, or wet as in a steam bath. Loss of tissue fluids under these conditions is made use of in order to lose weight. Sometimes several kilograms in water can be excreted this way. However this is only a temporary loss if normal eating and drinking habits are maintained. Since salts and other solids make up a good percentage of sweat content they must be replaced. Loss of the mineral salts, particularly sodium can lead to severe complications. One example is 'miners' cramp', for miners were susceptible to heavy sweating and consequent mineral loss. An increased salt and water intake is given to those workers at risk whose job causes heavy sweating. Loss of too much salt and water can lead to a fall in blood pressure and

dizziness which could be extremely dangerous, and is known as heat exhaustion.

HAIRS

Hairs grow from dermal structures known as
'hair follicles'. These are lined with epidermal cells which form an inner and outer
sheath. The part of the hair projecting from
the follicle is called the hair shaft. The
development of the hair follicle starts with
a part of the epidermis thrusting downwards
to meet a small portion of the dermis which
forms a hair papilla. The latter feeds the
growing hair and therefore controls its
growth. Food and nourishment essential for
its growth are supplied by the capillaries of
the dermis. A hair bulb is formed from the
cells of the epidermis in direct contact with
the dermal papilla which fit over the hair
papilla. The constant adding of new cells to
the base of the hair causes it to lengthen and
grow inside the follicle. Each hair is a slender
tube composed of an inner layer of medulla
and an outer layer or cortex. In man, growth
of hair continues for anything between 2–6
years, although it may be as long as 25 years.
This period of active growth and cell division
is called Anogen. The hair then enters a
transitional phase known as Catogen after
which it enters the final stage, Telogen. A
new hair may grow in the old follicle,
providing the root is healthy and the old and
new hairs may both protrude from the same
follicle for a few days. Impregnation of the
hair cells by a horny proteinous substance
called keratin cause it to die in much the same
way as keratin hornifies the protoplasmic
living cells of the skin. In the regions where
they grow thickly the hairs of the body form
a protective insulation. Air which is trapped
between the hairs reduces evaporation and
heat loss, but man, unlike his ancestral
animal origins, relies on clothing to keep him
warm, and not the hairs on the body. The
hair follicle is supplied with sensory nerve
endings which respond to touch and movement of the hair. Connected to the hair
follicle are the tiny involuntary muscles
erectores pilorum responsible for the hairs
standing on end as described earlier.

NAILS

Nails are the horny keratinous protective
covering of the last digits of the fingers and
toes and are extensions of modified epithelium. They grow from the matrix bed,
which is richly supplied with blood and
nerves. They are constantly being pushed
forwards so that they project beyond the
edge of the finger. The nail body itself has no
nerve or blood supply and can be cut and
filed to suit the shape and requirements of the
client. It is important for the beauty therapist
to have short nails so that she does not scratch
or catch the client with them.

Functions of the Skin

The skin serves the body as a protective and
useful two-way screen with several important functions.

PRINCIPAL FUNCTIONS OF THE SKIN

The principal functions of the skin are
1. *Heat and temperature control*—a major
   function.
2. *Protection*—a major function.
3. *Absorption*.
4. *Excretion and secretion*.
5. *Sense of touch*—a major function.

1. HEAT AND TEMPERATURE CONTROL

A great deal of the body's heat is distributed
by the circulatory system round the body.

Regular body temperature can vary according to (a) the time of day—temperature being higher in the evening, (b) age—temperature being higher in the young and active, and (c) small variations can be found in different parts of the body and on the surface of the skin. Usually the body temperature is taken in the axilla or under the tongue and is found to be normally 36·8°C. Any extreme of rise and fall in temperature could be dangerous. The sweating mechanism of the body, together with convection, conduction, and radiation of heat from the body helps to regulate the balance of heat loss and gain in the body, maintaining its temperature evenly.

SWEATING

Nervous mechanism of sweating is directly by nerve endings terminating in the epithelium of the sweat glands, and indirectly through a reflex stimulation of sensory nerve endings in the skin. The centre of regulation of sweating and heat is in the brain. Two marked effects are produced in the skin when the heat and sweat centres are stimulated. Firstly vasodilation in the capillary network round the coiled tube of the sweat glands in the dermis, causes a flushing and pinking of the skin. This dilation and widening of the blood vessels carrying more blood to the surface of the skin, brings more heat to the surface some of which is lost by convection and radiation. Secondly sweating accelerates the heat loss by virtue of the evaporation of sweat on the surface of the skin.

Quantity of sweat excreted depends upon the climate, but in a warm atmosphere such as on a typical English summer's day, about one pint is lost.

Insensible perspiration is the name given to the normal amounts of unnoticeable sweat which is evaporated by the heat of the body.

Sensible perspiration is the term used when a person is aware of producing large quantities of sweat, which are not readily evaporated, and may even drip off the skin.

FACTORS WHICH INCREASE SWEAT

Increased sweat production results in a *reduction of body temperature*.

Exercise: Muscle activity which burns up and oxidizes food, especially fats, produces heat and sweat.

Shivering is an involuntary attempt of the body to increase heat, in extremes of cold, or emotional situations.

Heat: Clothes increase and maintain heat production, and so does exposure to warm or hot temperatures above those of the body.

Emotional tendencies: Hormones released due to fear, excitement, and other causes into the blood circulation cause dilation of capillaries over the body and induce sweating.

Foodstuffs: Vinegar, curries and other such commodities have a dilatory effect upon the superficial blood vessels producing an increase of skin temperature and sweat. Hot foods and drinks are also other factors which increase the temperature of the body. Alcohol is well known for its effects on the capillaries.

Drugs: Vasodilation can be improved by certain drugs when circulation is poor, and there are side effects of some drugs which inadvertently increase body temperature.

Fevers: Fevers result in increased temperatures. Diseases such as rheumatoid arthritis and pulmonary tuberculosis can result in profuse sweating.

FACTORS DECREASING SWEAT
PRODUCTION AND INCREASING
BODY TEMPERATURE

Cold: Exposure to temperatures lower than the body will result in a close-down of the blood vessels near the surface of the skin.

This is called 'vasoconstriction'.

Rest: Lack of muscle activity will result in keeping the body cool. It is a well established fact that on a cold day vigorous exercise produces heat and sweating.

Age: As the systems of the body age, the dilatory action of the veins and arteries slows down. The lumen of these vessels becomes narrower and the circulation becomes sluggish. Poor circulation results in the body feeling cold, and the heat is conserved rather than lost. Therefore sweat production decreases as the sweat glands atrophy.

Diet: Cutting out all foodstuffs which cause vasodilation, will tend to reduce sweating. Therefore a carefully balanced diet which does not contain too many highly spiced foods, carbohydrates and fats is essential for a normal loss of sweat, so allowing the skin to retain its normal moisture, and not become dehydrated.

Disease: Certain diseases such as osteo-arthritis, diabetes, and low blood pressure, results in a decrease of sweat production.

Reversal of the sweat-producing factors can contribute to decreasing heat and sweat in the body. For example vasoconstriction (the closing down of capillaries) occurs on exposure to cold. The effects of certain drugs in the body can cause a lowering of body temperature. Nicotine causes vasoconstriction which ultimately affects the correct functioning of the heart and lungs. Marijuana commonly known as 'pot' or 'grass' also has the effect of lowering the body temperature which might prove to be harmful.

2. PROTECTION

There are many ways in which the skin serves to protect the body. Bacterial invasion is prevented by the dead horny layer and the slight antiseptic properties of sebum is thought to destroy certain bacteria. The cooling effect produced by sweating serves to protect the body from over-heating. Ultra-violet rays and heat rays are prevented from penetrating deeper than the epidermis because of its melanin content. When the skin is exposed to sunlight the melanin pigment production increases and darkens the upper layers of the epidermis. This provides protection of the skin, by allowing it to tolerate increasing exposure to light. Natural sebum may also serve to provide a filter against the sun's rays. Absorption of water and other fluids is prevented by the horny layer and cutaneous fat which tend to make the skin watertight. Vitamin D is formed in the skin from exposure to sunlight, and from this the bones are nourished. Due to its sensory responses to heat, cold, pain, stretch and so on, the body is protected from the dangers of the environment, by the living cloak of the skin.

3. ABSORPTION

Emphasis has been placed much too often on the absorption function of the skin, especially in the field of beauty. One of the most important roles of the skin is to repel and prevent foreign substances and bacteria from entering the body, so that in fact little absorption does take place although there is some. Materials such as iodine and mercury can pass through the skin. Minimal amounts of water may enter over the whole surface area of the skin and fatty substances through the hair follicles. The base of the Stratum Corneum forms a resistant barrier to electrolytes and these impede the movement of water. This can be altered in some way by the passage of an electric current, but such substances must be in concentrated form and will produce some local action, such as erythema. The size and solubility of the molecules is important in skin penetration and many molecules will simply be too large. A massage improves passage in this way. Emollient creams hydrate the Stratum Corneum only but if the skin is abrased, penetration is made easier. The head and neck are the easiest to penetrate and the soles and the palms are the hardest, due to the differing thickness of the Stratum Corneum.

4. EXCRETION AND SECRETION

Excretion concerns the elimination of waste products from the skin. Secretion concerns production of substances from the cells and glands of the skin. Excretion of waste pro-

ducts via the skin is considered to be minimal under normal conditions. Secretions usually refers to the sebum produced from the oil glands when relating it to the skin, which keeps it supple.

5. SENSE OF TOUCH

Of all the five senses in the body (taste, sight, smell, hearing, and touch) the sense of touch is without a doubt the most powerful. Some people regard this function of the skin as the most important. All over the body in the skin thousands of sensory nerve endings are geared to receive and transmit

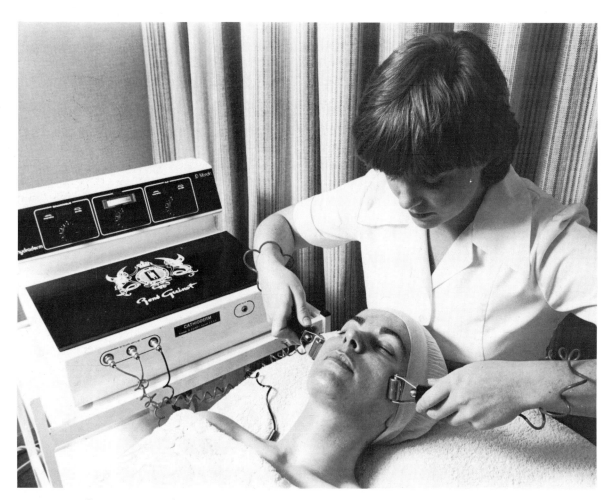

PLATE IE Iontophoresis treatment being given at the Lilian Maund School of Beauty

messages to the brain, making it aware of its environment. Sometimes the messages do not travel as far as the brain, for interpretation and reflex actions occur almost immediately at the level of the spinal cord in response to the stimulation of the nerve endings. In this way the body is protected from head to toe by the physical sensations which are always alert. But the sensation of touch is more than a registration of hot, cold, stretch, pressure, and pain. It is a silent language, and for the blind it is their eyes as well. Scientific experiments point towards the fact that people would die or at least be severely retarded if they were never touched, and of course being touched and touching start from birth. New born lambs cannot stand up until they are licked, and puppies are licked as soon as they are born in order to activate their nervous systems. So the sense of touch is needed and wanted and is the means by which so much can be expressed, and by which sensual impressions become embedded into the subconscious, remaining long after the others have faded.

Tactile, but not necessarily sexual, the sensation of touch is the best way to break down invisible barriers between people. A warm handshake, a friendly hug or kiss, is often used as a formal greeting between heads of states. Eskimos rub noses to greet each other, so incorporating the sense of smell as well.

Touching has been revived over the last few years as a new therapy, but it is as old as the hills, and taken for granted in much the same way. Every day people touch themselves and each other without thinking twice about it. Scratching an ear, leaning on a hand, smoothing face cream in lovingly or squeezing a spot hatefully, are all manifestations of this function of the skin. Pushing in a crowded shop, being squeezed against in a lift, patting an animal, tickling a child, stroking the aged who need so many reassuring caresses, all use the sense of touch with its two-way screen of receiving and transmitting.

For the beauty therapist, the sense of touch in her own hands should be developed by practising feeling different textures, temperatures and consistencies as well as the tissues, and structures of the body, particularly those delicate structures and textures of the face which are so irregular and varied in such a small area. In this way she will be able to relate the type of products, the method of application and the needs of the client's skin type, more efficiently and closely, transmitting at the same time the comfort, cheer and reassurance which is part of the treatment.

2. Skin Types

All over the world every woman has her personal skin problem. The 'normal skin' is rare and difficult to define. Very few women are lucky enough to have, let alone retain, the firm-textured and fresh, clear, bloom of a youthful skin. To-day any woman can acquire a beautiful appearance especially with help, treatment, and care from the beauty therapist. Each type of skin differs because it involves innumerable factors. Every one knows and accepts that the mind influences the body. It is not only a modern truism to say that mental happenings affect the reactions of bodily organs, it is medical and scientific fact. The results of these influences and problems are very much reflected in the condition of the skin, which can change from week to week and even from day to day. It is no easy task for those concerned in the care and treatment of the skin to build up a true detailed clinical picture of the individual's skin type overnight.

Superficial diagnosis of the skin types can be arrived at quickly by anyone, but this merely helps to sell cosmetics and other preparations, rather than being of true therapeutic value to the skin. The essence of beauty therapy lies in a thorough knowledge of the client, the methods employed when applying treatments, as well as the attitude and ability of the therapist concerned. Environment, atmosphere, social life, age, sex, occupation, diet, hormones, exercise, sleep, relaxation, the ability to cope with the usual stress and strains of everyday life, all play a large part in the final appearance of the naked skin. Beauty care with all the treatments and preparations in the world cannot preserve the skin from ageing, although it can help to aid and enhance its appearance.

When all the relevant information is sorted and sifted out and nothing has been left to guesswork or chance, the final conclusion, categorizing the skin types can be drawn. More is known today about the skin then ever before, so the descriptions of the skin types vary considerably. However the general focus centres around its sebum secretion and water content and from this the confused scene of skin types has been narrowed down, into four basic types. These four basic groups will be described as a guide for the beauty therapist to follow after analysing her client's skin. They are generalized enough to provide a basis around which treatments of the skin can be planned, and also to allow for the rapid change of fashion in cosmetics.

Four Basic Skin Types

Normal
Oily
Dry
Combination

1. NORMAL SKIN TYPE (Good skin)

Healthy pink glowing skin, neither shiny nor dull, firm to the touch and look, fine and even textured, no shiny areas, rarely develops spots, is unblemished, translucent, and lively.
Cause: correct metabolism, well balanced diet, age, correct skin care hygiene and nourishment, good elasticity in skin.

2. OILY SKIN TYPE

Open pores, discoloured sallow and dingy looking, tendency to spots and blackheads, shiny and greasy surface.
Cause: over-secretion of sebum. Incorrect metabolism. Too many fats and oils in diet, also carbohydrates and sugars can cause this kind of skin. Could be age, glandular. Insufficient cleansing and skin hygiene. Spreading infected spots.

3. DRY SKIN TYPE

Flaky, tendency to dandruff in the eyebrows. May be sensitive to reaction, and itchy, surface cracks and premature wrinkles form easily. Feels tight and stretched especially after washing.
Cause: Too little sebum, or sweat. Fluid content low in upper layers or non-existent, over-use of soap, detergents, degreasing agents, or skin toners and sunlight without due care and attention. May be lack of vitamin C in the diet. Central heating.

4. COMBINATION SKIN TYPE

Made up of a 'T' shaped panel (a blend of oily and dry skin) of grease across the forehead down nose and chin, gives general appearance of a greasy type of skin, although cheeks are quite dry. It is the most common skin type and found in many people.

SOME OTHER CLASSIFICATIONS

1. MOIST SKIN TYPE

Damp skin, due to over-secretion of sweat, could be due to nervous tension, metabolic disturbances, hormone imbalance, spicy, hot foods, disease, or fevers.

2. OEDEMATOUS SKIN TYPE

Swollen puffy tissues retaining fluid and water, perhaps caused by poor circulation and lymphatic flow, affected by extreme change in temperatures, premenstrual tension, too much salt in the diet, or damaged tissues.

3. DEHYDRATED SKIN TYPE

Lack of water in the tissues, may appear like fine orange peel, due to over-exposure to heat and sunlight, tissues have dried out, drastic dieting, reducing body fluid, drugs, illness.

4. FATTY SKIN TYPE

Tissues appear baggy due to fatty particles in the skin tissues, incorrect liver metabolism, faulty diet.

5. SPOTTY SKIN TYPE

Too much oil secretion, spots and blemishes on chin and forehead, perhaps blackheads too, often found in puberty and perhaps in the menopause when hormonal changes take place, may be due to faulty metabolism, incorrect diet, or reaction to drugs, pores open and texture coarse.

6. SENSITIVE SKIN TYPE

Appears transparent, rosier than normal, blotches easily may have allergic reactions, dry skins are sometimes sensitive, reddens quickly, may have tiny fine broken veins across cheeks and nose which are irreparable, it is easily irritated.

7. MATURE SKIN TYPE

This could be extra dry, lacks oil and moisture, has tendency to develop premature lines and wrinkles especially around the eyes and mouth, could be due to over-exposure in sun, or wind without sufficient protection, also due to age where elasticity is failing and firmness is lost, the underlying fat is shrinking and the skin loosens.

Factors to be taken into Consideration for Classification

I. CLIMATE AND THE SKIN

Complaints about the English climate are heard only too often, but it must be emphasized that it is that kind of damp climate which may help the typical English complexion with its own humidity. That is why in hot dry countries, and even in artificially dry hot atmospheres such as an overheated room, the moisture is lost from the skin at a faster rate than it can be replaced. The result can be one of withering, wrinkling, drying, and peeling, if this moisture together with the oil is not replaced in some way or another.

Desert climates which are hot and dry produce aged and dry skins, which could burn up if protection from the sun is not taken. Many fruits are left in the sun to dry in this kind of climate and the result of a prune summarizes best, the effect that this kind of climate can have on uncared for skin. In some desert climates the temperature may drop to below freezing, which provides a respite for the skin during the night. *Tropical climates* which are exceedingly hot and have a very high humidity content result in coarsened oily skins. The pores are open and the sweat never evaporates. White skins look sallow and unhealthy, dark skins although better able to cope with the sun's rays are also greasy and coarse. Many skins are acnified in this type of climate.

Sub-tropical climates are a little healthier than those of the tropics, for the humidity content of the air is not always quite so high and it is sometimes cooler. However the skin is subjected to an excessive amount of excretion and secretion and constant overuse of the glands and pores leads to enlargement. The tone of the skin does not have a fatigued appearance in this climate. Because of the variation in temperature range and humidity, it is less oily and spotty, but the tendency is for the top layers to dry out again and become parched.

Temperate climates consist of a mixture of everything and are those in which the four seasons are very distinctive. They are mainly cool and moist with few extremes of temperature and humidity. A normal skin would be that described as the 'English rose complexion'.

Arctic climates where temperatures are way below freezing point can be excessively drying. So drying in fact that living skin could burn rapidly if exposed without protection. This is the same form of burning as that found in hot countries, and produces a rapid drying out of the water content, but without sweating. Eskimos protect their skin with oil and blubber from the seals they catch. Freezing the tissues of the body is a common practice especially in America for surgical operations. Some surgeons have dubbed this method of work with the title of 'bloodless surgery', for the tissues are frozen and there is no blood shed.

Skin sensations are lost when they become cold and the circulatory system to that area is cut off. Therefore repeated and prolonged exposure to cold, resulting in poor blood supply, can eventually lead to a sloughing breakdown of the tissues and even gangrene. On the face, sores may occur due to poor under-nourishment from vasoconstriction, but the skin builds up a thicker and tougher immunity for protection against the cold winds of the arctic climate.

2. COLOUR OF THE SKIN

Skin varies in colour not only from person to person or from race to race but it varies in different areas of the body. Age, sex, climate, pigment, and inherited characteristics are responsible for the variations of colour between individuals. Racial colour is due mainly to climatic environment reacting on the pigment from the beginning of time, which eventually built up as genetic characteristics of the race. The variation of colour from one area of the skin to another is due to its melanin content, the blood vessels and also exposure to light, and thickness of the skin. Where the skin is thin it may appear to look pinker than where it is thicker. This is due to the blood vessels being nearer the surface and being rich in haemoglobin (red oxygen carrier). Those whose occupation causes them to remain indoors for long periods of time will appear paler and thinner skinned than those who work outdoors, and many night workers who rely on sleeping during the day acquire a 'night club tan' which means that they have unhealthy pale looking skins. Exposure to light, sun, and wind affects the skin's colour. The outside leaves of vegetables are always thicker and darker in colour and are said to contain more nutrients than the paler inner leaves, because of exposure to light and sun. In the white-skinned races there is less amount of the pigment-bearing cell, than in the darker skinned races. This pigment may be yellow, brown, or black and it is the pigment factor distribution which makes the different areas of the body lighter or darker. Ultra-violet radiation from the natural sun, especially, increases the activity of melanin and prevents deeper penetration of harmful rays into the underlying structures. Some areas have irregular patches of the melanin pigment and they may be manifested as freckles. Irregular deposits of melanin can also be quite disfiguring and this constitutes a disease about which little can be done, other than the expert use of cosmetics which may disguise this affliction if necessary.

Melanin is produced by pigment-bearing cells called melanocytes found in the epidermis. They produce colour granules of black or brown in their cytoplasm. A certain number of these melanocytes are found at the back of the eye and are responsible for protecting the retina.

Melanocytes protect the underlying structures of the skin, from the penetrating ultra-violet rays and heat rays, by increasing as a direct reaction on exposure to sunlight and darkening the skin's layers. Negroes produce a great amount of melanin, and exposure to ultra-violet rays darkens the skin more. Those incapable of producing melanin and have very white hair and pink eyes are called albinos, who incidentally have poor vision.

When people are very fair skinned they usually lack the ability to form much melanin. Since hair and eyes very often owe their colour to melanin, such particularly fair people are likely to burn in the sun rather than tan. A reddish brown pigment produces red haired types with similar skin colouring to those with fair hair. Dark haired people usually have skin rich in melanin. Melanin is not the only skin pigment. A yellow pigment called carotene also occurs in the skin. Ordinarily it is drowned out by the more deeply coloured melanin, but there are groups of people with skins rich in carotene and this results in a definite yellowish tinge to the skin. Thus three distinctive skin colour groups exist:

1. Black ⎫
2. Yellow ⎬ mixed colour groups.
3. White ⎭

Within each race can be found a number of different skin shades which must be taken into consideration when using cosmetics, and applying treatments. Bile pigments are carried by the blood and this gives the skin its jaundiced pigmentation, during infections or upsets of the liver. Everyone as a rule looks better for a healthy tan but the healthy effects of sunbathing and exposure to wind and sunlight are the subject of much controversy and have been over-stated.

3. EFFECTS OF SUNLIGHT

The effect of the sun's rays on the skin are considered to be most beneficial. Production of vitamin D occurs from a steroid present in the skin by the action of ultra violet light from the sun. The vitamin D thus formed and stored is absorbed into the bloodstream and ensures satisfactory development and maintenance of bone tissue, and proper utilization of calcium and phosphorous salts.

Ultra-violet rays produce the tanned effect by activating the pigment melanin in the skin. Some of its rays, the heat rays, can also burn the skin causing direct tissue damage. The tissues dry out, and erythema (pinking) may show as an immediate reaction to the heat rays, but the pigmentation found from the activated melanocytes may take up to one or two days to show. The skin thickens and toughens when exposed to sunlight. If neglected it can dry out and become dehydrated.

Skin cancer is caused through prolonged exposure to tropical sunlight. Small amounts of exposure with care, act as a tonic. On a sunny day people appear to be more cheerful, and look better when brown. Ultra-violet light therapy is used to dry greasy skins, in such conditions as acne, but this is not as beneficial as natural sunlight itself and may prove to aggravate the condition. It is also used as a sterilising agent. Most beauty salons and health centres offer courses of sunlight treatment to produce a healthy tan. Artificial sunlight does not always give the same tan as natural sunlight.

4. AGEING AND THE SKIN

Time does not only leave its trace on the skin alone. Every organ, tissue, and system of the body is affected. Physical disturbances and degeneration processes have been and are being studied by doctors, scientists, and psychologists constantly. Growing old implies that ageing is a gradual process, but changes in the body and skin can take place quickly within a short space of time. Everyone has heard the expression of 'growing white overnight'. Sometimes certain organs are at a more advanced stage of ageing than others, and some individuals are more mentally alert than others of the same age, yet physically appear older and vice-versa. Numerous people are endowed with a young looking skin all their life whilst others may have skin which will age prematurely by the time they reach thirty.

Many factors influence the ageing process and these must all be considered. Environment, social activities, diet, sleep, heredity, sudden shock, endocrine secretions, and the individual's ability to cope with, and adapt to, his or her life pattern are but a few of the internal and external factors which play an enormous role in affecting the ageing organism, and skin type. Statistics from group studies have shown that people do not age at the same rate or speed and that mental and intellectual attitudes in growing old also differ widely. However, one group test revealed that the individual tended to notice the physical onset of ageing in himself in the following consistent order:

1. Muscles, teeth, bones, back, limbs.
2. Failure of memory, sleeplessness.
3. Defective eyesight, hearing.
4. Skin, wrinkles, hair.
5. Fatigue.
6. Sexual organs.
7. Circulation.
8. Metabolism.
9. Digestion.
10. Kidneys.
11. Lungs (chest infections).

Conclusion: From this test it would appear that the heart is stronger and more capable of adaptation than it is given credit for and that people are more concerned with their functional abilities than their aesthetic attributes.

Despite the fact that so much research has been carried out on the living cells, no clear or precise conclusions have been drawn as to why man ages physiologically and chemically. Methods of arresting and slowing down the ageing processes have been devised, at least temporary measures, but as yet complete rejuvenation is as elusive as the proverbial pimpernel.

Because the skin is constantly subjected to a number of changes throughout the life span, the different stages of ageing should be examined briefly, so that a more complete picture of the ageing processes of the skin

can be drawn. Like a machine subjected to constant use and abuse, the skin becomes tired, worn and old. With lavish care and treatment the ageing process can be delayed. *Before birth:* at one month the embryo has developed one layer of skin.

The development of the dermis with a two layer formation commences during the second month. Four months brings the development of the sweat glands and by now it has seven to eight strata or layers with the sebaceous glands beginning to function by the time the foetus is six months. From seven months onward the baby is completely formed and the finest details of the skin, nails and hair are now perfected, being identical to those of the adult.

After birth: When the baby is born it is covered with a fine film of mucus, consisting of fatty substances and waste products formed from its different metabolic activities antenatally. Some babies' skin appears to be encrusted with a thin covering of dead dry cells, and the skin seems to be several sizes too big, withered and wrinkled. In the first few days of life it may also appear red and as the melanin content changes and the circulation copes with the outside environment, the redness fades. Although it is several weeks before the circulatory mechanism becomes properly adjusted to changes in temperature. As the baby flourishes and grows, its skin fills out. The skin of the baby and child is described as being the perfect flawless, ideal.

Five years to puberty: Sweat is produced naturally, between the age of five and seven years old and the little hands of children can very often be found to be hot, clammy and wet from this age onwards. The oil glands too may be secreting in small amounts, but it is not until puberty occurs and there is a hormonal imbalance or surge that obvious changes occur. The skin is replaced by stronger hair growths particularly in the axilla and pubic regions and the apocrine glands begin to function, the skin begins to lose its first beautiful bloom and its texture coarsens.

Puberty into adult: During this period of time the functions of the skin are subjected to the adjustment of the hormonal secretions. They pour into the bloodstream and activate an increase of sebum which brings about the variety of modifications seen in adolescent skins coupled with the accepted problems of emergence from youth to adulthood.

Adult to old age: From the age of twenty or thereabouts, the systems of the body are said to be fully grown and developed. Ageing of the skin is aligned with withering, and at exactly what point in time the skin commences to wither it is difficult to say, as ageing could be considered to start from the moment of birth, or even at twenty eight weeks when the life of the uterine baby is considered viable, should it be born at this stage. It is however from adulthood onwards that the different classifications of 'Skin types' are usually determined and drawn. From now on the skin begins very gradually to wrinkle and wither, and many modifications have already begun to show at twenty eight years.

Modification of ageing skin: Skin changes according to the various areas on the body. For instance fine wrinkles and lines appear on the face and body, where the skin is thinner, and it begins to hang in folds where it is thicker. This is due to the alteration of the underlying subcutaneous fat, and connective tissue which softens and becomes less firm. The papillary portion of the dermis becomes less undulating and the skin thins considerably. Arterioles thicken so that the nourishment to the skin is impaired. Veins on the hands may become more pronounced for example and those in the forehead may begin to appear as the venous circulation stagnates.

More keratin is produced due to further chemical changes, and the skin becomes dry, harder, and less resilient. Over the years the hair follicles and sebaceous glands atrophy with a gradually thinning out of the hair, and lessening of sebum secretion. The granular and prickle layers thin out and regeneration of new growth fibres in the skin lose their tenacity and it becomes stretched and thin. Melanin becomes distributed in concentrated patches, and gradually the skin may appear to be yellowish due to pigmentary disorders which may also occur as a result of the malfunctioning and ageing processes in other organs of the body. Dullness of the skin is a result of this withering revolutionary process taking place in the ageing skin with its final accepted appearance of old age. Yet there are many old folk with lovely colouring and smooth complexions, like those of the child.

5. SEX

For those whose concern is in dealing with beauty treatments, cosmetics, and hygiene of the skin a brief look at the differences in skin between male and female is of value, for the two are not identical except in basic structure and up to puberty.

Characteristic differences between the two skins are the responsibility of the endocrine glands and chiefly of the hormones secreted by the sex glands. Secretion of sex hormones occurs at the commencement of puberty (around 12) when activation of the sex glands really starts. It is these secretions which brings about the different characteristics in either sex. Small amounts of male hormone (androgen) are secreted in the female, and it is during puberty that the secondary sex characteristics occur. However in the male, due to male hormones affecting the functions of the skin, it is often thicker and coarser in texture and tougher to the touch. Generally the woman's skin retains more fluid due to her endocrine secretions and the subcutaneous layer of fat is denser, so that her skin is softer to the touch and appearance. Nearly all men have a darker colouring of the skin than women but the secretions of the oil glands is almost identical. During the female 'change of life' the sebaceous secretions lessen rather more rapidly than in the male. The sweat glands seem to be easily activated in the male and certain areas appear to be prone to more heavy sweating than others, such as the face and back.

6. EFFECTS OF TENSION ON THE SKIN

Tension spares nothing, including the skin. It is the root of many medical conditions which can manifest disorders of the skin, playing havoc with the sufferer. The skin can be affected by eczema, acne, allergies, sudden rashes, shingles, boils, styes, and many other conditions in both young and old alike. Several skin ailments directly stem from deep seated stress, long standing anxieties, and strain which have been tucked away out of sight into the subconscious until they erupt one way or another, like innumerable other diseases.

The beauty therapist or student may find it difficult to believe that problems, duties, lack of confidence, heavy pressures combined with other troubles may produce dramatic reactions in the skin, and contribute to the very reason why her client falls into one skin type and not another. For those who doubt this aspect about the skin the apparent simple reactions of blushing with embarrassment, sweating with fear, or blanching with shock, should clearly illustrate the body's automatic reaction to messages of tension which sweep through it, with no considered conscious thought or effort.

Of course not everyone reflects tension in the condition of the skin, but it is well to bear in mind that some skin types are a little deeper than at first sight. The role of the beauty therapist is not that of a psycho-therapist and so she should bear in mind that by no means does each spot or pimple, line or crease, dry or oily patch, mean that her client is wracked with problems or wrought with tensions. Part of her treatment is nevertheless to lend a friendly listening ear coupled with a cheerful, sympathetic and optimistic disposition, and to apply her knowledge, technique, and treatments in an intelligent manner.

7. RELAXATION

Exercises teaching her client facial exercises and to 'let go', instead of 'get going' would

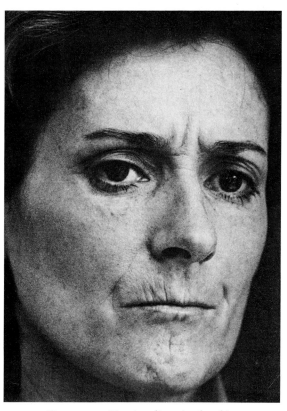

PLATE 2A   Tension lines in the skin

be a helpful way of promoting relaxation and improving the contours of the face, allowing those muscles which may register tension to relax. General relaxation should become a way of life, both for the therapist and the client.

8. WRINKLES, LINES, CREASES

Character lines: Sometimes these lines are tension in the underlying muscles due to the already mentioned reasons. Regular contraction of the facial muscles mainly produce the formation of the lines and furrows in the skin. On the whole, the lines coincide with the main creases on the face which usually follow the pull of the muscles, or which lie transversely across the muscle fibres. The skin does not have the properties of contraction and therefore cannot shorten as muscles do, so when the muscles contract the skin forms furrows, folds, lines, cracks, puckers, and crevices. The older one grows the more wrinkled one becomes, because the skin atrophies and constant wear and tear deepens the wrinkles or lines permanently. All muscles retain a certain amount of tension in them even at rest. This is called 'muscle tone', but if this natural tautness is increased by inner tenseness in certain areas, the skin is pulled with it and extra creases eventually begin to appear. The skin, like elastic, can stretch for so long but it cannot easily shorten, and spring back ironed out and straightened. When a particular expression is produced, several muscles may contract and sometimes long curved lines and folds occur in the skin, such as the crease from nose to mouth when smiling. Frowning produces a vertical ridge above the nose, unhappiness or discontent draws lines from the corner of the mouth downwards, whereas laughter produces the 'crows feet' around the outside edge of the eyes and happy surprise or astonishment produces the horizontal furrows across the forehead.

Over the years these well worn pathways of expression become deeply embedded. Unlike children, the soft tissues do not spring back into place, skin changes take place, and muscles lose their tone. All the muscles of expression give the face its character, individuality, and beauty. Certain Indian sects do not permit any extreme emotion or expression to be registered on the face so that it can forever remain 'ageless'. Their faces are serenely tranquil and their skins smooth, but what a lot they must miss if they never have a hearty laugh or indulge in a really good cry. Fortunately most men and women are able to adopt a more philosophical outlook about showing their age and feel that every line and each grey hair tells its own story and is well and truly deserved. Too much disguising and concern about concealing age can indicate a person's inability to face the inevitable fact that he or she is growing old, and they may well tend to look upon growing old as an unacceptable personal defeat.

9. BONE STRUCTURE

Muscle action alone and registration of emotions, the way people think, live, and look are not the only influences affecting these expression lines. A very great deal depends upon the bone structure of the face, and the individual physiological structure of the skin itself. High cheekbones (zygomatic bone) for instance can make a face seem fuller and less wrinkled, and a protruding jaw (mandible bone) keeps its line and shape longer.

10. FAT

Some skins retain the fat in the subcutaneous layer, which makes the face fuller and rounder, padding out what might otherwise be loose, redundant skin. This fatty layer may shrink as age progresses and its water molecules may dry out, or be lost through dieting. This latter can make even a young person look baggy, haggard, drawn, and old if the dieting has been too drastic. Fatter people always seem to look younger than thinner ones. Sometimes fat collects under the eyes giving the appearance of 'bags'. If the oil and fat of the upper layers of the skin dries out, the water content may be lost as the function of the grease in the skin is to provide waterproofing against loss as well as absorption.

11. ELASTICITY

The distribution of the bundles of white fibres which are tightly reinforced with elastic tissues in the dermis and connective tissue of the underlying structures are largely responsible for maintaining the youthful appearance in the skin. Cell regeneration slows down too and atrophy sets in leaving a flaccid pouchy skin. The skin begins to appear very thin and loose over the age of fifty.

12. COLLAGEN

This is the elastic type of substance which supports the skin. With age it weakens and thins out. Scientists are investigating this factor, and one day hope to provide corrective action and a solution. Collagen is becoming an increasingly popular ingredient in cosmetics, but it is doubtful if a molecule of this size can penetrate the Stratum Corneum.

13. NECKLACE LINES

These appear round the throat and are often revealing. At about thirty years, two neck bracelets appear as quite permanent fixtures and the skin begins to coarsen slightly and

may even show signs of crêpiness. At forty these line have extended deeper into the tissues and a third one begins to make its mark. Around this age also the jaw line slackens slightly and signs of 'double chins' are visible. The mandible begins to shrink with age. Over the bridge of the nose a horizontal crease may appear, and at forty five the creases across the forehead become apparent, and more extensive.

14. HYGIENE OF THE SKIN

It may seem superfluous to talk about hygiene to the beauty therapist but the treatments she gives to the client have to be followed through by the client, with elementary hygiene for them to be effective. Imparting a sense of beauty routine to the client should be included in the treatment and care of the skin by the beauty therapist as a home guide. Removal of cosmetics before going to bed at night is important, and if the client only uses soap and water she should be told to splash her face afterwards with cold water, which is always a tonic treatment for the tissues. The waste products of perspiration, dust and secretions formed during the night should be cleansed off again in the morning. The use of cleansing creams, milks, moisturizers and astringents will be dealt with in Chapter 6 (Complete facial treatment). Personal hygiene, fresh air, sleep, nutrition, relaxation, and other beauty care, contribute to the physical health of the body and make their mark on the skin.

15. SLEEP

Sleep is a great beautifier, but as yet not much is known about its chemistry which is only just beginning to be explored. Tests seem to prove that dreamless sleep, which may occur when sedatives and sleeping tablets are used, or in disturbed sleep, is not as restful as that in which dreaming takes place. Freud believed that dreaming was a safety valve allowing full expression for repressed and suppressed drives and impulses. Irritability, anxiety, and other symptoms have been reported from volunteers who were deprived of dreaming. Dreaming occurs during the deepest stage of sleep, of which there are four. Men are said to need less sleep than women, and about eight hours is an average amount. In the young very much more may be needed, in the elderly very much less or shorter periods more regularly may be required. New born babies almost sleep the clock round. All the tensions which are not released due to lack of the right kind of, or insufficient deep sleep, must manifest themselves in the outward appearance. Indeed they do soon show on the skin, so does impaired sleep, and so does the combination of both. The eyes appear as black pouchy circles and the skin looks pale, drawn and white. The total effect of lack of sleep is of general lethargy and sluggishness throughout the whole body. Sound sleep revitalizes and recharges all the systems of the body, including the skin, with vital energies, renewed and refreshed.

The main sleep inducers are warmth, relaxation, fresh air, comfort, and peace of mind, not forgetting clean teeth, body, and skin. To be able to convey all this to the client the beauty therapist should become an expert in it herself and watch those late nights. Beauty sleep before midnight has always been recommended.

16. EXERCISE

This plays its part in helping to maintain a good youthful body and complexion. Physical exercise either in the form of sport, walking, or keeping fit stimulates the flow of blood in the body. It is via the blood that nourishment and oxygen are carried to the different systems in the body. The walls of the veins and arteries need to be activated and exercised in turn by the action of the muscles. Working muscles cause respiration to be increased and deepen; this in turn increases the oxygen intake of the lungs and so into the tissues of the body. As a result of exercise the functions of the skin are maintained and improved. More sweat is excreted and the increased sebum from the sebaceous glands lubricates the skin, keeping it soft and supple.

17. EFFECTS OF COSMETICS, SOAP, AND DRUGS ON THE SKIN

The skin is a tissue which is of great interest to so many people involved in the world of cosmetics and dermatology. All the aspects and idiosyncracies are examined and studied in the minutest detail to find out what the effects of cosmetics on the skin are. One of the most important discoveries has been that it is primarily moisture and not oil which keeps the skin young looking, soft, and supple. The fats of the upper layers of the epidermis, the sebum of the lower, together with the products of keratinization responsible for the moisture content of the skin, are partly soluble in water and when diminished or destroyed by over washing with soap or by the application of the wrong kind of cosmetic can cause the skin's surface to become flaky, scaly, and dry. Researching the wide spectrum of beauty has produced many theories but few scientific facts and the subject is inexhaustible.

Allergy: Firstly the therapist should realise that the proportion of sensitive and intolerant skins to good cosmetics of high quality is small but she should be aware of the reactions that could occur in the skin, however rare. An allergic reaction manifests itself in several ways. Itching may be the first sign and symptom of a sensitive skin, on a small area. This may be followed by redness and more irritation. Eczemetous reactions may occur where the skin erupts and crusty sores form. Swelling and pin head type vesicles may occur, especially round the mouth. Some allergic reactions may occur when the skin is exposed to heat or one small component part of a product. In understanding allergy, the beauty therapist will find it necessary to look at the body's immunity, for allergy could be regarded as the body's immunity gone wrong. In the bloodstream can be found substances called antibodies. These are the protectors of the body against invading bacteria, foreign substances, diseases and anything which is harmful or harmless that may invade the body by accident or design. These invaders are called antigens and the function of the antibodies is to neutralize the antigens. In normal circumstances that is the end of the matter.

However, in the allergic person the antibody runs amok, for in addition to fighting and attacking the antigen it becomes attached to one or more tissues in the body. The antigen is now known as an allergen and when the tissue is next exposed to the allergen, or something very similar an allergic reaction sets up quickly and violently. Sometimes the sensitizing antibody may remain in certain white blood cells and is released to the site when the skin is penetrated or exposed to the offending antigen. First exposures do not produce allergic reactions. The cause of allergy from any particular cosmetic is usually one small molecular component part of it. In itself non-irritating but in the skin of some individuals it may attach itself to a protein molecule and together an allergic situation occurs.

There is no guarantee against allergic reactions to cosmetics, but all efforts have been made to minimize the risk, and before blaming a cosmetic for an allergy, other sources of sensitization should be ruled out. There is no answer to why one person will react to one ingredient and one to something else, both of which are probably quite innocuous. It is this very perversity that makes allergy so puzzling and difficult in producing a preparation which will injure no-one. Sometimes a cosmetic product can be used for years and then an allergic reaction may erupt. This could be due to change of environment, a new material or even soap or detergent changes, setting up a sudden explosive situation.

The American Medical Association has refused to permit the word 'non-allergic' to be used in conjunction with advertising American cosmetics, as they have decreed that no such cosmetic formula exists. 'Hypo-allergenic' coupled with 'Skin pollution' are the current terms used in conjunction with advertising some cosmetic preparations. In England the Trade Descriptions Act protects the public from similar claims, but it would be a difficult task to prove that any one cosmetic ingredient produced an allergy.

3. *The Cosmetic Materials*

Basic Beauty Wardrobe

Every beauty worker needs a basic beauty wardrobe for facial treatments. She will find that there are dozens of items which can be added to the list, but the following are portable essentials, only dependent upon a source of hot and cold water, a couch or chair, and a room for successful beauty treatments to be completed.

1. Cleanser (lotions, creams, etc).
2. Toner.
3. Moisturizer.
4. An erase stick or concealing cream.
5. Foundation.
6. Blusher for adding colour, or shading (rouges).
7. Highlighter for under the brows, cheekbones, etc.
8. Eyeshadow.
9. Eye liner.
10. Mascara.
11. Powder.
12. Lipstick.
13. Face masks and packs.
14. Cotton wool, paper tissues, foam sponge brushes of different sizes, orange sticks.
15. Blackhead expressor; tweezers.
16. Small bowl.
17. Hair band.
18. Terry towels.
19. Nail file; nail brush; soap; hand cream for personal use.
20. A large hand mirror.
21. Overall.
22. Scissors, tape measure, hair pins, and safety pins.
23. Suitable make-up box for above commodities.
24. Assortment of brushes. (*See* Figure 2.)

Make-up and its Contents

There are several kinds of ways in which make-up is used but basically it is for camouflage. Armed forces use make-up to hide them from the enemy, and perhaps to protect them with anti-repellent odours from insects, or from the sun with the use of sun-screens. Theatrical make-up disguises the actor and creates the new character he or she is to portray. Transvestites use make-up to portray themselves as members of the opposite sex, but most commonly make-up is worn by women in order to mask skin

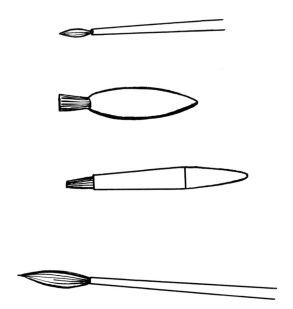

FIGURE 2   Assortment of brushes

imperfections and shininess, for protection, and to make themselves look prettier.

A thin layer of grease forms on the skin due to the activity of the sebaceous and sweat glands. Unless it is over-pronounced it is rarely noticeable in daylight. Under strong harsh lighting however it becomes much more apparent and is considered to be unattractive. The areas most affected on the face are the nose, upper lip, cheeks, chin and forehead. Sometimes the colour of the skin rightly or wrongly is considered to give away the constitution and way of life of the client which she wishes to hide, and it may even reflect the state of health. A yellowish complexion which should normally be a healthy pinkish colour, dilated blood vessels, a red nose, purplish spots on the cheeks, dark circles under the eyes, freckles and so on are a few of the blemishes desired to be camouflaged and hidden from view. Make-up can also be worn to accentuate good features in the face as well as mask the unwanted adornments.

Apart from the colour of the skin nearly everyone has lines and wrinkles reflecting change of expressions, moods or age. Small moles, enlarged pores (hair follicles), scars, and spots can be added to the list of blemishes. A woman wishing to be thought attractive will cover up all such irregularities, which she considers mar her beauty and appearance, so that she can present herself delicately masked to the world. It is not possible to achieve this without the expert use of make-up, and the beauty therapist.

COLOUR

Women buy coloured cosmetics purely for decorative purposes and not to produce structural transfigurations. Although bold use of colour and make-up can do this, it is usually a technique left for the stage. When choosing a colour scheme for the client, bear her own views in mind, her skin type, her hair and skin colouring, her features, and the clothes she wears. Most important of all, the client must be pleased with how she looks and feels when the make-up treatment is completed, despite current fashions, whether they be the natural or artificial look.

COLOURING AGENTS

In cosmetics the colouring materials must produce the required tone and intensity with the least amount of colouring matter or dye. This is because the same cosmetic preparations are usually used over a long period of time and some dyes may cause irritations of the skin despite the strict control by the authorities in the permissible products. The composition of the dyes may be such that certain impurities contained in them create skin allergies. Two groups of colouring agents are used in cosmetic dyes and pigments, both of which can be subdivided into natural and synthetic products. Natural dyes have been used for thousands of years. For instance a beautiful crimson dye extracted from the bark of the alkanna root found in southern Europe was used in ancient times to stain the skin. Chlorophyll, the green colouring matter obtained from the leaves and stalks of plants, has also been used over the centuries. A plant called 'lawsonia inermis' gave the ancient Egyptians henna for colouring the hair red and auburn. Carotene a yellow vegetable dye was found in carrots and tomatoes. Blue came from the plants woad and indigofera. Synthetic dyes are chemically manufactured mainly from coal tar to-day with over a thousand coal tar dyes being known. Natural pigments are found in naturally occurring earths such as rocks, or sandstones. These colours such as yellow ochre, brown (from the earth of Sienna in Italy) brick red (red bolus) dark brown (umber) have been used to colour the skin for as long as the vegetable dyes. They are considered to be harmless in the colouring of make-up and play an important part, providing that they are pure. As in all natural products their colouring is not completely fluent and can fluctuate according to the source of the earths. In the countries where the earths are heated strongly the pigments become burnt and yield new hues. Synthetic pigments are made from metal salts and elements and certain coal tar dyes. Many of the synthetic pigments are toxic and therefore unavailable for use on the skin. Lakes both natural and synthetic are colours made from compounds drawn from the dyes and pigments. Those prepared from coal tar dyes are frequently used in powders, lipsticks, and other make-up.

CHOICE

In choosing all coloured cosmetics for practical application, those which are found to stain the skin should be discarded, unless this is a quality specifically desired. The colour should be easily removable from the skin, but sufficiently stable to withstand the difference of temperature and light change, increased perspiration and oil secretion, and in some cases even insoluble in water especially around the eyes, or for blustery wet weather. After short or long periods of use any reddening patches of the skin should be observed which might suggest an allergy. Swelling and irritation of the eyes or any other form of irritation which suggests some vulnerability of the skin tissues to the cosmetic should be noticed and the cosmetic changed. Dryness may result when colours stain the tissues. Colouring agents should remain on the surface of the skin.

BLUSHER

Occasionally rouge is applied directly on the skin but is usually used over a foundation for adherence purposes. The essential function is to simulate the natural colouring of the cheeks or to add redness where it is lacking. Different names have been created for modern rouges, such as blushers, shaders and highlighters. The shaders are used to blot out or diminish undesirable features such as double chins, crêpey throats and necks, high foreheads or wide noses. These colours may range from pale pink blushers giving new life to faded skins, to dark browns casting shadows and creating hollows in shaping the features. Highlighters are usually concerned with paler colours white, cream, beige, perhaps pearlized with silver, or metalized with gold to exaggerate and emphasize good features making them appear more prominent and drawing attention to them. All the colours used should blend into each other smoothly without harsh lines being created where one ends and another begins.

POWDER COMPACT CREAM AND LIQUID ROUGE

Rouges can be purchased in various forms as with most cosmetic make-up products. Powder rouges are composed of the standard loose powder formulae plus dry lakes and pigments. Insoluble rouges have a tendency to stain the cheeks which is not desirable so that water soluble products are preferable. Compact rouge contains binders similar to those found in compact powders and adhere to the skin more. If dusting powder or rouge is fluffed onto the face the client's eyes should be closed to prevent small particles of powder flying into them and irritating them. The rouges contain a much higher colouring content than face powders but are basically devised in the same manner, all ingredients carefully pounded, mixed, and blended. Cream rouges are made from a fat, oil, wax, base with the colouring dissolved in it. A more natural appearance can be obtained by using these water-repellent rouges, as a continuous film on the skin can be formed compared with the applied powdered rouge. However because of the grease content they may show through the face-powder more quickly than the dry rouge but do prevent streaking from perspiration. Cream rouges are not suitable for greasy skins. Some cream rouges contain no water content and are technically known as 'anhydrous' products. Those which are made with water are called 'emulsified' products and comprise the vast majority of liquid rouge. Liquid rouges are highly favoured by some beauty therapists because of the ease with which they blend and spread smoothly onto the skin tissues, producing lovely effects. Special precaution in removing this type of rouge make-up should be taken because the colouring matter of these products may tend to penetrate the hair follicles or minute fissures in the skin. Cleansing cream normally takes care of this.

LIQUID MAKE-UP

These products are especially popular and together with liquid rouge are one of the easiest forms of make-up to apply. The covering capacity of these products is large and the result is a uniform matt appearance. Also the masking effect is stronger than with loose powders on other foundations. They can be used without powder, providing the face and neck with subtle tones. To test a good liquid make-up the beauty therapist must check that it does not cover the area too thickly, and will allow the skin to breathe. Smooth and easy application without rapid drying out is important, yet all dampness after application should be non-existent. If the powder settles at the bottom in a tube, bottle, or jar it is not a good sign. Neither should a crusty film form round the top. These products can be suitable for oily or dry skins depending upon whether they contain larger or smaller amounts of oil in their composition. Colouring agents used in them may dry the skin and special attention must be taken in cleansing. They also contain water, preservatives, humectants, surfactants, and perfume.

WRINKLE DISGUISERS

These are products, available on the market, which are in the form of a lotion. This is thinly applied to the offending wrinkles under the foundation and left to dry. Lines and wrinkles do seem to disappear temporarily. A superficial and mechanical stretching of the skin occurs as the protein matter of the content dries out. These preparations contain solutions of egg albumen and alcohol, or preserved solutions of beef albumen, and albumen from pig ovaries or placentas. The advertising claims are misleading and they are rarely found today claiming such fantastic results.

Face powder does not adhere to the skin well by itself and needs an undercoat, or foundation. These preparations can include creams such as a day cream, vanishing cream, foundation cream, or lotions, liquids, moisturizers, and even 'gels'. Each type of product leaves a slightly different effect on the skin, for instance with the simple vanishing cream, the film left is scarcely visible but sufficient to allow a following coating of powder to adhere to it if applied. All these foundations must improve the adhesion of the powder and provide a matt and dull effect on the skin. They may or may not tint it and mask it, and likewise may not always necessitate the use of a powder coat, without doing the skin any harm. They contain substances such as mineral oils, wax, lanolin, cetyl, alcohol, water, colouring agents, and perfumes. With additional ingredients such as turtle oils, almond oils, borax powder ingredients in varying ratios and formulae they can readily be transformed into massage creams, skin conditioners, emollients, or any named product available. Foundations are widely used and exceptionally popular. Thorough skin cleansing is especially important when this type of make-up is used because the pigments and lakes used in the colouring can set up small infections if any fragments are allowed to remain. Skin irritations and widening of the pores are more likely to occur through a careless cleansing routine. Powder should be cleaned off the skin thoroughly too, but it must be remembered that powder is only dusted onto its surface.

'Stick' foundations contain titanium dioxide which provides a good covering effect. These kind of foundations are found to be either soft or hard resembling a lipstick, inasmuch as they contain fat, wax, and oil also. They can be found in jars, tubes, or sticks.

The skin on the lips has an extremely thin corneal layer but with the germinal layer over-developed so that the rich blood vessels lie almost immediately beneath the surface showing the characteristic colour of the lips. Because there are no sweat glands and few if any sebaceous glands on the lips, they have a tendency to be dry, and can crack easily, especially in cold or dry weather. The lips receive their moisture from the saliva of the mouth. It is easy for foreign substances to penetrate the lip tissues causing further dryness, sores, and allergies. Lipstick or lip make-up is however the most popular of all the cosmetics used by women. Under all circumstances, with rare exceptions, she will reach for her lipstick before going out no matter how pressed for time she might be, or no matter what else she has to think about. The requirements of the client and those who use lipsticks are such that for the cosmetic chemist and scientist their composition and physical structure make them one of the most complicated of all the decorative preparations. There are various formulae and kinds of lip make-up on the market. Almost all of them contain crystalline and amorphous waxes, oils, fatty alcohols, and pigments. The use of natural waxes such as carnauba wax is expensive and causes such products to be highly priced. When choosing lipsticks, the beauty therapist should consider its appearance, its consistency, its behaviour when applying it and the properties of the deposited film left on the lips. For instance care should be taken that it doesn't stain the lip tissues, as they will become dry. It should soften the lips rather than dry them. The taste if any must be pleasant for the client, and its fragrance pleasing. Adequate covering of the lips is important and the film of lipstick should last as long as possible without having to be touched up. A coating of the lipstick

PLATE 3A   A model's complexion

should not be transferred to the teeth, which means that the lipstick must not be too greasy and soft. Over-softness may also result in crumbling during application and should not be dependent upon body or room temperature. Its colour should be built up by gentle pressure on application. Gloss is a matter of preference and fashion. Shine and glossiness is provided by paraffin oil which also acts as a lubricant. Also used is castor oil which helps to prevent the colour pigments from separating out. Counteracting the effect of some of the drying ingredients and substances used in lipsticks, fats such as cocoa butter, acetyl alcohol and lanolin which have an emollient effect are incorporated into their manufacture. Other various hydrogen-combined vegetable oils are also used in modern lipsticks. Cocoa butter causes a white coating to be formed round lipsticks. Modern cosmetics including lipsticks, often use silicones and synthetic substances. They are cheaper to manufacture and the effects of the product can be gauged more easily. Beeswax firms lipsticks and prevents oil leakage. Spermaceti, a white brittle substance found in sperm whales and used in the making of candles, is occasionally used in lipsticks to provide them with a soft touch on application. It may also counteract the use of beeswax which can make the product hard and dull. Carnauba wax, although a precious commodity, found in a wax-producing palm tree of tropical South America, hardens the lipstick and imparts an attractive lustre. Synthetic waxes such as ozokerite have almost the same effect as carnauba wax and increases the toughness of the lipstick. For colour, lipsticks rely upon a good balance of the lakes, pigments, and oils in dyes. A larger percentage of the dye in the lakes and pigments produces the 'indelible' and 'permanent' kind of lipstick but leaves lips stained after removal of the film. These lipsticks tend to dry and irritate the lips. However when a higher ratio of lakes and pigments is used and a smaller amount of eosin, the colouring of the lips is short lived but the effect is brighter and less drying. The stronger the colour, the colour content of the lipstick will be increased, and so more emollients are added to the lipstick to counteract the effect of drying out the labial skin. Even with the use of the best possible products on the market, the beauty therapist should be aware that with so many allergy-provoking substances, a cross sensitization could occur in this area. A change of colour in the same brand could set up an allergic reaction, so that from the point of view of skin care she must always be on the alert for untoward effects, especially when introducing new cosmetics onto different skins.

EYESHADOW

Accentuation of the eyes and brightening their whites are the main purpose of these commodities. At one time it was considered that women who wore eyeshadow wanted to be more than well groomed, they wanted to be noticed in particular by men. However, today eyeshadow is accepted as part of the cosmetic palette and just another means employed in enhancing another feature of the face, the eye. Make-up motivation is not studied too deeply by the majority of women to-day. It is considered to be part and parcel of appearing attractive and pretty for themselves and others. Eye shadows are applied usually on the skin over the eyelids and sometimes ring the underneath skin below. Pigments are contained in these preparations which must not come into contact with the eye, and careful cleansing must once again be emphasized with all products being used around the delicate eye tissue so that they are not damaged or irritated in any way. Some of the substances used in the manufacture of eyeshadows are similar to those used in lipsticks. Metal salts are added to give a metallic sheen and colour is often dictated by the fashion of the day. Several colours may be used and blended around the eye socket at the same time which produce some interesting and lovely effects especially for evening wear. Eyeshadows are made in powders, creams, gels, liquid, and lotion forms. Powder eyeshadow is popular but unless a foundation is used its clinging power is limited. A disadvantage in using powders is that particles of the eyeshadow may irritate the eye. However, much depends upon the good technique of the beauty therapist in application.

MASCARA

This is available like almost all the make-up preparations in different forms. It is intended to darken the eyelashes making them appear more lustrous and lengthy and so accentuating the eyes. Cake mascara consists of colours, fats, waxes, and oil in water mixtures which are deposited onto the brush. This is then applied to the eyelashes where it dries. Cream mascara, which is not frequently used, is similar to cream rouge being greasier than the cake mascara. Liquid mascaras are most commonly based on mixtures of oils, resins, and lampblack. Those with better waterproofing resistance are alcohol based but the alcohol can irritate the eyes if they come into contact with them. Again they need special attention in the removal. Colour again depends upon fashion.

EYEBROW PENCILS

Together with crayons, these are used to vary the thickness and shape of the eyebrows which can alter the complete impression of the face. At one time it was the fashion to totally pluck out the eyebrows and redraw them according to personal taste. These pencils and crayons are hardened creams, and waxes and produce a softer effect than mascara, on the eyebrows.

FACIAL CREAMS, LOTIONS, OILS AND MILKS

Mass production of skin creams of every description began as ingredients such as animal waxes, synthetic waxes, alcohols, sterols and silicones were added to the cosmetics which hitherto contained only vegetable or animal fats and oils. Mineral oils are still subject to controversy especially in Europe, and the benefit on the skin is in dispute, for it is thought that they can have harmful effects on the skin such as cancerous growths, dermatitis, and the production of comedos. Cosmetics are a complex industry today and because it is so closely connected with the preservation of the living cell in the youth and beauty of the skin as well as its enhancement, there must be many conflicting view points. Facial creams, lotions, oils, salves and emollients can be rather confusing inasmuch as each preparation may serve several ends. For instance a massage cream could be used for cleansing, a protective night cream, a sunscreen, an emollient, cold cream and even a foundation cream, despite its title.

Such products as cleansing cream must leave the skin feeling smooth, non-greasy, and silky. They must readily be able to cleanse the skin of stale make-up, grime, and waste products without penetrating its surface. Depending upon the ratio of ingredients they may be manufactured as liquids, milks, and oils. Whichever form they take they must spread easily at body temperature and soften quickly, producing no dragging sensation on the skin whatsoever. Liquids contain more water, milks contain casein, and oils have a high level of oil content in their formula. Cold cream is only slightly different to cleansing cream, being slightly harder and firmer in consistency. It should remain on the skin longer, both contain a high fat content but cleansing cream has more mineral oils resulting in a softer texture. Cold cream may contain lanolin making it an emollient and a more suitable massage cream. Lanolin is absorbed by the skin. Paraffin, white bees-wax, mineral oils, stearic acid, borax water, and perfume are used in the manufacture of all these kinds of creams. Almond oil, and olive oil may be incorporated into better creams and oils for the skin. Greasy skins require skin lotions which contain grease absorbing and drying substances such as triethanolamine, lauryl sulphate, dilute alcohol, milk liquid, water, and preservative. The exact formula of any one cosmetic product is not publicly known, but the beauty therapist can always contact the manufacturer directly to enquire about their contents.

FACE POWDERS

As well as improving the attractiveness of the skin in a general, over-all manner by diminishing shininess, face powders also compliment the natural skin tone and colouring. They also provide a smooth and matt velvety surface. Such a product requires the very maximum of preparation and for the would-be experimenters of fabricating this product it is not easy to produce a face powder which possesses a number of qualities in one. For instance it must spread well and cover the skin evenly. It has to wear well in hot weather without looking patchy through increased sweating. During blustery weather it must cling and be protective, maintaining at the same time the correct degree of opacity without needing to be plastered on. Neither should it streak in the rain. Colour must be variable

so that exact skin tones can be matched, and its perfume has to appeal to all, innocuously fading after perhaps half an hour. The quality of the powder and its consistency must be uniform under all conditions and for an indefinite period. If the powder is too opaque it can make the wearer look like a clown, yet if too transparent it may not mask the skin secretions or blemishes. The importance of not having to repowder frequently means that it must be able to last for a reasonable length of time under any conditions. These are a few of the concerns of the manufacturer who has all the knowledge and equipment at his fingertips. Even blending the powders is a job for an expert, and the beauty therapist should concern herself with choosing a good reliable brand, bearing in mind all the properties required. Oily skins having a stickier surface do not require such a high proportion of adhesive materials in the powder or cosmetics. Dry skins being less shiny and perhaps more cracked, fissured and wrinkled may require a finer powder with increased adhesive properties, but lower covering powers.

The most effective masking properties are found in zinc oxide and titanium dioxide. However if the covering power of the powder is too great, a deadpan mask-like appearance occurs. Usually only a light masking is required in order to blot out shininess, irregular colouring and blemishes. Light or heavy covering powders can be obtained, and also translucent powders which merely cut out shine, allowing the foundation colour to show through. Calcium magnesium carbonate and colloidal kaolin reduces or covers shininess, absorbing perspiration and sebum. It is essential to tint face powders as the white ingredients would result in a deadly pale complexion. Lakes or pigments are used as colouring agents. Dyes may be used in the manufacturing process but as these sometimes stain the skin are not always satisfactory. Lakes are not affected by light although some water soluble dyes for colouring matter are. The attractive velvet peach-like complexion which some women appear to have is due to ingredients which create a matting effect and adhere to the fine downy hairs on the skin. Rice starch, chalk, and special metal stearates produce this bloom. Improvement of adherent properties is brought about by the inclusion of zinc stearate, magnesium stearate, and colloidal kaolin. Its spreading powers or slip is provided by substances such as talcum, rice starch, special colloidal kaolin and chalk. If a powder is too heavy or dense it may be lightened and made fluffier by the addition of magnesium carbonate, amorphous silica zinc, and magnesium stearate. However, if it is too fluffy it may escape into the atmosphere and settle on the mucous membranes causing the client to sneeze, cough, or her eyes to water. Traces of fats, oils, and waxes may also be found providing waterproofing; perfume is also added.

Compact powder is similar to loose powder but is bound together in a compressed cake form. The binders are mixtures containing substances such as ammonia, stearic acid, starch, lanolin, and cetyl alcohol. As a result of the binding and pressing process this powder is rather coarser than loose powder and the effect on the skin is slightly different, having less need for a heavy foundation.

SKIN PERFUME

The application of perfume to the skin is nothing new. Despite the fact that in whatever shape or form direct application to the skin is not commended, it is out of choice that this method of perfuming the skin is employed. Certain perfumes irritate the skin and may change in fragrance after contact with it. The perfume of a face powder should only be delicate and its fragrance must linger on. Adding a perfume to the cosmetics, makes its use pleasanter for the wearer, as well as masking any unpleasant odour from the materials. The fragrance of the product very often governs the selection of the product by the beauty therapist for the client, and as the client is the wearer it is her considerations which are viable in the end. A cleansing product should never be heavily perfumed if at all, for the client may find it annoying, especially if it is a cheap perfume which is more than likely in such a product. Perfumes are considered to convey meanings. Each perfume conveys a personal message to the individual. If the beauty therapist is choosing a cosmetic and considering its perfume for her client, she must firstly ask herself about the fragrance, and then consider it in relation to the knowledge she has about her client's likes and dislikes.

Essential oils and synthetic aromatics provide the cosmetics with their fragrance. The perfume ingredient can cause an allergic reaction on the skin, and can actually produce discoloration. However, usually only small proportions of perfumes are added to the cosmetics.

Beauty therapists are using essential oils more frequently in the salons, and in 'aromatherapy'. These natural oils with their own particular perfume are extracted from flowers and plants and are thought to have beneficial effects on the mind, body, and skin.

Herbs and plant extracts have been used for thousands of years in many ways. Because the process of extraction of the oil essence from the plants is costly, treatments using them in their undiluted form are extremely expensive. Often only a drop or two of the essential oil is used and mixed with other massage oils or creams. In these cases it is perhaps for the benefit of their fragrance and odour alone that they are used, rather than the powers of healing, refreshing, soothing, rejuvenating, and relaxing with which they are supposed to be attributed.

'Aromatherapy' involves a specialized connective tissue massage which traces the pathways of the nerves and bones of the body with the finger tips. However, many beauty therapists find that their own conventional massage using these oils rather less economically produces equally favourable results. The choice of the oil depends upon the condition of the client to be treated and the property which that particular essential oil is thought to contain.

ASTRINGENTS, TONERS, AND FRESHENERS

These products cool down the skin, producing a refreshing sensation and helping to "close the pores". By irritating the skin, astringents cause swelling around the skin pores so that open pores look temporarily less obvious. Unfortunately skin pores can not be opened and closed at will and enlarged pores can not be prevented or permanently closed. They may contain antiseptic and disinfectant substances which kill some surface bacteria. If these agents are too strong the result is stinging and burning which can be most unpleasant especially if the skin contains any minute abrasions. Ethyl Alcohol is used, menthol and camphor for cooling. Hexachlorophene is a powerful antiseptic incorporated into the formulae of astringents and toners. Fresheners usually employ flower waters such as rose water. Witch-hazel is also an astringent. Perfume may also be added to this group of cosmetics.

Colourants can also be included to enhance the eye appeal of the product, although this is not vital.

Face Packs and Masks

One of the earliest forms of face packs was to apply the skin with hot and cold moist towels for several minutes. This produced a tonic reaction on the skin. The functions of these treatments, whether they be mud packs, honey masks, complexion clays or any other type of beauty mask, are synonymous. Special mud, bean flour, and milk still used in modern practices are left-over ideas as old as the hills, being joined by an ever increasingly wide range of other materials. Effective, if only temporary, they are enjoyed more than ever by both men and women alike. Fresh fruit, vegetables, whites of eggs, honey, herbal mixtures, kaolin, Fuller's earth, are but a small selection of some of the ingredients which are used in these treatments. However it is not wise to experiment in home-made ideas, for indiscriminate treatments could provoke allergic reactions in the skin.

EFFECTS AND USE

Firstly the sensation of application of the mask or pack produces a slight heaviness and a shock to the face, the sensation of which should be explained to the client. This is followed by the refreshing coolness as a direct result of the evaporation of the water content of the pack. As the pack dries out it creates an impression of warmth and tautness. A further stimulating effect may occur from the action of the active ingredients such as the enzymes in honey, fruit juices, or gases if hydrogen peroxide is used. Because the treatment relies on the deft skill of the beauty therapist and complete relaxation of the client for its total success, it has become an almost standard treatment found in beauty salons, saunas, and health farms. The full benefit of the 'do-it-yourself' type of face masks and packs is rarely achieved as it is much more beneficial for the client to sit back and relax and let the beauty therapist apply, mix, time, and cleanse it off the skin.

Absorption of superfluous grease and grime, surface skin, and waste products is another effect of the face pack. In addition there is an astringent effect of tightening the skin. Fullers' earth, colloidal china clay, wilkinite, and bentonite are used in face packs for their absorbent properties. The tonic effect producing the skin tightening sensations are brought about by the use of gums. Evaporation of moisture is permitted from the skin by the use of kaolin and starch ingredients. Waxes applied to the skin make it perspire. After the removal of the face pack the erythema continues to increase, reaching its maximum redness up to fifteen minutes later and fading away after two hours. If the face pack is incorrectly mixed or applied and is allowed to dry out too quickly skin burning can occur. This is most unpleasant and can happen if ingredients are not accurately measured or sufficiently mixed according to the skin type, especially on the neck where the edges of the pack may be applied too thinly. Its thickness must be uniform throughout. Depending on the skin type different kinds of packs can be applied to various areas. When the face pack has been removed, the increased circulation draws more fluid into the tissue spaces and they appear to 'plump' out. This is known as 'turgot' or 'turgence' which helps to minimize wrinkles temporarily. Other effects such as emollient, bleaching, and moisturizing are brought about by the inclusion of the appropriate substances in the formula used. Zinc oxide is used for mild astringency, helping to reduce minor inflammations of spotty skins. Witch-hazel has a refreshing effect, oil an emollient and soothing effect. Face packs made with oatmeal or magnesium carbonate are good for greasy skins. Herbal masks and packs are exceptionally popular in Europe. These are thought to have anti-inflammatory, enzyme stimulating and anti-bacterial effects on the skin. Some herbal oils are sage, thyme, peppermint, arnica flowers, rosemary, chamomile, euphrasia, and melissa. They are mixed with ingredients such as witch-hazel or flowers waters heated and then applied. Fruits and vegetables are used for their vitamin content but as the skin absorption is negligible these effects should not be stressed. In some cases it is now thought that moisture may be drawn from the skin into the fruit by osmosis. The enzymes in fruit may however produce a stimulating effect. All after-effects should be carefully noted for some ingredients may have irritating effects, espcially honey. Herbal packs may result in allergic reactions. Packs containing stimulating items should be patted on the skin gently, so that a strong hyperaemic reaction is not induced by any form of rubbing. Mucilagenous substances found in certain vegetable origins such as cactus, aloe, agave have a moisturizing effect. Lanolin, although it does not replace the skin's natural oils, is absorbed by the skin and will have an emollient effect if incorporated into the packs. Oils and fats also leave the skin feeling soft and smooth. Fresh milk has always been recommended by the medical profession to reduce skin irritations, and it can be incorporated into face packs for use on delicate skins. Comfrey roots containing sulphur would be helpful to acnified skins, as sulphur has excellent healing properties. Placenta extracts and hormones are still used with trepidation, although the effects are alleged to be those of rejuvenation, and popular in Europe. Face masks using different ingredients and applied with direct galvanic current are the specialization of many beauty salons and treatment centres. Yeast packs are used to

PLATE 3B   Peeling off a brush-on mask

stimulate skin respiration and their popularity has enjoyed a long life. It is rare that a yeast pack has provoked an allergic reaction but occasionally an infection may result

if it is not cleansed off thoroughly. Dry skins respond to the non-clay type of mask where moisturizing and emollient effects are produced. Bleaching masks contain lemon juice, hydrogen peroxide and Fullers' earth, but lightening the skin or discoloured patches cannot occur quite so easily. Gelatin and plastic masks refresh and invigorate the skin providing it with a cooling sensation. Glycerin, methyl cellulose, and water are the main constituents, and are combined to form a non-sticky transparent jelly. This usually dries out in about three minutes and is easily removed from the neck and face.

Effects of Cosmetics on the Skin

When the effects of cosmetics on the skin are considered, the functions of absorption and penetration of the skin cannot be forgotten. Absorption often refers to absorption into the blood stream, which if it were easily arrived at through the skin could be dangerous, so that penetration is really a more apt and fitting description. Penetration of certain commodities such as oils, acids, alkalis, alcohol, dyes, vitamins, hormones, drugs, and medicaments into the superficial cell layers of the epidermis does occur. Some more than others. Like absorption it is just as difficult and so many cosmetic items have to be formulated in such a way that they can, when necessary, aim at penetrating below the surface. Most cosmetics contain a mixture of many ingredients. Several ingredients may be common to them all providing a basic recipe. Each cosmetic ingredient can in turn be split up into several component parts, so that a simple vanishing cream isn't really simple. Any one of these parts of the finished cosmetic product may be absorbed or penetrated, and affect the skin, depending upon the quality, and proportion in the formula. Sometimes certain ingredients are used specifically to facilitate one major component part. Depending upon the effect required on or in the skin, the proportion and selection of ingredients changes and alters. Lanolin, an oil found in sheep's wool, is readily absorbed by the skin but in its pure form is difficult to apply.

With certain additions such as borax, water, mineral oil, petroleum jelly, wax, and a good mixing, a cream suitable for application to the skin can be made. The final processing of the cream is important in the final product. For instance it can be made to cleanse, moisturize, soften, or massage the skin. The chemical formulae of the individual potions and lotions available for the skin are secrets closely guarded by each manufacturer, but the aim and end product are the same, that is the well being of the skin by penetration, absorption, and application.

COLD CREAM

This cools the skin by the slow evaporation of its water content. Some absorption does take place in the uppermost dry layers of the skin allowing it to be stretched without tearing, so making it an excellent medium for massage. A greasy film is left on the surface of the skin.

CLEANSING CREAM

This does not penetrate the skin too deeply, for its main function is to spread easily at body temperature, removing and dissolving make-up, grime, dirt, and the superficial dead layer of skin without dragging. It should be easily removable from the skin with tissues or cotton wool and can be used in conjunction with hot water. Degreasing of the skin is not necessary as penetration is not required. Cleansing creams are capable of absorbing substances that soap and water alone do not clean off the skin.

CLEANSING LOTIONS

These clarify an oily skin and contain a much higher water content. Some are especially formulated for cleansing greasy skins where the superficial waste products of the skin may be more proteinous.

ASTRINGENTS, AFTER SHAVE LOTIONS

These affect the pores of the skin by rapid evaporation. The stinging effect which sometimes follows is due to the large quantities of antiseptics, alcohol, and perfumes added to these preparations. Alcohol causes a rapid reduction in the surface tension of the skin, due to the rapid evaporation of sweat, and heat. This cools the skin down and can degrease and dry out the superficial layers. The capillaries contract and the pores shut down because of the diminished sensible perspiration. Desiccation of the superficial layers of the skin may occur. Depending upon the strength of the antiseptic astringent substances, surface bacteria may be killed, and the protein content of the skin may shrink. Astringents can have a very harsh effect on the skin if they are too strong. Mild ones only should be used on the face.

The effect of the astringent does not depend upon the means of application like some cosmetic or toilet preparations and 'slapping' it on can eventually lead to an inflammatory condition of the skin causing degenerative changes of the sweat gland may be misconstrued as pore shrinkage. The beauty therapist should be aware that this is not 'astringency'. Deep cleansing treatments are very often followed with applications of astringents. Alcohol found in these products has a solvent effect on the grease of the skin drying out the oils, being readily absorbed.

Some astringents have a higher alcohol content and too frequent use on a greasy skin can result in increased oil production.

SKIN TONICS

Together with fresheners, these may be very diluted astringents and should be freshening and cooling to the skin without any harsh stinging effects. Evaporation on the surface of the skin is followed by dilation of the blood vessels which produces a stimulating tingling and refreshing effect. Fresheners may contain more ingredients such as rose water or witch-hazel than tonics and sometimes mild or strong alkalis are added to produce the cooling or stimulating effect required. They can be drying on the skin and will degrease the surface sebum and waste proteinous matter.

FACE PACKS

Like all the other cosmetics there are many varieties of face packs. Mud packs are the most familiar and are treatments which date back for thousands of years. Certain earths in ancient times were accredited with miraculous powers and today they are the most popular forms of facial masks given. According to the formulation of such mud and face packs, they can soften, degrease, cleanse, bleach, stimulate, refresh and tighten the skin. It depends upon the skin type as to which effect is required. If necessary the beauty therapist can apply small amounts of different packs to the face which may need more than a general treatment. When the effect of the pack is to produce profuse perspiration flushing out the impurities and any dirt from the pores of the skin they should always be applied with some form of heat. This is absorbed causing dilation of the capillaries and therefore increased sweat production. Psychologically the client feels that something is being done for her. Usually face packs are applied warm, or with some form of heat and warmth.

FACE MASKS

These come in varying forms but the ingredients are applied to absorbent materials which are cut out to the shape of the face. They can be impregnated with cleansers, astringents, oils, fresheners, honey, herbal mixtures, once again depending upon the effect required on the skin can be either warm or cold. Both the face packs and masks produce a pleasant tightening sensation on the skin when drying out.

MOISTURIZERS

Moisturizers and vanishing creams are readily evaporated from the skin but leave a fine film of emollient which reflects light. This has the effect of a sheen on the skin, making it look slightly dewy. The gentle evaporation produces a cooling sensation, temporarily closing the pores and the substances left on the skin makes it feel soft, supple, and humified. Depending upon the ingredients and the ratio used the dry superficial layers may absorb a proportion of the moisture contained in the preparation like a sponge, and regain its translucency for a while.

Both moisturizers and vanishing creams provide the skin with an aqueous film, onto which make-up such as powder may be applied, as a base foundation.

FOUNDATIONS

These can be in liquid, cream, or powder form with similar properties to those of the moisturizers and vanishing creams. They are usually used to provide the powder with better adhering powers. According to the particular job to be done and the skin type to be suited, some foundations give a glow and an irridescence to the skin, providing it with the means to disguise blemishes. A smooth, matt, and sometimes tinted surface is provided for the follow on make-up, or in some cases it can be used completely on its own.

Foundations are not intended to be absorbed into the skin but should be able to spread quickly and evenly over its surface lying and setting in its place perfectly until removed at a later stage.

SKIN FOODS AND EMOLLIENTS

The description 'skin food' is a little misleading for it implies that the skin cells can be fed and nourished and therefore would not cornify and die. If this were so, the function of the skin essential for life, would be impaired or at least altered. However the cells of the skin can be influenced in a desirable manner by so called nutrients, helping to delay dehydration. The application of skin foods incorporating fatty substances and moisturizing agents may be absorbed into the outer cell layers, keeping them soft, supple, and moist or may provide the skin with a moist film which helps to retain its own humidity, so that the external condition and appearance of the skin is improved. In this way these kind of creams and emollients are designated with their general title of 'skin food'. Nutrients and nourishment are other slight misnomers often linked in connection with certain creams.

These kind of skin foods also lubricate and condition the skin and may help to delay the onset of wrinkles. Lanolin is one of the finest materials which most closely resembles the natural skin lubricant, that of sebum. Lanolin extracts are commonly used in most cosmetics but they do not seem to possess the same properties as pure lanolin. However when appreciable quantities of lanolin are used the cosmetics seem to be sticky, and its characteristic odour cannot be disguised even in smaller quantities. Lanolin, has another serious drawback in that it has been found to cause comedoes or blackheads on otherwise normal skin.

The value of lanolin lies in the fact that it can hold moisture and can penetrate the superficial cells of the skin providing an excellent two-way barrier. Almost identical to the final fatty substances found in the superficial layers of the epidermis which lubricate this area, it is a most desirable ingredient in any cosmetic, especially those which purport to 'nourish and feed' the skin, having proved efficacious for many years cosmetically and medically. Skin foods can be classed as those which contain lubricating substances, vitamins, hormones, or other creams containing miscellaneous additives, such as proteins. Emollients soften the skin and consist of fatty substances which alter the surface of the skin structure so that it may develop a fattier superficial layer.

VITAMIN CREAMS

In the treatment of open wounds or in dry cracked areas, creams containing vitamin A found in cod liver oil have proved to be invaluable. Granulation of the skin is promoted and the damaged areas heal quickly. Lesions in the skin are thought to improve with creams containing vitamin F when there is a deficiency of this vitamin in the body, which is rare. Vitamins C and D have also been found to aid healing in bruising and wounds even when a deficiency does not exist. Certain eczemas of the skin are improved with vitamins of the B complex group and have cured chilblains and other skin diseases which may be a direct result of vitamin deficiency. These conditions require oral doses of the vitamins but they should only be prescribed by a doctor, or at least before taking vitamins he should be

consulted. Definite evidence of the value of vitamins applied to intact healthy skin is not yet fully substantiated, yet there is no reason to dismiss these cosmetics as valueless, if and when the vitamin content is absorbed by normal skin.

FAKE TANNING CREAMS

These are really skin dyes which only affect the top two dead layers of the skin, the Stratum Corneum and the Stratum Lucidum. Most contain Dehydroxyacetone as their active ingredient. The pigmentation does not offer sun protection in the same way that the migration of melanin does, by darkening the skin and thickening it. The effectiveness of the fake tanning creams depends upon the number of applications and the normal colour of the skin. If the base ingredients are of poor quality, allergic reactions may occur. The creamy content of the preparations disguises the fact that they can have a drying effect on the skin once the creamy aqueous film has been removed. Sometimes the chemical reaction on the skin produces a strong fishy odour.

POWDERS

These have a drying effect on the skin but have little clinging power. They provide unfavourable conditions for germs. Some powders contain mild antiseptics but these are mainly used in body dusting powders. Allergic reactions may be activated with some powders if perfumes are used in them and some cause a pigmentation of the skin. Again this may be due to the perfumed chemical. Purity of powders is important as to the effect on the skin. Those made from slate are not as pure as those from special soils found in certain parts of the world. Functionally a face powder should impart a smooth peach-like bloom and finish to the skin, hiding any shininess due to sebum, secretion, or the sweat glands. If perfumed, its pleasing odour should radiate, the psychological value of which is considerable. Some powders may be used merely to mask skin defects, and others for the characteristic smooth feeling when applied. The slippery easily spread powders are used as an excellent medium for dry massage. Depending upon the constituents used, as is the case in all cosmetics, so the effects differ. For instance powders made out of rice starch whilst imparting an excellent velvety bloom to the skin, become sticky and may clog the pores. They also cling to and accentuate the fine down on a woman's face, which otherwise would be unnoticeable. Chalk powders do not always slide smoothly on to the skin and may be more drying than others. Face powders may also provide the 'colour' to the skin. The colouring constituents can in turn result in drying or pigmenting the skin, and they can tone down florid complexions. Liquid, compressed, and cake powders are also used, producing similar effects on the skin; this is usually a matter of individual choice but is directly related to the skin type.

LIPSTICK

The effect of using a lipstick is usually to accentuate the good points and disguise the bad ones of the lips. At the same time it imparts an attractive colour which is in keeping with the other cosmetics and even the clothes the client wears. Sometimes lipsticks may produce a moist effect, or a shiny glossy look. They can completely alter the facial appearance when applied skilfully. Generally women who use lipsticks regularly, rarely suffer from cracked chapped lips, so they have a protective function as well as being decorative. They are considered to induce a sense of mental comfort, as in the case of other cosmetics.

ROUGE, SHADERS, HIGHLIGHTERS

These can be powder, liquid, or in cream form. The effects should be soft and natural on the face, adding colour or masking and accentuating the features of the face. Depending upon the constituent parts of the formula they may also dry the skin by a degreasing action or appear to moisturize it by leaving a fine greasy film on the surface.

MASCARA, EYESHADOWS AND EYELINERS

These are all used to improve the appearance of the eyes. They can be non-soluble in water and must not be toxic or harmful to the eyes. Creams, powders, and liquid forms can be obtained but very often current fashion dictates the form of the day and also the colour, but it is advisable to use whichever is most suitable for the client's skin.

SOAP AND DETERGENTS

Dirt on the skin is supposed to be one of the major causes for any eruptions which may occur. The public are forced to become pre-occupied with cleanliness and hygiene by the number of advertisements concerned with soap and detergents. Both soap and detergents have very powerful degreasing effects on the skin. These cleansing agents if used in excess not only remove grease in an effort to remove bacteria and dirt, but weaken the skin's protective powers at the same time. Caustic soda, which is very alkaline, dries out the skin and removes its natural sebum, altering the skin's normal acidic reaction. Most soaps and detergents use caustic soda. Addition of antiseptics, perfumes, and colouring agents can cause further sensitization reactions. The skin can become inflamed, blotchy, and dry. Allergic reactions can be set up in other parts of the body especially round the eyes if the fingers carry an allergen which may react with some product or ingredient on the face. When discussing hygiene with the client, the beauty therapist should stress a careful choice of soaps and that washing twice a day is not excessive. More than twice may produce fissuring of the skin through which harmful bacteria may then pass.

WATER

Cold water produces a temporary arrest of vasodilation of the blood vessels in the skin, which produces a contraction of the skin pores and a tonic effect. If the whole body is subjected to cold water a rise in blood pressure may ensue. This could counteract the drop in blood pressure after heat baths. The respiratory centres in the brain are stimulated because of the sudden arrest of respiration which is then followed by a gasping inspiration. Warm water induces a sense of relaxation and comfort. It may also stimulate the sweat glands and cause profuse sweating which could cleanse and open the pores of the skin by ridding them of impurities, grease, or grime. Powder can be removed by water, and hot or warm water may remove other cosmetics but not satisfactorily on its own. Water can be used as the main medium for electrically operated massage baths, steam baths, and in facial cleansing equipment.

HERBS

Along with health, the beauty scene is shifting to what has been termed 'natural' beauty, so that both health and beauty are taking on new dimensions in its current movement to return to a natural look.

DRUGS

If the client is taking a course of drugs for any purpose, the beauty therapist should be aware of the matter, and modify or stop treatments accordingly. Sometimes drugs can produce certain skin reactions.

4. *The Client's Face*

A great deal has already been mentioned about the role of the beauty therapist and her part as an artist. Little has been said about the subject matter on the canvas, that of the client's face.

From the earliest possible moment the client's general impression must be observed by the impartial beauty worker. She must regard her client as an individual despite the fact that followers of fashion often achieve the opposite effect. Very often the external appearance of the client will reflect the client's view of herself and enable the beauty therapist to form an immediate insight about her. The client's opinion of herself will not coincide with that of the onlooker. It may even change from day to day according to her mood. On the whole it is difficult for the client to be self critical and observe herself objectively. Different lights and mirrors also alter a point of view. Some accepted beauties may be over-critical, however, and feel that some minor defect, unnoticeable to others, ruins their appearance. Others also may feel that only defects are obvious. If the client lacks confidence she requires her confidence and self concept to be built up. On the other hand if she considers herself to be attractive she requires this confidence to be reinforced.

General Observation Points

1. Overall impression of client.
2. Skin type.
3. Skin texture.
4. Age.
5. Any blemishes (crows feet, freckles, moles, thread veins).
6. Any skin infections.
7. Colouring.
8. Face shape.
9. Bone structure.
10. Any facial hair.
11. Personality.
12. Social standing.

General Face Shapes

HEART SHAPE

Usually has a wide forehead with the face tapering to a long jawline, rather like an inverted triangle. The head needs width at the cheeks and jawline. Medium length hair is the most suitable with a side fringe. *Make-up aim:* to reduce width across forehead emphasizing jawline.

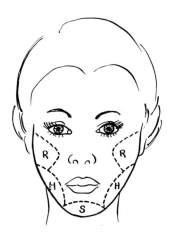

FIGURE 3　Heart shape

SQUARE SHAPE

The forehead is broad corresponding with an angular jawline. This shaped face should have a little height without width and the hair should taper well towards the jawlines. The client should avoid straight lines, flat tops, and short cuts.

Make-up aim: to narrow the forehead and jawline reducing the squareness of this bone structure.

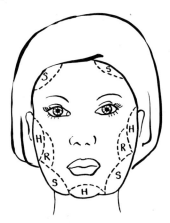

FIGURE 4　Square shape

ROUND SHAPE

The face is usually short and broad with full cheeks and rounded contours. Width at the top of the head should be provided with height from the hair which should be worn close at the sides. A slanting fringe if any.
Make-up aim: to slim the appearance.

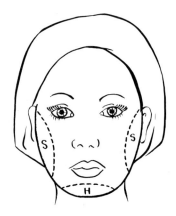

FIGURE 5　Round shape

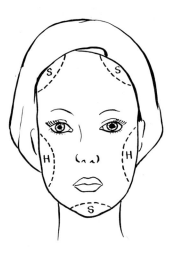

FIGURE 6　Oblong shape

OBLONG SHAPE

This face has a narrow shaped frame. A side fringe with short hair should be worn and assymetrical styles should be worn.
Make-up aim: to create an impression of width and shorten the face length.

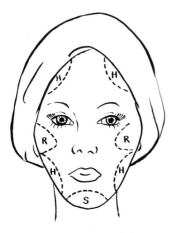

FIGURE 7   Diamond shape

DIAMOND SHAPE

The forehead in this bone structure is narrow with the cheekbones extremely wide, tapering to a narrowed chin. A central fringe should be worn with the hair full below the cheeks but flat at the cheekbone line.

Make-up aim: to minimize the width across the cheekbones.

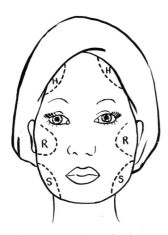

FIGURE 8   Triangle shape

TRIANGLE SHAPE

The forehead is narrow and the face gradually widens to the angles of the jaw which are broad and prominent. The hair should be swept off the forehead to create an illusion of width with a reverse flicking fringe. It can be worn long round the sides of the face, or short above ear level.

Make-up aim: to create an impression of width across the forehead and to narrow the jawline.

OVAL SHAPE

This shaped face and bone structure is generally considered to be the ideal shape. The chin tapers slenderly from a slightly wider forehead. All styles look good.

Make-up aim: to accentuate natural shape.

FIGURE 9   Oval shape

Shapes of Specific Features

LIP SHAPES

Thin lips can be increased by curving both the upper and lower lips gently adhering to the natural shape.

FIGURE 10   Thin lips

47

Thick full lips can be narrowed by keeping inside the lipline and using a darker shade centrally. The outside corners should be sharply emphasized.

FIGURE 11   Thick full lips

Small mouth can be enlarged by building the sides out of the upper and lower lips extending the corners.

FIGURE 12   Small mouth

Drooping mouth can be uplifted at the corners by building them up with colour.

FIGURE 13   Drooping mouth

Thin upper lip follows the natural curving of the upper lip building up its outside line.

FIGURE 14   Thin upper lip

Thin lower lip can be built up by extending the natural curve to balance the upper lip.

FIGURE 15   Thin lower lip

Cupid's bow shaped mouth with a full centre can have the outsides built up.

FIGURE 16   Cupid's bow

JAWLINE SHAPES

Every aspect of the face is scrutinized, The jawline and neck are especially important. All foundation should be carried evenly down the jawline throat and dressline to avoid any demarcation line. The beauty therapist observes the following shapes of jawlines.

BROAD JAWS

These are minimized by the use of a dark shader starting from the temple area down and over either side of the angle of the mandible bringing the centre of the face into sharper contract so creating a more balanced width.

NARROW JAWS

These are highlighted to create an illusion of width.

ROUND AND SQUARE JAWS

These are receded again by shading or a darker foundation being used on their width. This helps to provide an oval look to the face so balancing it.

CHIN AND NECK SHAPES

PROMINENT CHIN

A dark foundation or shader should be used on the chin, sometimes a touch of rouge can be equally as effective.

RECEDING CHIN

A lighter foundation or a highlighter will make it appear more prominent.

DOUBLE CHIN

A double chin or loose skin should be thrown into shadow with a dark foundation or shader.

THICK NECK

This needs to be shaded.

THIN NECK

This should be highlighted to create an illusion of roundness and prominence.

NOSE SHAPES

LARGE OR PROTRUDING NOSE

This is made to look smaller by applying dark foundation or shader blending it smoothly into a lighter foundation on the sides and cheeks. It can look retroussé by applying a highlight on its tip. Cheek rouge must be kept away from this nose shape.

THIN SHORT NOSE

This is widened by applying a lighter foundation or highlight down its central bone. Stopping at its tip, the foundation should blend into its sides fading into a darker cheek foundation.

BROAD NOSE

This is made to look narrower by shading the sides of the nostrils and the septa.

THIN LONG NOSE

This is broadened by applying a highlighter or light foundation down its centre and nostrils to above its tip which is shaded.

SNUB NOSE

This is made to appear more prominent by highlighting the septa between the nostrils and its length.

FOREHEAD SHAPES

LOW FOREHEAD

This is given an impression of depth by highlighting it with a lighter foundation or a white highlighter, particularly on the temple bones.

PROTRUDING FOREHEAD

This needs to be minimized by creating an impression of fullness in the rest of the face. The forehead, eyelids, and upper part of the nose are shadowed with shaders or a darker foundation.

EYE SHAPES

Small eyes can be enlarged by applying the shadow to extend above, below, and slightly beyond the eye.

FIGURE 17   Small eyes

FIGURE 18   Round eyes

Round eyes need lengthening by taking the eyeshadow past the outer corner of the eye. *Close set eyes* need the shadow applying upwards from the outer edge of the eye.

FIGURE 19   Close set eyes

FIGURE 20   Wide set eyes

Wide set eyes should have the shadow applied on the upper lid nearest the inner side. *Protruding eyes* can be minimized by blending the eyeshadow carefully over the prominence of the bulge on the upper eyelid and outwards towards the eyebrow.

FIGURE 21   Protruding eyes

FIGURE 22   Hanging, heavy lidded eyes

Hanging, heavy lidded eyes should be shaded evenly from the eyelash line into the crease and socket of the eye and over the heavy lid.

EYEBROW SHAPES

The shape and size of the eybrow will depend upon the shape of the face and the effect required.

OBLONG SHAPED FACE

The eyebrows should be shaped almost horizontally and only as far as the outside corner e.g. straight eyebrows.

ROUND SHAPED FACE

Arched eyebrows are needed to create an illusion of narrowness extending as far out to the cheek bones as possible. The shaping commences immediately above the inner corner of the eye, e.g. arched eyebrows.

SQUARE SHAPED FACE

The eyebrows need to be highly arched on the outside to try and create an oval impression, e.g. angular eyebrows.

TRIANGLE SHAPED FACE

Extra width at the forehead is needed and eyebrows should only be slightly arched, extending low, e.g. arched.

NARROW FOREHEAD

This requires a low arch.

HIGH FOREHEAD

This requires a high arch.

CLOSE SET EYES

These appear further apart if the distance between the eyebrows is widened and their length is extended. The reverse procedure narrows wide set eyes.

SHAPE SIZE

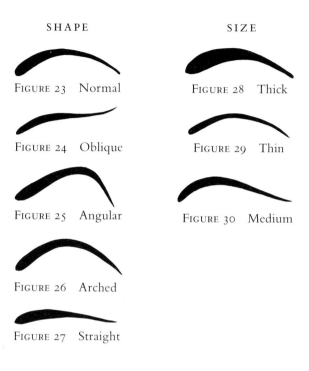

FIGURE 23 Normal

FIGURE 24 Oblique

FIGURE 25 Angular

FIGURE 26 Arched

FIGURE 27 Straight

FIGURE 28 Thick

FIGURE 29 Thin

FIGURE 30 Medium

Ethnical Differences

When considering the aspects of different types, consideration of treatment must be made in respect of each racial group. Cosmetics which may suit an Anglo-Saxon skin will not produce the same results on a Negro, Indian, or a Chinese skin for example. Generally speaking negro skins are oilier and coarser than most other skins and have a richer blood supply so giving out more heat. Japanese skins are paler than Chinese skins which are yellow tinged in colour. Fortunately during recent years cosmetics have been manufactured catering especially for all groups of people bearing in mind their requirements. It is advisable to use these ranges of preparations especially in make-up so that clown-like effects are avoided, and the beauty of each race is properly enhanced.

Colour and Corrective Make-up

Good and bad facial features can be played up or toned down with the use of the right-make-up. Usually the make-up employs the method of accentuating an area with highlighters or a lighter shade foundation cream, and shading or shadowing an area with shaders, shade blushers, or a darker foundation.

HIGHLIGHTS

Highlights are produced when a lighter colour is used than the general foundation bringing out the areas to be emphasized, or creating an illusion of width.

SHADOWS

Shadows are formed when a darker colour is used than the original foundation so subduing areas needing to be minimized throwing emphasis elsewhere.

N.B. Whenever different colours are used as in two foundation tones, highlighters or shaders, care must be taken to blend them perfectly into each other so that no harsh lines can be detected between them. This rule applies to the use of eyeshadows and rouges where several colours may be used in a very small area.

COLOUR PERFECTION

Colour perfection can only be achieved when the make-up flatters or is complementary to the skin tones, the eyes, and the hair. All aspects of the client's face must be viewed including her profile as well as full front face.

AGE LINES

Creases round the mouth and crows feet can be softened by making the area appear fuller. This is achieved by the use of a lighter coloured foundation or highlighter applied over the area. The crevices appear to be lifted out and less noticeable. Care must be taken not to allow too heavy distribution of foundation to settle in these areas.

FRECKLES AND MOLES

These can be faded into obscurity with the use of a good covering foundation cream, or a blemish stick or cream which is slightly denser. This latter must tone exactly with the rest of the foundation otherwise it will stand out.

THREAD VEINS AND HIGH COLOURING

These can be disguised with a foundation which has a green tone blending it into the rest of the make-up, or by the use of a green coloured moisturizer.

A face powder which had a blending in it of green can also be used to tone down florid complexions.

DAYTIME MAKE-UP

Daytime make-up should be natural, lighter and more casual.

EVENING MAKE-UP

Evening make-up can be exotic, exaggerated, and bolder, taking into consideration the dress to be worn, the occasion, and lighting if possible.

Cleansing the Skin

The skin is highly resistant to infection and is an important defence organ of the body. However this defence can be weakened by the application of certain chemicals to the skin and its solvent properties must be such that the debris, make-up, and grime of the atmosphere are removed without depriving the skin of its natural oil film. The skin will also be soiled with secretions from the sudiforous and sebaceous glands as well as the natural debris from dead skin cells which must also be cleansed away. The concentrated sebum forms collectively over the sebaceous ducts and is not always cleansed away by the solvent effect of a cleansing cream or lotion. Emulsifying processes are also involved so that water soluble and dispersible waste materials are emulsified away due to a chemical reaction taking place on the skin. The cream must spread easily without any dragging of the facial tissues and all traces removed with a simple application of warm or hot water leaving the skin feeling clean and fresh.

To counteract the loss of natural oil on the skin the classic cleanser contains small amounts of emollient materials. Soap and alkaline substances are also used which may alter the skin's natural acidity. This has a tendency to make the skin feel taut and dry if used in excess.

Although the skin cleansing has no deeper effect on the underlying tissues of the skin and the functions of it, it is not considered a purely superficial treatment. Together with the facial massage cleanse, stimulation of the circulation occurs. In this way the skin can be said to be nourished and fed. Shedding of the external epidermal dead cells results in slight absorption of the nutrient properties contained in a good skin cleanser, and allows the skin to respire properly. The health and condition of the skin is improved and maintained by the increased flow of blood. This is caused by the mechanical stimulation of massage or the application of any form of heat. In turn broken-down tissues are helped to be repaired, and infections are healed more quickly. Impurities are removed and the germinal layer is stimulated. Therefore, in care and treatment of the skin, skin cleansing has a vital influence on its appearance, its ageing, and its functions.

Six Basic Aims and Principles of Treatment

1. CLEANSE

This rids the skin of all dirt particles and make-up. Prevents clogging of pores and infections which may ensue as a result. Stimulates the circulation.

2. TONE

After a thorough deep cleansing, this closes pores to prevent further invasion and refines the texture of the skin, 'shrinking' the pores.

3. MOISTURIZE

This creates an impression of succulence in the skin, and helps to prevent it drying out as well as trying to increase moisture content.

4. NOURISH

An emollient is supplied to the surface of the skin making it feel supple and soft and helping it maintain its elasticity. Superficial wrinkles are discouraged by increasing the circulation, using massage, and an emollient cream.

5. FIRM

Attempt to tone up the skin through an increased circulation and tighten the skin using suitable preparations, cream for massage, toners, and astringents for the skin.

6. APPEARANCE

To create an improved appearance with or without make-up.

Ageing of the Face

Several factors should be considered when discussing the ageing face. The signs and symptoms of the ageing face are visible by the appearance of wrinkles, fine lines, folds in the skin, dropped facial contours, thinning and toughening of the skin, and loss of pink colour in the skin. Water is lost from the skin and loss of nourishment from an impoverished blood supply causes it to dehydrate and even atrophy, losing its youthful bloom.

AGE GROUPS OF THE SKIN

16–20 YEARS

This age group has a firm compact skin with no permanent lines or wrinkles. The tissues are plumped and rounded without any signs of puffiness. Sometimes there may be a tendency to spots or acne when the skin is more likely to be coarsened, oily, or greasy. Usually the texture is smooth, fine, and firm.

20–30 YEARS

This is the age where all signs of chubbiness have disappeared and where women enjoy the best of bloom in their skin. Colour is healthy and glowing, contours are firmly chiselled and defined. Any trace of lines are unnoticeable even though fine lines begin to form towards the thirties.

30–40 YEARS

Signs of ageing have begun to make their mark especially on the neck. The jawline is still firmly definable at first but soon shows positive signs of ageing. The skin colour starts to wane. The facial tissues begin to lose their fatty layer and tiredness creeps into it. Creases and wrinkles remain after the expressions forming them have disappeared. Elasticity of the skin is decreased and it starts to look a little baggy. There is a tendency to puffiness of the eyes and even high colour in the cheeks. Coarsening of the fine texture may have occurred especially round the nose, chin, and forehead.

40–50 YEARS

There is still a strong good definition of features. Creases and wrinkles are now permanencies. The jawline shows signs of jowls and permanent double chins. Elasticity of the skin is by now greatly reduced and it begins to look very baggy. The widening of pores spreads to the cheeks and some women due to hormonal disturbances find that an adolescent skin occurs, i.e. spotty and greasy. The skin has begun to thin out and may even look papery towards the fifties. Blemishes such as broken veins take the place of the high colour, and the skin looks sallow.

50–60 YEARS

The skin although coarse appears even textured again but dry. It is loose and thin. The eyes are lined and puffy giving a narrower impression. Round the edges of the lips the skin begins to be uneven and its firm definition is disappearing. Lines and cracks appear all over but are not too deeply embedded.

60–70 YEARS

At this age the skin looks soft and pappy. It is very thin and there is little underlying fat protecting it. Darkened patches may appear pigmenting it. The throat, neck, and chest are very wrinkled and crêpey. There is little if any secretion of oil, and perspiration decreases.

Client Type and Requirements

REQUIREMENTS

Requirements for the client vary according to her age group and skin type. Nearly all women are fairly equal mixtures of different types, the following types give a general picture of each.

RELAXED AND CALM

Client will respond to all treatments based on the physical aspect of the skin, i.e. age, colour, and type. Their skin is smooth and firm without tension lines.

NERVOUS AND TENSE

Client requires reassurance in the form of soothing treatments combined with slow relaxed manipulations using much effleurage and stroking.

The atmosphere must be relaxed and there should be no element of rush about any of the treatments. Stimulating treatments should be avoided. Their skin looks taut, shiny, and coarse.

UNRELAXED AND RESTLESS

Clients require short unhurried treatments. There should be no time lag between the treatments which must be carried out in a relaxed manner. Stimulating treatments requiring deep slow massage manipulations are important. Usually they are thin people with dry skins and pale colouring.

TIRED AND WEARY

Clients require toning treatments which should help to revitalize her and create a sensation of well-being. The aim is to stimulate the clients interest in herself, and not let her drift into far-away thoughts. Their skin looks pale, exhausted, and droopy.

CONFIDENT AND CAREFREE

Clients are usually talkative and active. They require vigorous exotic treatments with stimulating massage manipulations. Their skin may be found to be of good colour, thick and elastic, showing firm contours.

JOLLY CHEERFUL

Clients tend to be over-weight with a fatty skin which is soft and smooth. They require stimulating treatments encouraging the flow of lymphatic fluid, and toning treatments.

Observation Points when recognizing Skin Types

1. DRY SKIN

A dry skin is recognized by:
(a) The surface is often scaly and there may be a tendency for dandruff in the eyes.
(b) Tightness after washes with soap and water.
(c) There is a tendency to have an extra sensitivity.
(d) The epidermis may be very thin in dry skin.
(e) Premature wrinkling occurs because it seems to have less elasticity than normal skin.

CLIENTS HOME CARE REQUIREMENTS

1. Cleanse with a cream or oil cleanser—never soap and water. Remove cream with damp cotton wool.
2. Use a very light skin tonic or rose water applied on damp cotton wool.
3. Use a rich night cream.

In the morning the client must re-cleanse, remove cream, and tone as before. Apply moisturizer most suitable for dry skin type liberally.

MAKE-UP

The client should be advised to keep away from extremes of temperature and use make-up suitable for a dry skin condition, i.e. all cream-based products.

2. OILY SKIN

An oily skin is recognized by:
(a) Shiny surface.
(b) Tendency to blackheads and spots.
(c) May appear sallow and dead looking.
(d) Open pores.
(e) The epidermis may tend to be thicker.

CLIENTS HOME CARE REQUIREMENTS

1. Cleanse the face with soap and water, or a liquid cleanser may be used. A sponge or complexion brush can also be employed.
2. Instruct the client to tone the face and

neck by rinsing first with warm water and then with cold. Any infected areas should be dried with paper tissues and the rest of the face patted with a towel.

3. An astringent should be applied with a piece of cotton wool, and allowed to dry. In the morning the cleansing and toning procedure must once again be followed.

MAKE-UP

If there is any infection, medicated make-up is advisable otherwise a protective base should first be applied followed by liquid based make-up.

3. COMBINATION SKIN

A combination skin is recognized by:

(a) A 'T' shaped panel; the forehead and centre of the face having all the appearances of an oily skin.

(b) The rest of the face has the characteristics of a dry skin with slight sensitivity on the cheekbone area.

CLIENTS HOME CARE REQUIREMENTS

Cleanse the face applying the oil and dry skin techniques.

MAKE-UP

The client must be instructed to use appropriate make-up preparations, applying astringent-based ones to the greasy areas.

4. NORMAL SKIN

CLIENTS HOME CARE REQUIREMENTS

1. Wash face and neck with soap and water, or she can use a suitable light cleanser.
2. A light skin tonic can be applied.
3. Application of a good moisturizer should follow.

4. Make-up based on cream.
   A light night cream is advisable.

5. SENSITIVE SKIN

A sensitive skin is recognized by:

(a) Tendency to blotching.
(b) Rashes may be apparent.
(c) May be prematurely wrinkled.
(d) Thread veins are seen more frequently on this skin type.

CLIENTS HOME CARE REQUIREMENTS

1. Face and neck should be cleansed with unperfumed or non-coloured cleansers. Traces should be removed with damp cotton wool. Milk cleansers are most soothing for this skin type. Light massage only for those with broken veins.
2. A good creamy non-astringent moisturizer should be used.

MAKE-UP

Non-allergic and unperfumed make-up should be used.

GREASY AND DRY AREAS

Can be established by pressing a clean piece of paper tissue gently over all the areas of the face. Oily patches will mark the tissue and dry areas will not. A plot of these areas can be made on the clients record card, by charting a blank drawing accordingly. Thus correct treatments and cosmetics can be applied.

The Muscles of the Face

Certain muscles of the face are attached to the bones of the face and head only at one end, the insertion. Other muscles are attached entirely into the facial skin alone. When the muscles contract they cause the surface of the skin to be drawn into the direction of their pull. Sometimes the skin is pulled at right angles to the muscles also. They contract in response to external stimuli received by one or other of the five senses. The contraction of these muscles because of the effect on the skin produce different expressions and are known as the muscles of expression. Lines, wrinkles, and folds in the skin are very often formed as a result of their contraction; these eventually remain apparent even in total relaxation.

Every contraction and corresponding expression resulting from it can reveal the general character of the client, and very often her innermost feelings. The saying that 'the face is the window of the soul' is therefore justified. Even the slightest response to external stimuli can betray hidden thoughts and feelings. Normally only great conscious effort prevents the response in contraction of these muscles and results in a 'poker' face. Because expressions indicate a state of mind it is always advisable for the beauty therapist to keep sight of the client's face when giving any treatment. Expressions indicating untoward effects can then be seen immediately, and steps can be taken to rectify them instantly. The frequency of muscular contractions eventually results in permanency of the lines of the face. Therefore the older the client the deeper and more permanent the lines, furrows, and wrinkles will be. Although the action of an individual muscle creates its own expression, several muscles usually contract to produce a combined overall expression. This may register different feelings at once, such as horror and laughter, or surprise and laughter, and so on. Some muscle fibres eventually contract and shorten causing puckering of the skin whilst others become over-stretched and lengthen causing skin slackening. It is important to understand the layout of the muscles of the face for all forms of facial treatments especially for massage and electrical treatments.

THE CHIEF MUSCLES OF FACIAL EXPRESSION

ACTION	POSITION
Occipito Frontalis Two parts: (a) draws the scalp forwards, wrinkles the forehead, raises the eyebrows and skin over the bridge of the nose. (b) Occipital part draws the scalp backwards Two parts together draw the scalp backwards, register expression of surprise, horror, and fright.	Forehead to over the scalp and nape of neck. (*See* Figure 31.)
Corrugator Supercilli Draws the eyebrows downwards and inwards producing vertical creases in middle of the forehead. Causes frowning.	At the corner of the eyebrows, near bridge of nose.
Orbicularis Oculi Closes the eye in sleeping or blinking. Causes 'crows-feet'.	Circles the orbit of the eye around eyelids.
Pyramidalis Nasi Draws down the inner angle of the eyebrows producing wrinkles over bridge of nose.	Along the bridge of the nose.

contd. page 58

57

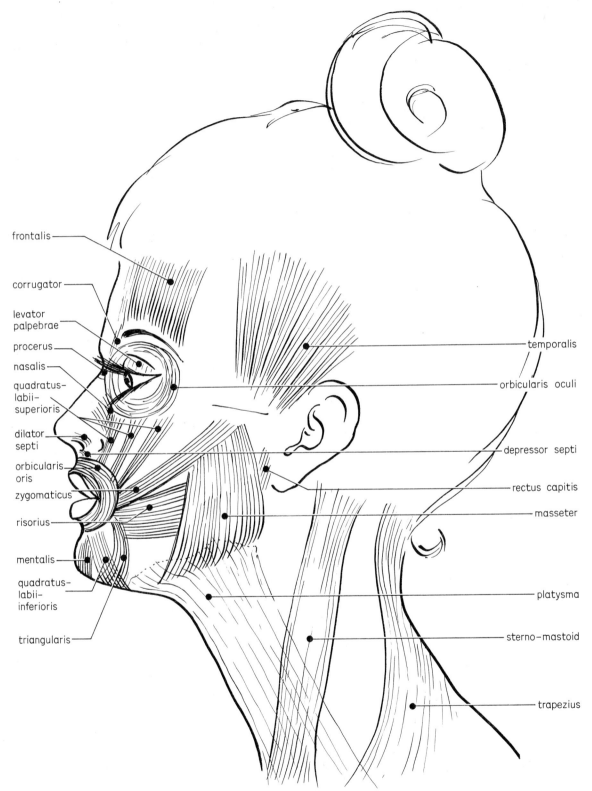

frontalis

corrugator

levator
palpebrae

procerus

nasalis

quadratus-
labii-
superioris

dilator
septi

orbicularis
oris

zygomaticus

risorius

mentalis

quadratus-
labii-
inferioris

triangularis

temporalis

orbicularis oculi

depressor septi

rectus capitis

masseter

platysma

sterno-mastoid

trapezius

FIGURE 31   Muscles of the face

ACTION	POSITION
Orbicularis Oris When strongly contracted purses the lips, compresses lips.	Circles around the mouth.
Masseter Raises the lower jaw used in chewing.	In the cheeks.
Temporalis Raises and draws the lower jaw backwards.	Sides of temple above and in front of the ear.
Buccinator Puffs out the cheek as in blowing.	Lower cheek, above jawline.
Depressor Labii Superioris Depresses lower lip and turns mouth downwards.	Below the lower lip and jaw.
Platysma Helps to draw down the lower jaw and lip, in an expression of horror. Wrinkles the skin of throat and neck.	Along the jawline over the front and sides of neck out to points of shoulders.
Trapezius Lifts and raises the shoulders as in shrugging.	Large triangular shaped muscle at back of neck, in between the shoulder blades.
Mentalis This raises and pushes up the lower lip, causes wrinkling of the chin as in doubt or displeasure.	Above point of chin, and its tip.
Risorius Produces a broad laughing smile.	Across sides of cheek and mouth from in front of the ear.
Zygomatic Major Draws the mouth upwards and backwards as in laughing.	From the cheek bone downwards to corner of mouth.
Zygomatic Minor Draws mouth sideways into a wistful smile.	Situated below the major muscle.
Levator Labii Superioris Draws lip upwards and dilates the nostrils.	Over the upper lip.
Sterno-mastoid Turns head from side to side. Bends head sideways and produces nodding movement.	On the side of the neck from below the ears to the sternum.
Pectorals (major and minor) Move the shoulder joint and narrow the chest.	Across upper part of chest out to shoulders.

5. *Focus on the Eyes*

The Structure of the Eye

The eye is the organ of sight. It is a special sense organ, and is supplied by the optic nerve. It is situated in the orbital cavity and is spherical in shape being approximately 2·5 centimetres in diameter. The intervening space between the eye and the orbital cavity is filled with fatty tissue which together with the bony walls helps to protect the eye from injury. It has three coats, the contents of which do not concern the beauty therapist.

MUSCLES OF THE EYE

There are six muscles of the eye which are responsible for moving the eyeball and are voluntary muscles. They are:
1. The medial rectus.
2. The lateral rectus.
3. The superior rectus.
4. The inferior rectus.
5. The superior oblique.
6. The inferior oblique.

All of these muscles originate in the bony wall of the back of the orbital cavity and have their insertions in the sclera, which is its outermost covering, lying underneath the transparent membrane known as the cornea.

THE ACCESSORY ORGANS OF THE EYE

Because the eye is such a delicate organ it has structures which protect it:
1. The eyebrows.
2. The eyelids and eyelashes.
3. The lacrimal apparatus.

1. THE EYEBROWS

The eyebrows arise from the skin over the two arched skin protuberances lying above the bony eye orbits on the frontal bone. Numerous hairs form the eyebrows which protect the eyes from sweat and dust.

2. THE EYELIDS AND LASHES

There are two moveable folds of skin above and below the eye. On the free edge the eyelashes grow. The lids are composed of a thin covering of skin in which muscle fibres comprise a main part. These muscles close and open the eyelids (orbicularis oris and levator palpebrae superioris). A delicate lining of the eyelid called the conjunctiva is reflected over the front of the eyeball. When the lids are closed it becomes a closed sac and protects the cornea and the front of the eye. The' function of the eyelids is to ward off anything which will harm the eye.

3. THE LACRIMAL APPARATUS

This comprises a complicated system of glands, ducts, sacs, and other structures which basically provide the eye with its tears and moisture. Their function is to bathe and wash the eye, and even disinfect it due to their composition, finally draining into the tear duct and into the nasal cavity.

Eye Treatments

DARK SHADOWS

CAUSE

Anaemia.
Lack of sleep.
Poor digestion.
Lack of fresh air.
Excess starch and sugar in the diet.

TREATMENT

Ice packs, or tonic water packs placed over the eyes for fifteen minutes will help to lessen the shadow effect temporarily, prior to camouflage make-up. A concealer cream or blemish stick should be applied lightly, followed by the normal make-up routine.

TIRED EYES

CAUSE

Eye strain such as reading in bad lights or for too long.
Bright lights and glare.
Lack of sleep.

TREATMENT

Relaxing facial massage with emphasis on the eye massage. This should be followed by eye exercises, after which moist, cold eye pads can be applied to the client's eyes for ten to fifteen minutes.

PUFFY EYES

CAUSE

Retention of fluid (kidney complaints).
Overstretched skin around the eyes.
Dropped contours.
Too heavy night cream.
Allergic infections.
Crying, lack of sleep, eye-strain, physical deterioration.
Fatty deposits around the eyes.
Age and hereditary factors.

TREATMENT

When it is sure that no medical condition exists, treatment may be given.

Warm olive oil packs may be applied first, prior to a general facial massage. Clean off the oil thoroughly with hot towels. Apply cold water or ice cold witch hazel pads on the eyes for ten to fifteen minutes. Apply the whipped white of an egg around and on the eyelids for only five minutes, removing with cold water. Re-apply mild tonic pads for a further five minutes. Pat dry gently with tissues.

CROW'S FEET

CAUSE

Expression lines.
Dry skin.
Ageing processes.
Screwing up the eyes for varying reasons.

TREATMENT

Massage using gentle circular kneadings and tapping manipulations with a light cream.
Egg pack may be used.

Olive oil pack with gauze and warm oil, taking care to prevent the oil from seeping into the eyes, or from cooling.

Eye relaxing exercises may be given.

Moisturizing cream must be used before applying make-up. A lighter coloured foundation or erase stick may be applied to camouflage shadows under the eyes. *Faradic current* may be applied with the disc electrode around the eyes but with insufficient current to cause muscle contractions, only the tingling sensation must be felt.

SPECIAL EYE EXERCISES

1. Head held straight, ask client to blink gently ten times and then open her eyes wide.
2. Ask the client to keep her eyes as wide open as possible and turn them to the extreme right. This position should be held for ten counts.
3. The eyes should now be turned to the extreme left, and this position held for ten counts.
4. Ask the client to turn the eyes back to the front, still wide open, blink ten times and then relax.
5. Ask the client to look into the right corner of her eyes, and then down to the left. Repeat to upper left corner and then down to the right.
6. Ask the client to raise the eyes upwards, and then downwards five times each.
7. Tell her to look at the bridge of her nose and then follow the sides of it to the tip, and back again.
8. Six blinks.
9. Finally ask her to circle her eyes round first in one direction, then the other.

EYE TONIC

Follow the eye exercises by placing eye pads soaked in ice cold witch-hazel or rose water on the client's eyes. The client should be reclined and relaxed completely. Keep the eye pads wet and moist by constantly applying more ice cold fluid from a squeezy plastic bottle. Do not over-soak the pads otherwise it will run down the face and make the client uncomfortable. Leave for between ten and fifteen minutes, after which the eyes will appear whiter, brighter and more sparkling. Proceed with make-up.

Eyebrows

SHAPING OF EYEBROWS

Before shaping the eyebrow it is important to recognize the natural shape. The eyebrow follows the curve of the eye socket and this can vary greatly from person to person. The eyebrow should begin in line immediately above the inner corner of the eye, its arch should reach its highest point immediately above the outer edge of the iris. To find the eyebrow length, the beauty therapist should measure a line perpendicularly from the outermost corner up to the brow. (*See* Figure 32.)

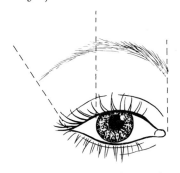

FIGURE 32   Measuring eyebrow length

Eyebrows frame the face prettily. Bushy eyebrows can make a client look older. Too thin eyebrows, however, can give a hard look to the client's face.

METHODS OF SHAPING

1. WAXING

There is a school of thought which considers waxing to be a suitable and an efficient way of shaping the eyebrows. However the extreme delicacy of the tissues should be borne in mind before embarking upon such a method. Also the close proximity of the eyes should be considered as the wax could seriously damage the client's vision should it stray into this area. If wax is used small strips are applied as in the method for leg waxing. A fine brush is used and one small strip is sufficient for each eyebrow.

2. ELECTROLYSIS

Whilst this method is permanent after 2–3 treatments on each hair it is sometimes quite painful, depending on the clients own pain threshold and the skill of the operator. Some schools of thought may also consider the proximity of the eye and the frontal sinuses to contra-indicate this treatment. It is inadvisable permanently to shape the eyebrows to a certain fashion, and generally few clients are prepared to spend the time for this lengthy procedure.

3. DEPILATORY CREAMS

Are not popular in beauty therapy because the skin round the eyes is extremely sensitive. Strong chemicals such as those used in depilatory preparations could cause an allergic reaction, proving to be dangerous to the eye itself if accidental exposure occurred.

4. RAZORING

Should never be used, because this leaves the points blunt making them appear thicker and darker.

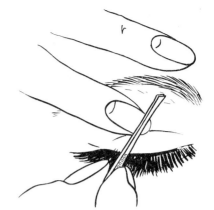

FIGURE 33 Eyebrow shaping with tweezers

5. SCISSORS

May be used to trim thick and bushy eyebrows but not for shaping. Great care must be taken when using scissors near the eyes.

6. TWEEZERS

Are the most favoured method employed by the beauty therapist for shaping the eyebrows. (*See* Figure 33.) It is a simple, clean; quick and painless way when performed correctly.

METHOD OF EYEBROW SHAPING WITH TWEEZERS

1. Prepare client and trolley.
2. Select correct and suitable shape for the client's face.
3. Brush eyebrows first against the growth and then with growth back to natural line.
4. Apply hot towel.
5. Wipe sterile tweezers over with surgical spirit. Wipe skin with antiseptic pad and place illuminated magnifying glass in position.
6. Pluck out the hairs quickly in the direction of their growth, being careful not to catch the skin, especially when using automatic tweezers.

7. Start at the bridge of the nose, if the hairs need plucking here, as the skin is less sensitive in this region. Work outwards to the tail of the eyebrow. Keep checking that both eyebrows match in thickness and shape, by brushing into shape after every few hairs have been plucked out. The eyebrows must always follow the curve of the eye and only the sparse growth of hair from under the eyebrow arch should be removed. Hair on the natural upper eyebrow line should never be removed.
8. Pat the area after shaping with a skin tonic, or a mild astringent to close the pores.
9. Finally brush the eyebrows into the new shape.

N.B. If the client does not pluck her eyebrows regularly, gradual shaping should take place over a series of treatments, otherwise this tender skin may become sore and inflamed. Puffiness may also result with too drastic a first treatment. Eyebrows should be shaped and maintained every two weeks.

EYEBROW COSMETICS

There are various methods of applying cosmetics to the eyebrows to emphasize their colour.
1. Eyebrow pencil.
2. Eyebrow shadow.
3. Eyebrow liner.
If necessary the eyebrows can be bleached or tinted up to the desired colour.

APPLICATION

Whichever method is used, care must be taken to simulate the natural hair. The therapist must never draw hard lines. Soft, feathery strokes emphasizing the arch most resemble the natural hair.

64

CHOICE OF COLOUR

The main fault with eyebrow cosmetics is that the eyebrow is made to appear hard. This creates a harsh, severe, and ageing look in the face. So both in choice of colour and application of the chosen colour, care is needed to achieve a softly defined brow. The colour resembling that nearest to the hair should be chosen. Black brow colouring is only suitable for clients with black hair, and then not always.

HAIR COLOURING	COLOUR OF PRODUCT
Blonde	Brown or Grey
Light Brown	Brown or Grey
Dark Brown	Brown
Grey	Grey
Auburn	Brown or Auburn
Black	Black or Brown

EYEBROW AND EYELASH TINTING

Natural blondes may have a distinct advantage over darker women so far as unwanted hair is concerned, because fair hair doesn't show up as heavily as dark. Blonde women often suffer, however, from a bald and ill-defined look about their eyes when they are not made up. Eyebrow and eyelash tinting is popularly requested in beauty salons both from the older and younger generations. Special eyelash colouring preparations are available and should be used. Great care must be taken to avoid colouring matter entering the eyes. Splash with cold water and seek medical help in case of accidents.

REASONS FOR USE

1. Extremely light coloured brows and lashes.
2. To match hair colour change.

3. For use in summer when mascara is a nuisance and likely to smudge when swimming.
4. For a client who is allergic to mascara.
5. To make lashes appear longer.
6. For a busy client who has little time to apply mascara.
7. To give a more natural shape to the eyebrows instead of eyebrow pencil.

CONTRA-INDICATIONS FOR USE

1. Skin diseases.
2. Eye disorders or diseases (redness, swellings).
3. Allergies.
4. Sensitive skin.
5. Immediately after eyebrow plucking.
6. Contact lenses.
7. Nervous clients, such as the elderly who may blink.

PROCEDURE FOR EYELASH TINTING

Test for allergic reaction An appropriate test should be carried out before each treatment as the client may suddenly develop an allergic reaction to the dye which could be quite serious. If the eyebrows are to be tinted as well then this usually takes less time, about one minute. It is better to repeat the treatment than to dye the brows too dark as this will give a hard appearance to the client.

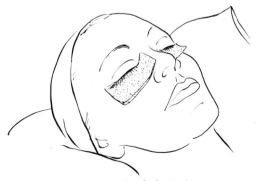

FIGURE 34   Eyelash tinting

1. Cleanse the area to be treated thoroughly, then use a mild tonic water to ensure that all grease has been removed.
2. Check for contra-indications.
3. Smear a small amount of vaseline around the skin edge of the hair to prevent staining the surrounding skin. Use a blunt brush to apply the vaseline or face cream coat, taking care not to touch the roots of the hair lashes or brows.
4. Place a pair of thin cotton wool or lint pads cut to the curved shape under the eyes. Make sure they are moist enough to stay in place or cream the under sides so that they fit snugly under the lower lashes. (*See* Figure 34.)
5. Mix the tint according to the instructions in a small non-metallic bowl. Different products require different mixing so always check instructions first. A liquid tint may run slightly so that a cream or gel type may be preferred by the beauty therapist, to prevent it from running into the eyes.
6. Use either a brush or an orange stick tipped with cotton wool to spread the tint evenly, over the upper and lower lashes. Work from the roots to the tips of the lashes.
7. Cover both eyes with pads of lint to stop the client from opening her eyes. It also keeps the tint warm, speeding up its action. Leave for five to ten minutes.
8. Remove pads together with the pad shapes, firmly wiping off surplus cream from the outside corner to the inside.
9. Any surplus tint can be removed with a water-moistened pad of cotton wool.
10. Place two moistened pads of cotton wool over the eyes and leave for a further five minutes. This helps to relax the eyes.
11. Tissue dry after removal.
12. Proceed with further make-up.

65

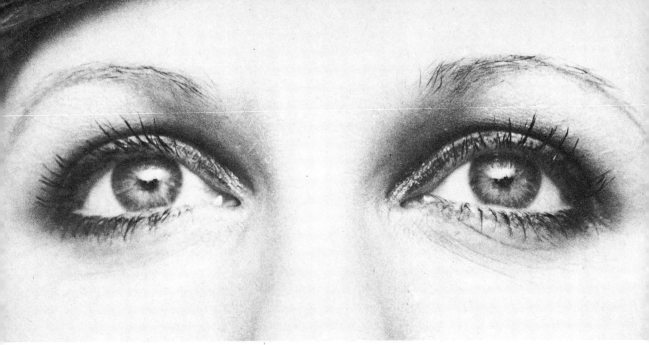

PLATE 5A   The eyes

The eyebrows can be tinted at the same time, smoothing the tint along from the nose edge outwards.

N.B. In the case of tint going into the eyes, wash with cold water immediately, using an eyebath to dilute its action.

False Eyelashes

CHOICE OF EYELASHES FOR EYE TYPES

TYPE   Upward slanting eyes.

EYELASHES   Medium eyelashes to sweep the cheeks, plus lower lashes.

TYPE   Downward slanting eyes.

EYELASHES   Medium length lashes on upper lids, longer length on lower lids.

TYPE   Wide set eyes. Need bringing close together.

EYELASHES   Natural medium lashes uneven in length.

TYPE   Small close-set eyes. Need an illusion of width to enlarge them.

EYELASHES   Filmy, feathery lashes, longer at the outer corners. The lower lashes should be emphasized likewise.

TYPE   Deep set eyes. Need drawing out.

EYELASHES   Extra long fine eyelashes with upturned tips. Lower lashes should also be added.

EYELASH CURLING

Special eyelash curlers can be used on the eyelashes when made up, as this helps to hold the curl. The beauty therapist should curl the eyelashes from the front, asking the client to look slightly downwards. Another method is to roll the eyelashes over an orange stick whilst applying the mascara. False eyelashes may be recurled this way.

DIET

Diet for healthy eyes is important. Food-stuffs containing vitamin A should be included in the client's diet. Although food does not affect vision as such, night blindness can occur if vitamin A is lacking. Fresh citrus fruits should always form part of the diet as well as tomatoes, fish, and carrots.

APPLICATION OF FALSE EYELASHES

These should be applied before eye make-up although a little mascara may be used beforehand. The eyelid should be dry and free from grease to ensure adhesion. There are two kinds of fixative.

I. SELF ADHESIVE

This is applied some ten to twenty minutes before application of the lashes and then allowed to set. Adhesion should then be retained for several applications of eyelashes without further necessity to replenish.

2. ADHESIVE

This fixative is applied immediately prior to the lashes being placed into position and it is still moist when it contacts the skin. Although it may be white in colour it dries colourlessly.

APPLICATION

The glue of either type is applied in a fine strip to the base of the false eyelashes. Take care that it sufficiently covers either end without protruding and peeling. Also it is important to keep it off the lashes to avoid them sticking together and sticking onto the client's lashes. This can be painful when they are removed.

Tweezers or an eyelash holder are used to place them gently into position. The client's eyes are closed and the false eyelashes are placed immediately over the roots of the real lashes. Press the false lashes into place along the eyelid, checking that they are secure. Lift the eyelid and slightly roll it back over the base of the lashes. This blends both sets of eyelashes together. Allow them to set for a few minutes before further make-up is applied. The same technique is used for applying single lashes, or lower lid lashes.

INDIVIDUAL EYELASH APPLICATION

Artificial eyelashes are a feature of modern make-up and many women feel undressed without them. The service of applying a semi-permanent type of individual false eyelashes has become increasingly popular. It takes thirty minutes to apply them, and should last approximately up to six weeks the normal cycle of growth. Some salons offer a weekly touch-up service to replace lost ones. Many hairdressing salons offer this service to clients.

PROCEDURE

1. Prepare client and trolley.
2. Decide with the client the type of eyelash most suitable. Observe her face and eye shape before the final choice.
3. Working from behind the client, who should be reclining (as for facial treatments) ask her to open her eyes and look ahead but slightly downwards.
4. Apply the extra strong adhesive, to the individual false eyelash.
5. Using tweezers, place this on top of the root of the natural lash as close to the lid as possible.
6. If the eye waters, ask the client to sit up, and then continue again.
7. Check both eyes to see if they match.
8. Apply the lower lid eyelashes from the front, in the same way as above.

Eye Make-up

THE CIRCLED EYE

The eyeshadow is taken beneath the eye and lower lashes. The colour may or may not be the same on the top and lower lids, but it should be of the same intensity.

THE RAINBOW EYE

Several pastel shades are chosen and lateral bands of colours are drawn from the lashes to the brow.

THE CHIAROSCURO EYE

Shading in beiges and browns replaces colour.

THE MONOCHROMATIC EYE

One strong colour only is used together with mascara.

ORDER OF MAKE-UP

1. Cleanse the face and tone.
2. Apply moisturizer.
3. Apply foundation, contour make-up, and rouge.
4. Apply loose powder.
5. Eye make-up.

ORDER OF EYE MAKE-UP

a. For a dramatic effect begin with a socket line. Brown or grey shadow is usually used but any colour coordinated to be the darkest colour on the lid, is drawn from the inner to the outer eye corner. It is then blurred slightly with the fifth finger.
b. Apply the lid shadow (eye colour should be considered) from the inner to outer corner. From the base of the lashes it should extend to the bottom of the depth socket line.
c. Next use a pearly beige highlighter or a pearlized shadow that compliments the lid colour, or alternatively use white powder shadow. Smooth this on immediately under the eye brow to the top of the depth line, concentrating on the brow bone and blending all make-up so that harsh lines are not visible.
d. Do not use any eyeliner if it is not needed, otherwise use brown, grey or a deeper shade of the shadow and draw a thin line.
e. Mascara is applied next. First on the top of the lashes, and then on their underside and on the lower lashes. When applying to the lower lashes, place a piece of tissue between lower lashes and lid to prevent smudging onto the skin.
f. Eyebrow pencil or shaper follows last.

DAYTIME EYE MAKE-UP

This should be light, considering the colour of clothes, hair, and eyes. Heavy false eyelashes should not be worn.

EVENING EYE MAKE-UP

This should be more adventurous. Browns and greys will disappear under electric light and are better for daytime use. Colours can be stronger and brighter for evening wear. Jewelled eyelashes or even sequins fixed on and around the eyes would be exotic for special occasions. Gold or silver flecked eye shadow catches the light prettily at night and looks most effective.

MAKE UP FOR CONTACT LENSES

This should be non-greasy to prevent the minutest speck from entering the eye and blurring vision between the lens and the eye. It is preferable to ask the client to remove her contact lenses before make-up as slight pressure over the eyes could cause discomfort and pain. The lenses can be applied before powdering but the eyes should be kept closed to prevent any specks of powder floating onto the lens. Eyeshadows used with a brush and clean water are the best method, and eyelash tinting is recommended for clients who wear contact lenses, otherwise the beauty therapist should use a waterproof mascara.

PLATE 5B   The eyes

MAKE-UP FOR GLASSES

Powder make-up is best for clients who wear glasses. If false eyelashes are applied, the beauty therapist should recommend short, thick ones as long ones are not appropriate under glasses. Bright eyeshadow flatters the eyes under glasses. Preferably the blue and turquoise shades rather than neutral ones, and highlighter below the brow widens out this area. Eyebrows should not be too thin but brushed high and arched naturally.

Long sighted glasses sometimes make the eye look pin headed. The aim of the make-up should be to enlarge and lengthen the eye. Colours should be very clear. White pearly shadow should be avoided as it reflects on the lenses. Muted pastel shades are preferable. The eye socket can be accentuated with a dark shadow which should be smudged softly at the edges. A slight touch of a light pearlized shadow applied just above the lower lashes accentuates the lashes and softens the look of the eyes. False eyelashes should be used but if not, apply several coats of mascara to both upper and lower lashes. Care must be taken not to allow them to touch the lenses however. If eyeliner is used, apply it from the centre of the eyelid to the outside corner, not from the inside corner.

It should be softened and extended at the edges of the eye.

Short sighted glasses tend to enlarge the look of the eye, distorting it. In the over forties, when long sight is more common, the make-up is used to disguise wrinkles and baggy eyelids. Bright powdery eyeshadows accumulate in the folds of the skin and should be avoided. Liquid eyeshadows in muted shades and colours should be used. These are best when pearlized. An exaggerated eye socket is ageing. Highlighting effects should be used above the cheekbones. Individual false eyelashes are effective with dark mascara applied to the lashes. If the glasses are tinted, black mascara should be used. Eyeliners must be used sparingly and never beyond the eyelid corner, especially if the eyelids are baggy. A light coloured pearly pencil can be used to outline the lower eyelid.

69

BROW BONE AND EYE MAKE-UP

This bone defines the shape of the eye. For instance a protruding bone creates a deep set look to the eyes. Therefore before applying make-up to the eye area, the general shape and size of the brow bone is considered. The main considerations are whether it is fleshy or bony, if it should be highlighted or shadowed and whether it requires attention drawn to it or not.

LOWER EYELID

This is the area immediately below the eye. The lower eyelid has a complementary effect on the upper eyelid. When make-up is applied to it, it gives depth and an overall finish to the appearance of the eye.

1. SHADOWS

Shadows beneath the eye require a lighter foundation or a suitably pale colour.

2. PUFFY EYES

Puffy eyes need to be shaded with a darker colour of foundation.

EYELINER

REASONS FOR USE

1. To alter shape of eyes.
2. To make eyes smaller.
3. To alter position (e.g. wider, closer).
4. To make eyes appear slanting, or rounder, etc.
5. To elongate or widen the eyes.
6. To accentuate the eyes.

FIGURE 35   Surrounding lines

FIGURE 36   Extended lines

LINES

Lines drawn beneath the eye make the eye appear smaller and more enclosed. Broad dark lines make the eye appear smaller although some small eyes are completely lost without an outline strongly defined.

When drawn to surround the eye (*See* Figure 35), eyeliner makes the eye appear smaller; when the eyes are already small, lines surrounding the eye will give it a clear definition.

Eyeliner drawn in an extended line beyond the eyelid corner will give the eyes an elongated appearance (*See* Figure 36).

SOCKET ARCH

This is shadowed softly or severely according to the person's taste with colour or colours of choice. It accentuates the depth of the eye and again adds contour to it.

6. Order, Method, and Technique of a Complete Facial Treatment

Salon Procedure

Mobile beauty therapy involves home visits to the clients and compromises have to be made whenever necessary, but it is a very popular and welcome service for the busy housewife. Wherever possible, the ideal should be aimed for with regard to equipment, preparation, and client consideration. The beauty therapist should be able to adapt herself and the treatments, based on the same principles as those found in a well-equipped and successful beauty salon.

In a salon, it is the receptionist who will probably be the first person to greet the client. It is her personality, attitude, appearance, and approach which will convey the initial vital impression of the salon.

Appointments should always be checked, although treatments do overlap unavoidably sometimes. This may be due to the client arriving late or over-booking of appointments and other unforeseen circumstances. If the client has to wait, an explanation should be made, or in the case of home visiting beauty therapists, a telephone call explaining the delay would be appreciated. The receptionist could then take the client's coat before showing her to a chair.

RECEPTION AREA OR WAITING ROOM

Comfortable chairs, current magazines, newspapers, and books should be provided in an area where there are no treatments at all in progress. Warm but well ventilated, this area should provide a soft, relaxing atmosphere.

TREATMENT ROOM

The room or area in which the client is to receive treatment should be prepared before the client enters for treatment. This involves general cleanliness and tidiness of cupboards, shelves, and floors which should be regularly washed and cleaned with disinfectant. Drips on and around bottles and jars should be wiped away immediately. To ensure that bacteria are not transferred from one client to another, as well as cleaning off sticky material, the equipment must always be sterilized between each treatment. This necessitates a plentiful supply of linen, needles, electrodes, etc., to ensure that they are always readily at hand.

STERILIZATION

There are several methods of sterilizing equipment like tweezers, spatulas, needles, and electrodes. Linen, of course, must be laundered in boiling water temperatures. All this must be done beforehand, ready for use when the client arrives.

1. ULTRA-VIOLET RADIATION

This can be used and the equipment such as tweezers can be wiped with alcohol, spirits, or washed first to clean off any adhering substances. Care must be taken not to allow the ultra-violet rays to fall on to the therapist's eyes, therefore store the cabinet either above or below eye level. The sterilizer or ultra-violet lamp should be turned on for three minutes prior to use in order to stabilize the rays and bring them up to maximum intensity. After that, the instruments should be left for twenty minutes in the light. There is a disadvantage in that the equipment should ideally be turned over into the rays exposing all sides.

2. BOILING WATER

This is essential for laundering towels, gowns, sheets, and pillowcases but usually is impractical in the salon unless there is a separate laundry room with washing and drying machines. Small stainless steel sterilizers such as those used in hospitals are simple and easy to use. They will hold bowls, glass electrodes, needles, tweezers, and all equipment which should be sterilized easily and practically. Small items which may be readily lost in the water can be placed together in a bowl and lowered into the water which is then brought up to boiling point for twenty minutes. The equipment can be left until ready for use, or removed and covered with a clean towel on a nearby trolley, or put away. For the beauty therapist who wishes to use the boiling water method of sterilization without the sterilizer, the same purpose can be served simply by boiling up the equipment in a large pan for

twenty minutes. It is an advantage to tie small pieces together with a band. Caution against scalding from steam should be taken when opening the sterilizing equipment and in using the boiling water. The equipment must be cool before use on the client.

3. CHEMICALS

Chemicals are another popular method often used in beauty salons. Jugs of chemical solution into which the tools can be placed are a handy method. These solutions should be changed regularly and the precise instructions recommended for use should be followed. Sterilizing cabinets very often incorporate the use of formaldehyde. These, like steam or water sterilizers, require a power point for electricity for running purposes. An electric element in the cabinet heats up the chemicals, producing fumes which rise into the cabinet killing all bacteria. Five minutes is the recommended length of time taken to sterilize the equipment completely. Care should be taken not to allow the fumes to escape into the atmosphere as they can sting the eyes of the operator, therefore always use in a well ventilated room. Brushes can be conveniently sterilized with this method. Ten per cent eusol or dettol solution can be used in the sterlilizing trays or jugs and the equipment is immersed in them for at least twenty minutes before they are removed and dried for use.

PREPARATION OF THE TROLLEY

Preparing the trolley may take ten minutes so this must be done before the client arrives. The beauty therapist would therefore be wise to have briefed herself with a look at a list of the day's clients and treatments to avoid delays and waste time. Ultimately, if she is well organized, her clients will benefit and unnecessary breaks in treatment will not occur. A silent running trolley, preferably with a compartment drawer, is ideal.

TROLLEY LAYOUT

1. Place a tray on the trolley or on a table near to the couch.
2. Towels, hand towels, spare pillows, should be placed on the lower shelf.
3. On the tray place cleaner, astringent, tweezers, cotton wool, massage cream, massage powder.
4. Tissues and all other commodities including make-up if required for the treatment by the tray or in the drawer.
5. Client's record card.

PREPARATION OF COUCH AND CLIENT FOR FACIAL TREATMENT

1. A massage couch of the right height and width should be opened out on which a

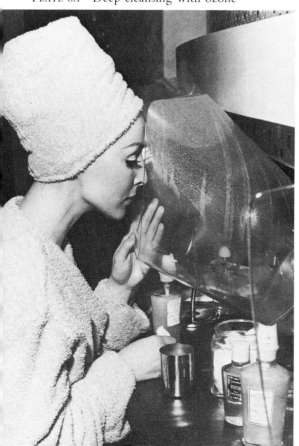

PLATE 6A   Deep cleansing with ozone

blanket and then a sheet are placed, with pillows nearby.

2. The beauty therapist now shows her client to the couch.
3. The client is asked to remove all jewellery from her ears and neck and any clothing which may obstruct the face and neck treatment. A gown should be available if required.
4. Client is asked to lie down face upwards and a towel is wrapped around her feet.
5. The sheet and blanket are turned up over the feet, followed by one side and then the other side, so that she is wrapped up cosily like a cocoon. A pillow may be placed under her knees if required for further comfort and one to support her head. At the neck edge of the client the sheet and the blanket are turned back and a towel should be tucked across the join. This looks neat and avoids soiling the linen and clothing.
6. Cover the client's hair with a towel, crêpe bandage or hair band, drawing it back off the hairline so protecting it. The client is now ready for the treatment to commence.
7. The beauty therapist should wash her hands at this stage and should have neat, short, and clean finger nails. Her overall must be freshly laundered with sleeves above the elbow and her hair should be tied back. Ample use of a good deodorant by the therapist is essential.

ORDER OF WORK FOR A FACIAL TREATMENT

1. Check hands are washed.
2. Apply cleanser to neck and face, avoiding lips and eyes.
3. Remove make-up (upward movements) using paper tissues or damp cotton wool.
4. Apply cleanser to eyes and lips.
5. Remove with damp cotton wool.

73

6. Apply small amount of cream to face and neck, give deep cleanse massage movements.
7. Remove surplus cream, make-up, grime and dead skin cells with tissues or damp cotton wool.
8. Apply cream.
9. Facial massage.
10. Remove surplus cream with tissues.
11. Apply hot towels and steam if required.
12. Shape eyebrows if required at this stage or remove blackheads if necessary.
13. Apply face pack.
14. Apply astringent.
15. Proceed with make-up routine.

The main points of this list will now be dealt with in greater detail.

Technique and Method of Cleansing

I. SUPERFICIAL CLEANSE

(a) Wash hands.
(b) Take cream out with spatula onto the back of the hand
(c) Apply cleansing cream to the entire face and neck. First cleanse the eyes and lip areas separately. Remove cream with damp cotton wool. (Or alternatively the eye and lip areas can be cleansed last.)
(d) Remove cream from over the entire neck and face with paper tissues or damp cotton wool.
(e) Apply cleansing milk or cream to the entire face and neck. Give the following deep cleanse treatment.

2. DEEP CLEANSE

(a) Slide fingers down from the mandible to the sternum. Stroke fingers up the sides of the sterno-mastoid. (See Figure 37.)

FIGURE 37   Deep cleanse 1

(b) Cleanse the chin area with alternate hands with stroking movements above and below jaw line. (See Figure 38.)

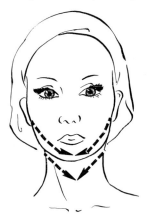

FIGURE 38   Deep cleanse 2

FIGURE 39   Deep cleanse 3

(c) Circular kneadings follow from the chin to the corners of the mouth, continuously to the corners of the nose and then out-wards along the zygomatic cheek bones to the temples. (*See* Figure 39.)

(*d*) From (*c*) slide the fingers from the temples across the forehead and down either side of the nose. (*See* Figure 40.)

FIGURE 40   Deep cleanse 4

(*e*) Circular kneadings are given round the base of the nose. (*See* Figure 41.)

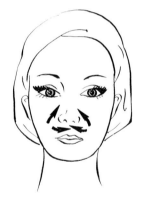

FIGURE 41   Deep cleanse 5

FIGURE 42   Deep cleanse 6

(*f*) From (*e*) slide the fingers and hand out-wards across the cheeks and up to the forehead. (*See* Figure 42.)

(*g*) Circular finger kneadings are next given transversely across the forehead with one hand. (*See* Figure 43.)

FIGURE 43   Deep cleanse 7

(*h*) Circular finger kneadings follow in a zig-zag manner over the forehead, re-peated both ways. (*See* Figure 44.)

FIGURE 44   Deep cleanse 8

FIGURE 45   Deep cleanse 9

75

(i) Circular stroking around the eye area follows from the middle upper corner and three tapping movements above the eyebrow completes the deep cleanse. (*See* Figure 45.)

Surplus cleansing cream should be removed with damp cotton wool or hot towels. A piece of cotton wool soaked in witch-hazel can be tapped briskly over the whole face. Finally, wipe over the whole face with a fresh piece of cotton wool.

Massage

It would be unsatisfactory and quite pointless to describe the massage procedure without first mentioning briefly some of the aims and effects of massage. Massage, whether it is given manually or electronically in one form or another is the common denominator in all beauty treatments. Without the physiological effects and benefits that massage has on the skin and underlying structures, the physical value of many beauty treatments would be considerably reduced. There are several techniques of massage which are used in beauty salons and training schools. It should be borne in mind that the massage should not be too strident or deep.

AIMS AND EFFECTS OF FACIAL MASSAGE

1. By stimulating the blood circulation the tissues are nourished and fed. Oxygen is brought to the area by the blood, waste products, and carbon dioxide are carried away. This helps to cleanse the skin and rid it of impurities. The oxygen is essential for cell regrowth and metabolism and so the skin is stimulated.

2. With an increased blood supply, heat and warmth of the skin and area massaged is promoted. This in turn causes an increase of sweat and sebum secretion in which the pores of the skin are opened. Through the pores with the aid of sweating, impurities, dirt, grease, and waste products are removed and so the skin is cleaned, lubricated and appears healthy and glowing.

3. The top outer layers of dry skin are loosened by massage and cleared away from the surface, allowing the fresh healthier growth to emerge and breathe freely.

4. Increased oil secretions help to maintain the water content of the cell layers so improving the moisture content of the skin. This returns to the skin its dewy bloom and youthful texture, if only for a short time, and the ageing can be said to be delayed.

5. Maintenance of the skin's elasticity is aimed for, by stimulating the stretch nerve endings in the skin which respond by a reflex contraction. Thus, apart from feeding and nourishing the elastic fibres of the skin, the skin is toned up in this way. Sagging skin may tighten and double chins may be alleviated. The formation of wrinkles and lines are hoped to be delayed.

6. The underlying muscles are fed, nourished, and stimulated by the increased blood supply. In a similar way to the skin, sagging muscles are toned up and the contours of the face can be improved or at least further ageing of the face, chin and neck can be delayed for a while. Massage helps to prevent further atrophy and malfunctioning.

7. Increased blood supply to the area promotes absorption of external 'nutrients' by making the skin more receptive and translucent. With the increased blood supply, an exudation of tissue fluids takes place which can fill out the sagging epidermal layers.

8. The tissues are lifted and the effect of gravity is counterbalanced.

9. By using certain manipulations, depletion of excess fluid in the tissue spaces can be encouraged, so removing puffiness and bagginess.

10. Promotion of relaxation is of tremendous value in attempting to rejuvenate the skin. Tired eyes are rested and nerves are soothed and refreshed. The total effect on the client is that of producing a sense of well-being and invigoration. The eyes appear brighter and the skin glows.

CLASSIFICATION OF FACIAL MASSAGE

Facial massage falls into two classes:

1. *Stimulating massage* is one in which the manipulations are deeper and quicker, but it is still relaxing.

2. *Relaxing massage* is one in which the movements are lighter and slower, but the tissues are still stimulated (the percussive manipulations are excluded) by means of the improved circulation.

BASIC FACIAL MANIPULATIONS
(Movements)

1. Circular finger and thumb frictions or kneadings.

2. Stroking and effleurage, digital and palmar.

3. Tapping, digital or point hacking (some call this slapping).

4. Knuckling.

5. Scissoring.

6. Shaking and vibrations.

TECHNIQUE OF MASSAGE MANIPULATIONS

1. CIRCULAR FINGER AND THUMB FRICTIONS (thumbing)

These are small continuous circular movements performed with the whole padded palmar surface of the finger tips or thumbs. The tissues are pressed down on to the underlying structures and rotated in a circular direction. On relaxation of the fingers, they travel on gently circulating a new area of tissue. The pressure emphasis is aimed towards the lymphatic flow.

2. STROKING AND EFFLEURAGE

Both palmar and digital stroking, and effleurage are relaxed sliding, soothing movements with the padded palmar surfaces of the fingers and thumbs. Effleurage always moves towards the lymph glands, stroking may not do so and can be used as a linking movement between manipulations maintaining the continuity and flow of the massage. Sometimes the whole padded surface of the hand may be used. Here the hand should be completely relaxed and drawn with even pressure over the skin, moulding to the shape. Stroking and effleurage must not be too deep otherwise dragging of the skin may occur, but it can be firm or light. Contact throughout the facial massage is maintained with the use of this manipulation which is extremely soothing in effect.

3. TAPPING, DIGITAL HACKING OR POINT HACKING (flick-ups)

These are stimulating movements performed with one, two, three or four fingers using the palmar surface. The fingers gently tap the area in rapid succession. Digital hacking allows the fifth finger to strike the area first. Emphasis is placed on lifting the tissues and structures in an upwards manner, towards the therapist who is sitting above the client's head. The moment the fingers have touched the part, they are lifted from it and the movement is repeated. Tapping and hacking are excluded in a relaxed massage.

4. KNUCKLING

The fingers are lightly curled and flexed into the palm of the hand and the dorsal aspect of the middle phalanges and distal interphalangeal joint (last knuckle joint) is used of either one, two, three or four fingers. The movement consists of small circular, rotatory kneadings lifting the tissues in an upward direction. Care over bony points should be taken as the skin tissues could be damaged and it can be uncomfortable on these areas. This manipulation is not included in a relaxed massage.

5. SCISSORING (zig-zag frictions)

Scissoring is another manipulation like frictions, kneading, and knuckling, which requires gentle pressure. These movements are sometimes referred to as petrissage. With scissoring the tissues are gently 'wrung' from side to side by the action of the padded palmar surface of the end digits. The index and middle fingers of both hands are separated as in a V shape and placed in opposition to each other, the middle and index finger of one hand linking into the opposite two. Gentle pressure is applied to the tissues with both sets of fingers towards each other. This causes the structures to be lifted and lightly twisted from side to side. They are then relaxed and the fingers move rhythmically on, covering all the area. Scissoring is only applied to areas where there is an underlying flat surface of bone against which the tissues can be pressed, i.e. the forehead.

6. SHAKING AND VIBRATIONS

These manipulations are coarse or fine trembling-like movements of the hands, fingers or finger tips. The palmar surface is used. They are placed on the area to be treated and lifted and relaxed with rapid succession. They are excellent for promoting relaxation mainly affecting the nerves, and in the facial massage used over the cervical vertebrae and over the exit of the facial nerve.

POINTS TO NOTE IN FACIAL MASSAGE

1. The client must be warm, relaxed and comfortably supported.
2. Atmosphere should be quiet.
3. Talking should be discouraged but if conversation does take place it should be calm and quiet.
4. The client's eyes should be closed.
5. Continuity of massage must be maintained throughout with stroking.
6. When placing the hands on or removing them from the skin, a light but firm touch should be cultivated.
7. A systematic procedure must be followed.
8. The therapist must be comfortably positioned and personal hygiene impeccable. Bad breath, body and tobacco odours must be non-existent.
9. Cleanliness is essential.
10. Nails must be short so that scratching is eliminated, and the hands well cared for and supple.
11. Breathing into the client's face, should be avoided
12. Choice of the right cream is essential to ensure that the hands are able to glide and move smoothly whilst massaging.

STANDARD FACIAL MASSAGE

1. Effleurage and stroking begin the facial massage. Place the hands and fingers'

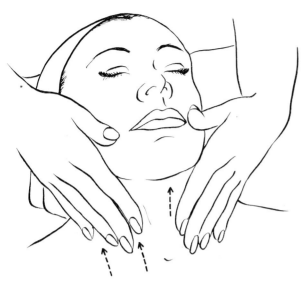

FIGURE 46   Effleurage to the neck

palmar surface along the clavicle, fingers pointing towards the sternum. With a gentle but firm movement draw them outward in the direction of the shoulder, covering most of the area above and below the clavicles. Maintaining contact, turn the hands so that the fingers now point out to the shoulders and slide them inwards along the upper borders of trapezius to the back of the cervical vertebrae, and neck. Once again turn

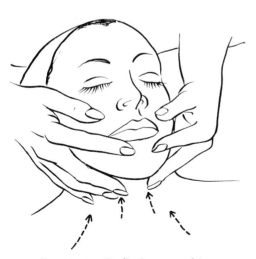

FIGURE 47   Preliminary stroking

the hands so that the finger tips point towards each other and follow the contours of the jawline (*see* Figure 47) forwards and down covering the sides of the throat and neck, to finish with the hands lying across the clavicle. This triangular shaped effleurage is repeated three times.

2. Thumb and finger kneadings are given from the point of the shoulder across the upper borders of the trapezius to the base of the neck, and occiput.

3. Six running vibrations are given at the base of neck along trapezius.

FIGURE 48   Thumb flicking

4. Stroking movements with each hand lifting sterno-mastoid and platysma from the sternum on the left up to the mandible, continue over the facial muscles, and temple across the forehead to the opposite temple. This is repeated to the right side of the face using both hands separately. The return stroke must be light, ensuring that contact is not broken. The contours of the face are strictly adhered to by relaxed smooth, gliding hands, and fingers. These movements are repeated three times.

5. Finger or thumb kneading along the line of the jaw and mandible is now given starting from the centre of the

chin using each hand evenly to either side, and returning to the centre in the same manner.

6. Thumb flicking in an upward flicking manner over the same area using both hands or the thumbs to each is repeated continuously eight times. (*See* Figure 48.)

7. Move with a connecting stroking manipulation and one hand to either side of the face up to the forehead. Starting with both hands on the right side from the centre of the forehead, stroke upwards to the hairline, lifting the tissues from the eyebrows and moving to the right temple in sixteen strokes. (*See* Figure 49.) Eight half moon strokes using the padded finger tips are given from the outside corner of the eyelid to its inner corner. Eight light strokes are given under the eyes, from outside to inside. This is followed by thirty-two stroking movements lifting the brows to the hairline moving across to the left temple. Here the eye movements are repeated and sixteen stroking movements of lifting the brows, back to the centre follow.

FIGURE 50   Scissoring

8. Three strokes circling the eyes outwards from the inner and upper corner is followed by three circles from the inner and lower corner in the opposite direction. Very lightly three circles of finger kneading using the third fingers are given in both directions.

9. Finger or thumb kneadings are next given starting from the centre of the forehead out to the right temple with both hands working together in a zig-zag like manner across the forehead to the left side and back to the centre. All areas of the forehead should be covered with this double manipulation.

10. Scissoring follows on the forehead starting from the right working across the tissues to the left, back to the right and finishes on the left again. (*See* Figure 50.)

11. Scissoring is repeated over each eyebrow.

12. Lifting the mandible and jaw line follows. The fingers of one hand are reinforced by the fingers of the opposite hand and are placed under the chin. The beauty therapist lifts her elbows upwards and lifts the muscles and tissues of the chin and jawline with a firm even pressure.

FIGURE 49   Stroking the forehead

13. Contour Brace follows by anchoring the thumbs of each hand either side under the chin. The fingers and palms of each hand respectively, slide with firm pressure outwards and up over the chin and across the cheeks to the temples, tracing the contours of the face.

14. Full Face Brace is next given. The palms of the hands are placed over the cheeks, the fingers pointing towards and lying over and under the chin. A gentle but firm pull is exerted on the tissues and the hands are moved upwards with a delicate pressure.

15. Point Hacking from the centre of the chin to the right side, across to the left and then back to the centre is the next movement. (*See* Figure 51.)

16. Tapping, a light stimulating movement follows in the same direction.

17. Knuckling is next given using the right hand on the right side supporting the head with the left hand. This movement commences from the centre of the sternum across the pectoral muscles and around the right deltoid, proceeding along the upper borders of trapezius to

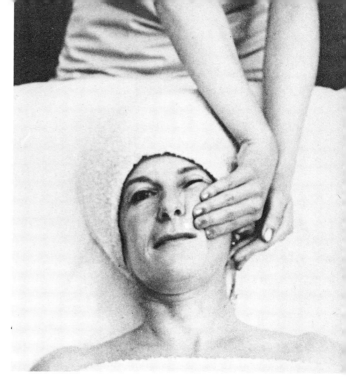

PLATE 6B Lifting

the occiput. It is repeated to the other side, before being given with both hands to the sterno-mastoid muscle from the sternum to the mastoid process behind the ear, and from underneath the chin along to the lower ear. This movement is continued lightly across the cheeks

PLATE 6C Contour brace

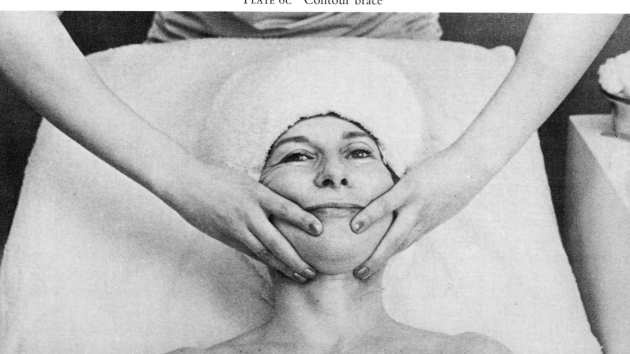

and around the laughter lines of the eyes, across the forehead and generally covering the whole face.

18. Effleurage and stroking movements are given (*a*) from the centre of the forehead out across the temples following the contours of the face under the ears down along the side of the neck to end in the supra clavicular glands. (*b*) from the bridge of the nose outwards across the cheeks to end in the same glands. (*c*) across the chin to end behind the ears. (*d*) the movements as in number 1.

N.B. Effleurage and stroking should be interspersed freely throughout to link up all manipulations, making the massage continuous and fluent.

EFFECTS OF THE FACIAL MOVEMENTS

1. The platysma and sterno-mastoid muscle are lifted. The lymph flow is stimulated as the movement is directed towards the lymphatic glands above the clavicle and in the side of the neck. (Supra clavicular and cervical lymph glands.) It relaxes the client and accustoms her to the touch of the beauty therapist.

FIGURE 51 Tapping, or point hacking

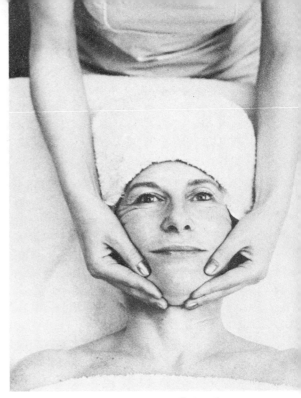

PLATE 6D Full face brace

2. These manipulations relax the trapezius by helping to loosen any tight area of muscle, break down adhesions or tension nodules between the muscles, bones and connective tissue. The circulation is also increased.

3. Stimulates the nerves in the neck and also the facial nerve so that its functions are maintained.

4. This movement counteracts for a short while the action of gravity and lifts the muscles upwards. It is also a soothing relaxing manipulation, following the course of the lymphatic fluid flow to the glands. Alternate stretching and relaxing of the tissues during the movement helps to tone up the skin.

5. Masseter muscle is lifted, and adhesions between the bones and muscles may be removed. It also stimulates the blood to the area rapidly.

6. Orbicularis oris is stimulated and the skin is stimulated and toned by a rapid increase of blood to the area.

7 and 8. The stroking manipulations on the forehead are soothing and relaxing. The frontalis muscle is lifted together with the superior part of the orbicularis oris. All these movements on the forehead and around the eye help to erase the wrinkles, lines, and creases from the skin and muscles.

9. These manipulations are stimulating to the muscles and skin, with a localized increase in the blood supply, which nourishes and feeds the tissues encouraging the granular layer of the skin to regenerate and grow.

10. Loosens the frontalis muscles on the forehead helping to remove the wrinkles. Also has a stimulating effect.

11. Lifts and stimulates the brow area and brings nourishment to the area by way of the blood.

12. The flow of lymph towards the lymph glands in front of the ear is encouraged and waste products will be speedily absorbed. The effect of gravity is counterbalanced, as the tissues are lifted.

13. Masseter is lifted particularly, together with the other facial muscles.

14. Platysma, sterno-mastoid and all the

facial muscles are lifted firmly.

15 and 16. Percussion in this area is given to try and break down fatty tissue, increase the circulation, tone and stimulate the muscles, skin, and nerve endings, and improve the jawline contours.

17. Stimulating to muscles and skin tissues, the circulation is improved and the facial structures are fed, nourished, and toned.

18. All waste products and increased tissue fluids are encouraged to flow towards the lymph glands. The increased blood supply is directed finally away from the head towards the venous flow, so preventing dizziness or headaches which may occur due to the increased circulation to this area.

Hot Towel and Steaming Procedure

Although hot towelling has been superseded by the use of facial steamers, they are still an excellent method of opening the pores and are frequently used, especially for those whose budget does not rise to an electrical steamer.

HOT TOWELS

The towels are soaked in hot water and carefully wrung dry. The beauty therapist must test the heat of them on the inside of her arm before attempting to place them on her client's face. They are then quickly and neatly folded and, providing the client's skin sensation is normal, placed on her face leaving only the nostrils, mouth, and eyes free. Two pads of cotton wool soaked in witch-hazel can be placed on the client's eyes during both the hot towel and steaming process. This serves to protect the eyes and also refreshes and relaxes them. When the towels on the face have cooled after about two to three minutes, they are quickly re-

PLATE 6E   Hot towelling

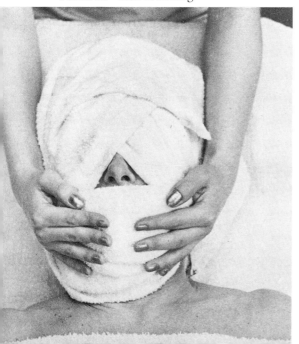

83

placed by fresh ones. Up to ten minutes is allowed for hot towelling treatment. They are then removed wiping away any surplus grease. Eyebrow shaping, or the removal of black and white heads, may follow here.

STEAMING

There are varying kinds of steaming machines available on the market. Some are designed for the production of ionized water vapour for general facial treatments, entailing either steam vapour treatment alone, or combined steam and ozone treatments. The unit comprises a rectangular shaped metal case, the interior of which houses an ultra-violet arc tube, switch mechanisms, and pilot lights. A removable glass vessel accommodates the heating element. The construction is such that the steam vapour produced is directed through a nozzle opening which faces the client. Incorporated in the vapour circuit is the ozone producing device which is extracted from the ultra-violet light, and is superimposed on the steam vapour. The switch panel on the external surface of the casing has two switches, red for the vapour and blue for the ozone. The ozone switch is only brought into action after the steaming has commenced. It is turned off before the infrazone or water vapour unit, which is left running for several minutes afterwards. The water content of the vapour unit must be constantly filled before use to prevent the heating element burning out the machine. Care must be taken to avoid scalding and spitting of the steam.

METHOD OF USE

1. Check that the tank is filled with water. In no circumstances should chemicals be added as this would give rise to the danger of liquid being discharged instead of vapour.

2. Plug in the socket making sure that all wires are carefully out of the client's way and that the unit is standing firmly in position, with the nozzle directed away from the client at this stage.

3. Turn on the red switch so heating the water.

4. When the vapour starts discharging commence production of the ozone by switching on the blue switch. The ultra-violet arc tube should strike and the steam vapour changes into a bluish white cloud.

5. Whilst waiting for the water to heat check that the client is comfortably settled. Soak two pads of cotton wool in witch-hazel and place on the client's eyes. The eyes should be protected and kept closed if witch-hazel pads are not used.

6. Position the apparatus so that the client receives an even distribution of the vapour.

7. The distance between the discharger and the skin depends upon the effect required
    (a) Greasy, pale, faded, and dry skins, 20 centimetres away for 20–30 minutes.
    (b) Average normal skin with fine closed pores, 25 centimetres away for 15–20 minutes.
    (c) Sensitive skin, 31 centimetres away for 10–15 minutes.

It is important not to exceed the stated length of time or distance. Most manufacturers will have a leaflet of precise instructions but much depends upon the beauty therapist's sense of judgement and skill.

EFFECTS OF VAPORIZATIONS

1. Opens the pores and enables the skin to excrete waste products, grime, grease, and dirt which may be clogging them.

2. The ozone from the ultra-violet helps to sterilize and dry out greasy skins.

3. Vaporized only treatments help to stimulate the oil glands and moisturize the skin.

4. The circulation is increased causing the skin to sweat and rid itself of impurities.
5. Increased circulation leaves the skin soft and glowing.
6. Comedos can be expressed more easily after the treatment has been completed. The skin should be wiped gently and either a toner to close the pores, or witch-hazel applied, by means of soaking cotton wool and patting it all over the face to close the pores, or a face pack can next be applied which will close the pores.

Face Masks

I. FOR A NORMAL SKIN (or combination skin if 2 separate packs are not mixed)

Recipe: 1 part light kaolin.
1 part Fuller's earth.
Method: Mix with witch-hazel into a smooth paste, apply, and leave for 15 minutes. Remove with hot towels.

2. FOR A DRY SKIN

Recipe: 1 part light kaolin.
1 part magnesium carbonate.
Method: Mix with rose water, apply, and leave for 10–15 minutes. Remove with warm towels.

3. FOR AN OILY SKIN

Method: Mix witch-hazel and Fuller's earth to a smooth paste. Apply, and leave for approximately 15 minutes. Remove with hot towels.

4. FOR A SENSITIVE SKIN

Recipe: 1 part kaolin.
2 parts magnesium carbonate.
2 parts calamine powder.

Method: Mix with rose water, apply, and leave for approximately 8 minutes. Remove before completely dry with warm towels.

N.B. Put cotton wool over eyes. Remove excess with cotton wool.

KAOLIN FACE PACK

This pack is used for a congested troubled, spotty skin. It is especially beneficial for those suffering from comedos or acne. The effects are to draw the impurities to the surface by increasing the circulation. Greasy skins should be treated with the kaolin mixed with witch-hazel. For dry skins rose water is used, and when treating a normal skin the mixture is bound with water. If too much liquid is used when mixing the kaolin it will be runny and take longer to dry. Too little causes rapid drying. The beauty therapist must use her own judgement when mixing these kind of packs about the precise quantities of materials required.

APPLICATION

1. Prepare client for treatment.
2. Using a spatula mix the pack in a bowl until it is a smooth paste.
3. With a spatula apply the pack to the entire neck and face avoiding only the eye area and lips. Begin the application from the base of the neck, making sure that it is evenly spread, and that the edges do not thin out. If they do, too rapid evaporation of the moisture content may occur, causing a burning sensation and even producing discolouring of the skin.
4. If desired, position the heat lamp parallel to the skin, away from and never directly over the client, to hasten drying. The lamp must be placed at least 60 centimetres away from the area and up to

five minutes only given. Cover eyes with cotton wool soaked with cold water.

5. After 20 minutes when the pack should be completely dry, it is cracked gently with the fingers.

6. Remove the pack with warm dampened cotton wool, or face towels, wiping off all traces thoroughly.

7. Wipe face over with suitable freshener for further treatment.

FULLER'S EARTH PACK

This pack is used to whiten, soften, and smooth the skin. Once again witch-hazel is used for greasy skin, rose water for a dry skin and water for a normal skin.

APPLICATION

As for the kaolin face pack.

SULPHUR FACE PACK

Sulphur has been found to cause blackheads and therefore its use as a face pack should be avoided. However, sulphur has excellent drying qualities and use can be made of this if the sulphur is only applied to actual spots. In this case it would be mixed with witch-hazel. It does not dry out but remains tacky.

APPLICATION

As in the previous kaolin packs and using a spatula for application but removing the pack completely with hot towels.

MUD PACK

This pack is used on all skin types to cleanse and brighten it. It leaves the skin looking fresh, clear, and is particularly beneficial on sallow, sluggish, or grimy looking skin producing a clean healthy glow. It can be used often, at least once a week. (Special muds are used.)

APPLICATION

1. Prepare client by cleansing and massaging face if desired.

2. Using a spatula, mix the mud with a little warm water to make a smooth paste.

3. Apply with a brush over the entire face and neck area, commencing from the neck end, avoiding the eyes and lips.

4. Place cold water pads, or witch-hazel pads to the eyes.

5. Leave for 20–25 minutes.

6. Remove with hot towels, thoroughly.

7. Apply astringent.

8. Proceed with make-up or other treatments.

YEAST PACK

Yeast is used for cleansing the skin, softening and generally improving its appearance. Care must be taken when mixing the ingredients to use only a few drops of the chosen liquid, otherwise it will become too runny and will not remain on the skin. It can be mixed with witch-hazel, rose water, or water according to the skin type.

APPLICATION

As in previous packs but especial attention must be paid to its removal with hot towels, otherwise any small particle of yeast left adhering to the skin could ferment and cause an infection.

Make-up Procedure

There are many varied reasons for applying cosmetics to the face and these have already been discussed. The face should be thought of as a canvas and the beauty therapist the artist at work on it. Consideration should be given to the age, way of life, skin type and general facial structure before application commences. Good and bad features should be noted carefully. The skin and hair colouring will influence the shades of cosmetics chosen. No matter what the problems are, whether of structure or colour they can be easily camouflaged or corrected providing they are recognized in the first place. Therefore the face should be studied critically and truthfully to enable the fullest justice to be done to it. The skin must be scrupulously clean and all hair removed from face and neck before application commences. Never hurry the application of make-up.

LIGHTING

A good light is required which should fall directly onto the face about to be treated, casting no shadows. If the make-up is to be worn during the day then it is essential to use natural daylight. Evening make-up must consider the effects of artificial electric light, but clear white light should only be used whilst making up.

MIRROR

A 'true' mirror must be used and one of a suitable size if the client is to be made-up in front of it. Some mirrors of poor quality can distort the images and must not be used. Using a mirror helps to show the 'picture' of the client from a different angle, especially when the make-up artist works from behind the client's head.

GOLDEN RULE GUIDE FOR MAKE-UP

1. *Greasy skins:* use fluid make-up, non-greasy and astringent based.
2. *Dry skins:* use cream make-up with moisturizer, or moisturized fluid make-up.
3. *Congested skin:* use medicated or specialized make-up.
4. *Sensitive skins:* use non-allergic make-up, cream or fluid, nothing heavy, preferably with a moisturizer.
5. *Normal skins:* use any make-up.
6. *Combination skins:* liquid or fluid make-up but with moisturizer on dry areas.
7. *When* a client requires a make-up treatment the beauty therapist must:
   (*a*) notice what she is wearing, (or going to be wearing).
   (*b*) what make-up she is wearing, if any.
   (*c*) establish the foundation colour exactly, and details of all other colours.
   (*d*) remember that on older clients, light make-up, eyeshadow and blushers, with no mascara on the lower lids should be the rule.

ORDER OF MAKE-UP APPLICATION

1. Cleanse.
2. Moisturizer.
3. Foundation.
4. Highlighters, blushers, shaders, eyeshadow.
5. Powder.
6. Eyeliner.
7. Mascara or eyelash lengthener.
8. Eyebrow pencil.
9. Lipstick.
10. Powder type, rouge, or eyeshadow.

The colour of the skin pigment depends on the light which illuminates it. Natural daylight is composed of all the colours in the electro-magnetic spectrum and illuminate the face very clearly. Day time make-up should be natural and softer looking than evening. Strong electric lighting as found in the theatre is much more intense than ordinary domestic lighting. Make-up colours should therefore be stronger for evening lighting. Artificial white light may be made up of many hues, any one of which may be stronger than the other. If the coloured hues or rays fall onto pigment which is able to reflect them, the colour of that lighting effect is seen. But if it falls onto the pigment which absorbs the rays then the pigment colour is distorted. Sometimes all, or nearly all the colours in the lighting rays are absorbed and the result is almost black. For instance yellow street lighting distorts the pigment colour of the skin and make-up.

If the beauty therapist knows the possible light into which her client will be going she can adjust the make-up colours accordingly.

EFFECTS OF COLOURED LIGHT ON MAKE-UP

Pink makes all colours warmer except blue and green shades which appear slightly greyer. Warm tawny shades should be used for shading the face and blue and green eyeshadow should be avoided. Rose coloured lighting is flattering to nearly all skins.

Red alters all make-up turning yellow into oranges and ruddy tones into browns. Rouges fade into the foundation shades. The foundation shades therefore must be darker in colour with a corresponding change of rouge colour to match.

Straw make-up exposed under this lighting appears warmer, violet eyeshadows may become grey. Adjustment is unnecessary.

Amber turns foundation colour and rouges slightly yellower, and makes blues and greens fractionally greyer. Darker foundation with more pink or red tones should be used, together with a stronger rouge.

Green: all colours are darkened, with the red taking on a deep brownish shade. Lighter shades all round should be used.

Blue has the tendency of turning make-up grey, and any red in the make-up looks purple. Pinky tones should be avoided with rouge kept to a minimum.

Violet: all foundation shades become much pinkier or redder in a violet light, or one in which violet dominates. Yellow turns orange. Brown shades do not alter but rouge appears deeper. Bright green eyeshadow becomes greyer. Red tones in cosmetics should be avoided.

SKIN TONE	FOUNDATION, POWDER, COLOUR
Fair (pink or white)	peachy, honey pink or beige shades.
Medium (rarely pink) neither dark nor light)	peach or beige with pink tint
Dark	tan or olive slightly tinged with pink
High colour (red)	beige or green toned
Oriental	ochre tints with slight pink trace
Suntanned	tan shades with yellow or ochre tinge.

N.B. Powder one shade lighter than foundation.

PROCEDURE OF MAKE-UP APPLICATION

1. Client should be relaxed in a massage chair.
2. The back of the chair must be lowered

sufficiently so that her neck is straight but not stretched.

3. The operator should be sitting comfortably behind the client's head, so that she can stretch her arms and hands to meet in the hollow at the base of the client's throat. (If the chair is too low a strain is thrown on the beauty therapist.)

4. Alternatively the client can be placed in a relaxed, head supported, sitting position with the therapist sitting on her right, slightly to one side and in front of her.

5. Ascertain skin type, and choice of foundation.

6. Choose colour of make-up.

7. Proceed with application.

MAKE-UP PALETTE AND BRUSH

The back of the left hand may be used as a palette on to which the make-up is placed from its container. A wooden spatula can be used for removing small quantities out of jar or pot containers. Tube make-up can be squeezed directly on to the back of the left hand (or vice-versa if the beauty therapist is left handed). Liquid make-up should be used from the palm of the hand. From here she can blend and soften the make-up and apply it to the areas as she wishes with her fingertips. Alternatively a fine brush or dampened make-up sponge may be used combined with fingertip blending.

MOISTURIZER

All skins need a moisturizer of some kind. The choice will depend upon the skin type. The purpose of a moisturizer is:

1. To form a protective film on the skin.

2. To enable cosmetics to be applied more easily.

3. To help make-up last longer.

4. To protect the skin from the elements especially when make-up is not being worn.

5. To try and replace moisture content of the skin.

6. To try and prevent moisture loss from the skin.

7. To form a cushion between the skin and make-up.

PLATE 6F   Applying foundation using the back of the hand as a cosmetic palette

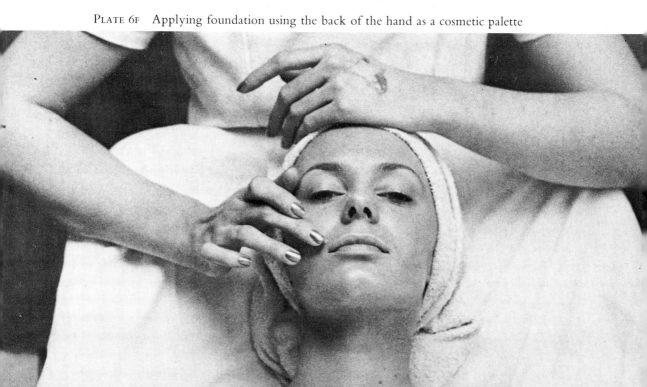

1. Apply moisturizer to back of hand.
2. Using working hand remove sufficient amount with pads of middle and fourth finger, replenishing when necessary.
3. Stroke it gently on to the neck and throat smoothing it upwards to the chin.
4. Apply further moisturizer over the chin, cheeks, nose, eyes and forehead taking care to cover all areas evenly with a thin smooth layer.
5. Wipe surplus off hand and fingers with a paper tissue.

FOUNDATION

The choice of foundation will depend greatly on the skin type, and care must be taken in ascertaining correctly the client's skin category (follow the golden rules). Once this has been decided the correct foundation colouring must be chosen. Although generally speaking the foundation colour is chosen to match or nearly match the skin's natural tone, it need not necessarily match the skin identically. It can be used to complement the natural tone. For instance a sallow skin may need a warmer, pinker tone or a honey colour. On the other hand too pink a foundation on a sallow skin may look incongruous. Electric light tends to distort colour, so a good strong natural light should be used if possible. The foundation is the flat colour background base ready for highlighting and shading.

APPLICATION

1. Apply a small quantity to the back of the non-working hand.
2. Using all the fingertips of the opposite hand or a moistened cosmetic sponge squeezed dry, apply the foundation all over the face, starting from forehead, nose, cheeks, chin, back to the hairline, move to under the eyes over the lids and between the eyebrows.
3. Check the area around the nostrils, in the creases of the chin, over the jawline and finally covering the neck and throat and under the chin.
4. The total effect should be that of a complete and even wash with no hard lines anywhere. It can be applied generously thickly or thinly as desired. Check for patchiness also.

HIGHLIGHTERS, BLUSHERS AND SHADERS

There are few clients who possess perfect contours and features. Highlighters, blushers, and shaders are used to fake certain attributes. The basic shape and structure must be taken into consideration but it is at this stage that the beauty therapist's artistic tendencies come into their own.

Highlighters are paler than the foundations. Up to three shades lighter foundation may be used also. Shaders are darker tones and blushers give warmth and roundness to an area. They may also be used as warm shaders. Highlighters are sometimes white or off white, and even irridescent preparations will accentuate areas, making them more prominent. Shaders up to three times darker than the foundation, or a shadow preparation or shadow blusher, diminish areas and detract attention by fading them away.

Careful shading and highlighting can produce delightful effects. Highlights can be used to erase deep lines or clefts and lift dark shadows beneath the eyes. They are also effective and flattering on the cheek bones and accentuate hollowed temples. Blushers and rouges add warmth and contour to a face. Shading and highlighting can also produce ageing if unskilfully applied. Theatrical make-up uses this technique to age characters.

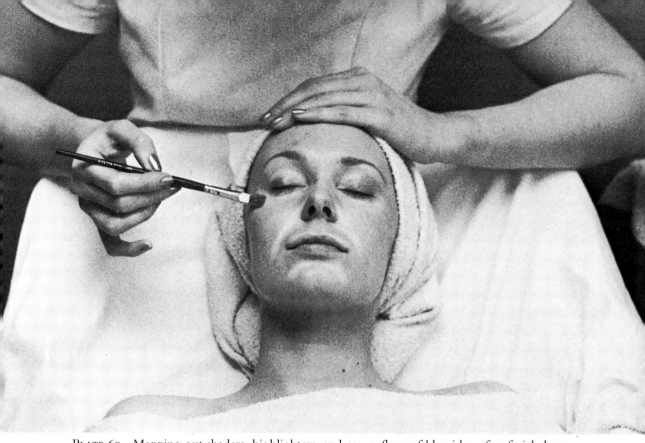

PLATE 6G   Mapping out shaders, highlighters, and camouflage of blemishes after facial cleanse

PLATE 6H   Applying eyeshadows

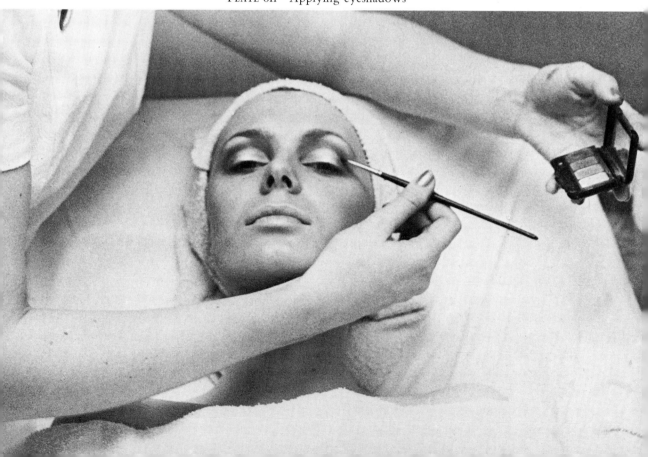

Chin: to make a chin more prominent, highlight it on its tip. Shade it on its tip with darker tone or blusher if chin is too long, or round it if it is too pointed.

Jawbones: apply highlight from below ear forwards towards the chin almost at a right angle to it if jawline recedes. Soften a prominent jawbone with shader or blusher.

Neck and double chin: shade them out if neck is scraggy or double chin is obvious, making them recede.

Nose: to make a nose appear thinner highlight the front part of it and apply a dark shader to the sides. To make a nose appear snub, apply a shader at the base of the lobe between the nostrils and stroke it sharply upwards off its tip. If the nose is too narrow, a thin light straight line should be applied from bridge to prominence to widen it.

PLATE 61   Patting on face powder for a matt finish

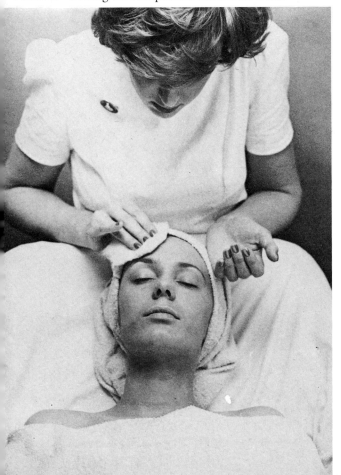

Cheekbones can be given an illusion of curving if the hollows below are shaded. This reduces the effect of a fat face. Hollows can be emphasized by shading below the cheekbones but care must be taken not to produce a haggard effect. When the hollows need to be lifted they should be highlighted. Cheekbones can be highlighted and highlight blushers can be applied. Rouge can be applied along the bone.

Eyebow bones: apply required colour to the prominence of the bone and eyelids according to the effect required. Usually it is highlighted (*see* Chapter 5 for further eye make up details).

APPLICATION

1. Apply the preparation to the back of the hand if necessary.
2. Use one or a combination of finger tips, dampened sponge, or brushes.
3. Blend the shadows after all the mapping out has been completed, and then highlight the areas.
4. Check that both shaders and highlighters are smoothly patted and blended evenly into the base foundation and each other leaving no harsh dividing lines. All edges must be gradually faded into each other.
5. Check that both sides of the face are symmetrical.

POWDER

Loose powder is used to set up the make up. The client can always retouch with compressed powder when necessary. The choice of colour depends upon the foundation used. Generally a powder one shade lighter is used. Translucent powders stop the shine and are ideal, for they do not alter the lighting and shading of the face, and allow the full effect to show through. A darker powder can create a smudgy look.

APPLICATION

1. Dip applicator, cotton wool, or down powder puff into powder.
2. Fluff it onto the surface lightly with a patting action. Stroking or smearing must not be attempted. Attention must be paid to avoid eyes and mouth.
3. Brush off excess lightly.
4. Dampen a piece of cotton wool in water and press it gently over the make-up to set it.

EYELINER

Lines drawn beneath the eyes make them appear smaller and more enclosed. Dark lines will also make the eyes smaller when drawn on the lower lid.

It is wise not to apply eyelines to an elderly client as it is rarely suitable for the skin, or eye types. Eyes become narrower, puffier and more watery with age.

Eyeliners are a point of fashion and consideration must be taken as to whether they are fashionable or not, and also as to whether the client wishes them to be applied.

There are various types of eyeliners:
1. Block.
2. Crayon or pencil (rarely used).
3. Cream.
4. Liquid.
5. Waterproof.
6. Non-allergic.

APPLICATION

1. Dampen brush and coat it from the container.
2. Apply from inner to outer corner of closed upper eyelid, near to the eyelashes in required shape.
3. Apply to lower lid under the eyelashes as closely as possible to the edge.

MASCARA

There are various types:
1. Block.
2. Cream.
3. Spiral brush or comb brush.
4. Waterproof.
5. Lash lengthening (filaments).
6. Non-allergic.
7. Liquid.

Mascara can be applied to all clients. Powder may be applied between the coats to achieve thickness and body. A clean dry mascara brush, or eyelash comb can be used to separate the lashes after application. Mascara is applied to both upper and lower lashes (less pronounced, if at all for the elderly client).

CHOICE OF COLOUR

Dark colours are the rule and black looks effective on blondes.

Hair colour
- Blonde – Any colour.
- Black – Black, navy blue, brownish black.
- Brown – Any dark colour.
- Auburn – Any colour.
- Grey – Grey blue, brownish black.

APPLICATION

1. Brush eyebrows free of any powder.
2. With dampened brush apply colour to the superior surface of the eyelashes first.
3. Coat the under surface of the lashes from inner corner to outer edge.
4. Apply colour to lower lashes.
5. Dust with powder carefully if desired.
6. Apply second coat only to the under surface of upper eyelid lashes.
7. Separate eyelashes if necessary when dry.

N.B. Turn to Chapter 5 for further information on eye make-up and treatments.

93

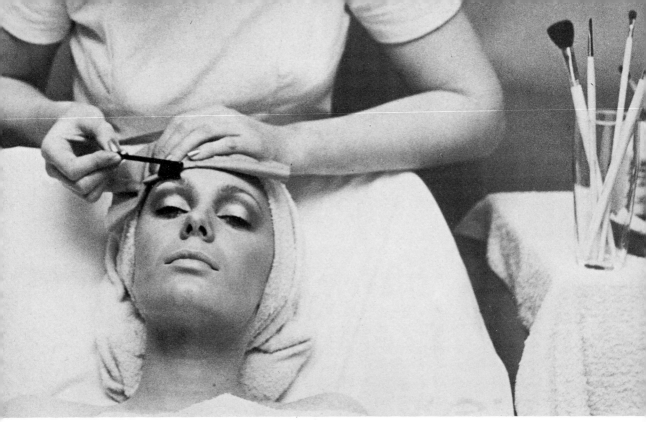

PLATE 6J   Brushing the eyebrows

PLATE 6K   Applying false eyelashes

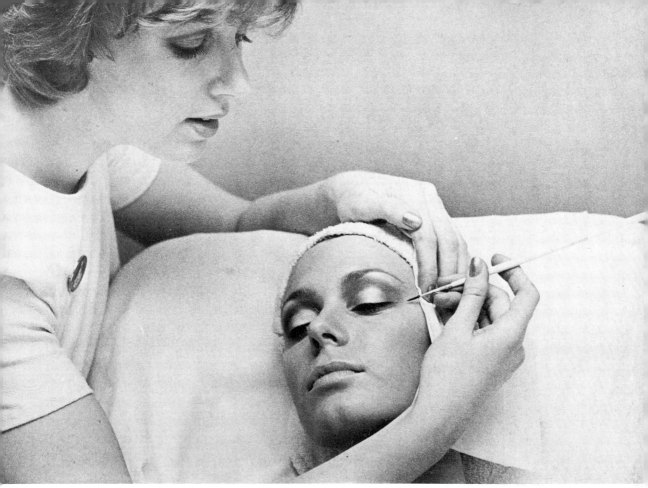

PLATE 6L   Eyeliner application

PLATE 6M   Applying mascara to lower lashes

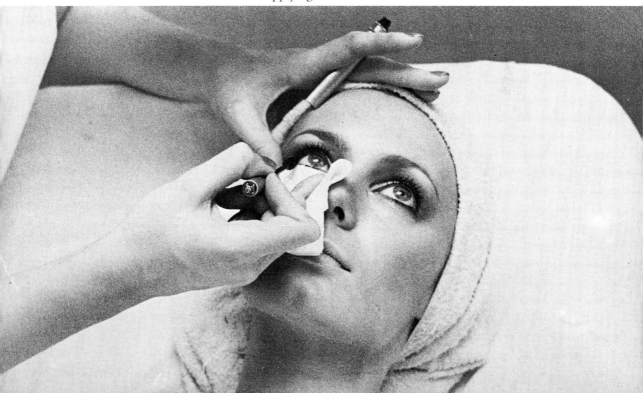

The application of the lipstick is an extremely important part of the complete make-up. It adds balance and contour to the face. An otherwise perfect make-up can be made or marred by the application of the lipstick. Sometimes clients prefer to wear no lipstick at all.

CONSIDERATIONS

1. *Lip, shape and size.* Take into consideration all the lip defects. Dark colours will make lips seem smaller and lighter, bright colours will appear to enlarge them. Two or more shades may be used to alter the shape and achieve the desired result. The lipstick may or may not be applied within or without the natural lipline. Most women look better when the lipstick is applied to the natural shape of the lips.
2. *Colour of the lips* may depend very much on the skin and hair colouring when the shade is chosen. The client's colouring must be related to the lipstick colour. Many people are able to wear several shades but usually there is one which is more flattering than others. 'Blue' lipsticks must never be applied to clients with florid complexions or broken veins. Orange and yellow tone lipstick draw emphasis to sallow and dingy skins. Pale shades should not be applied to clients with poor teeth or a bad skin. Beige lipsticks require strong skin tones. Darker colours will make the lips seem smaller, lighter ones will enlarge the size.

APPLICATION

1. Outline the lips with the lipbrush straight from its container.
2. Fill the lips in with the colour with small strokes.
3. Blot the lips with a tissue, (or powder).

4. Re-apply further lipstick.
5. Apply gloss coat if required.

ROUGE

Powder rouge is applied after the face powder and follows the zygomatic bone, keeping away from the eye region but fading off into the temple, or depending upon the shape of the face, and the effects required.

TREATMENT CONCLUSION

At the conclusion of the treatment remove the hairband from the client's hair checking that there is no make-up visible on the hair line. Help client to dress by handing back her clothes and jewellery and taking away the towels, unwrapping the sheet and blanket and removing the trolley.

Corrective Make-up

BIRTH-MARKS

There are two kinds of birth-marks. One which is cellular and appears as a mole, wart, or small beauty spot. The other is vascular and of the port wine stain variety. Both can be disfiguring and cause much mental anxiety and distress to a greater or lesser degree.

TREATMENT

1. Prepare client. Talk to her about the blemish and explain how easily she can cover up the mark herself at home. The make-up may appear slightly thicker on one side then the other but this is scarcely visible.
2. Examine the skin and note the colour of the mark, and the skin.

3. Match the skin tone as near as possible with the correct erase stick, or blemish concealer cream. There are several excellent products on the market for this purpose in many shades. Some of them are also waterproof, so that the make-up can last safely for the whole day before being removed with special removing cream.
4. Fill in carefully any pit marks on the surface of the stain with cosmetic putty used for fashioning false noses. If there are raised areas try to build up the area gradually so that it appears smooth.
5. Apply concealer cream over the area until it is blotted out starting from the centre and working outwards overlapping the edges onto the normal skin.
6. Continue with normal make-up applying moisturizer only over the unblemished area, but the foundation base over the stains or warts.

SCARS

Scar tissue is depigmented and paler than normal skin. It has no elasticity and nerve supply and is sometimes shiny and stretched looking with puckered edges. In negroes the scar tissue is raised and is called Keloid tissue.

Usually scar tissue can be covered with make-up, using a concealer cream when necessary.

Indented scars can be filled in or smoothed out with special nose putty. It should be applied so that it blends in with the surrounding skin. The colour is then brought up to the shade of the skin with a darker base before applying the general foundation.

Bad pit marks left from acne can also be filled in like this before the make-up is applied in the normal way.

Climate Considerations

HOT HUMID CLIMATE

Aim: to prevent the make-up from running down the skin. Oil based foundations cannot be worn in extreme heat and humidity.
Make-up: ideally a stain type of make-up is best, applied over a moisturizer. Lipsticks and rouges should be of the variety which give colour and definition to the face without fear of their running. The gel type is most suitable.

HOT DRY CLIMATE

Aim: to prevent premature ageing of skin when exposed to dry heat.
Make-up: both a moisturizer and moisturized foundation should be worn. This helps to avoid drying out of the skin and wrinkling due to the heat. A rich nourishing oily cream should be used in treatments. To help prevent the lips from burning, moisturized oily lipsticks should be used.

COLD DRY SUNNY CLIMATES

Aim: to prevent the coldness of the atmosphere and rays of the sun from producing broken veins and a weathered skin.
Make-up: should consist of creams which moisturize and protect the skin, allowing it to tan safely.

COLD SEVERE CLIMATES

Aim: again the skin must be protected from dehydrating and becoming weather beaten and ageing prematurely.
Make-up: rich, heavy protective creams should be used to nourish and protect the skin. Moisturizers, heavy cream foundations and even barrier creams can be applied.

7. Modifications and Special Facial Treatments

Consultation with Client

Before any treatment can be commenced, the client must be given an examination and consultation. The causes of any skin conditions should be identified and when necessary the client should be referred back to her doctor if there are any unrecognizable conditions or any which need medical treatment.

Client's skin is examined as to:

1. Whether it is oily or dry.
2. If the skin is coarse or fine textured.
3. If there are any cracks, lesions, pimples, discolouring, blackheads, and so on.

A course of treatment is then decided upon and a record card is filled in. This should state the name, age, and marital status of the client. Her address and telephone number are required together with that of her doctor. Occupation, children, and any recent illnesses are of importance. All treatments are recorded in detail on this card each time the client attends, together with reactions to the treatment and good and bad effects. Naturally in the case of untoward effects, the treatment is modified or changed. All treatments commence with the preparation of the client and equipment, as stated for a complete facial treatment in Chapter 6.

Usually a facial cleanse precedes all facial treatments although there may be no necessity for a full facial massage.

Skin Types and Treatment

DRY, FLAKY, AND WRINKLED SKINS

PLASTIC AND WAX FACE PACKS

Recipe: 50g Paraffin.
              50g White beeswax.
              25g White petroleum jelly.
              3 drops tincture of benzoin.

Method:

1. Melt all ingredients gently over boiling water and stir together. It should not be too hot. Test on skin before use.
2. Prepare client (cleanse skin, etc.).
3. Apply the pack to the face and neck with a brush and leave for 20 minutes.
4. Crack and remove and immediately apply rose water.
5. Continue and complete facial treatment.

The effect of a wax pack is to stimulate the sebaceous glands thus lubricating and softening the surface of the skin. The sweat glands are stimulated and impurities are removed.

Nutrients are brought to the skin by the increased circulation which removes waste products, consequently improving the condition of the skin.

GELATINE FACE PACK

The shapes are cut out of the gelatine to fit the facial areas. The individual pieces are wetted and dampened until they become soft and pliable. They are then pressed into place on the skin avoiding the eye area, and left for 20 minutes. The gelatine is peeled off quite easily. Apply mild astringent after wards.

N.B. Care must be taken not to stretch the skin when removing the above two masks.

MILK PACK (dry, aged, wrinkled, and under-nourished skin)

Recipe: almond meal and milk.
Method:
1. Prepare client using a simple light massage.
2. Mix almond meal and milk to form a paste.
3. Apply to face between layers of gauze and allow to dry for 20 minutes.
4. Remove the pack.
5. Sponge the face with warm milk.
6. Close the pores with rose water.

EGG YOLK PACK

Water is not used on the skin when this treatment is to be applied.
Recipe: yolk of egg.
6 drops of olive oil.
3 drops of benzoin.
Method:
1. Prepare the client with cleansing and facial massages, removing excess cream before applying the pack.
2. Mix all ingredients together with spatula, frothing thoroughly and apply to neck and face, avoiding eyes and lip area.
3. Leave for maximum of 20 minutes.
4. Remove as much as possible by peeling.
5. Soak cotton wool in almond or olive oil and remove remainder (warm the oil if preferred).
6. Remove excess oil with paper tissues.
7. If required apply make-up without moisturizer or foundation as the skin has absorbed sufficient oil.
Use these masks once a fortnight.

SLUGGISH SKIN

APPEARANCE

Yellow, lifeless, and dull with open pores and a thick epidermis.

CAUSE

Poor circulation and a bad diet. Very often the sudiferous and sebaceous glands are underactive. The client usually has little if any exercise and tends to neglect her skin. (Often older skins are sluggish.)

TREATMENT

The following treatments can be given:
1. High frequency.
2. Infrazone.
3. Massage.
4. Vibrators.
5. Vacuum suction.
6. Facial exercises.
7. Facial–faradic stimulation.
8. Infra-red lamp.
9. Face packs, suiting the skin type.

HOME CARE

Instruct the client to cleanse with a stimulating cleanser and massage with a complexion brush if desired. Face splashing with cold water is beneficial. Toners should be tapped on to the skin. Facial exercises should be practised. Fresh air and general exercising is helpful.

GREASY SKIN FACE PACKS

STRAWBERRIES AND GAUZE

Method: crush and pummel the strawberries and place between the gauze. Apply to the face and leave for 20 minutes. Remove the mask and wipe away excess fluid with witch-hazel. This has a tonic effect on the skin and acts as an astringent, drying out excess oiliness.

WHITE OF EGG AND LEMON JUICE

Method: Beat the white of egg together with the juice of a lemon. Apply it directly to the skin with a spatula. Leave it for 20 minutes, remove all traces with cold towels. Apply astringent.

PLATE 7A   Orange and cucumber juice mask

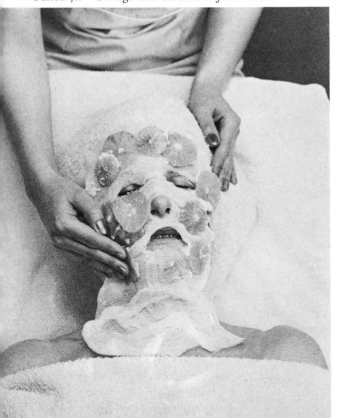

CUCUMBER AND FRESH FRUIT JUICE

This is an astringent toning face pack used on greasy skins.
Method: Pummel the cucumber and mix with orange or lemon juice. Apply between gauze pads and place on the face and neck area omitting the eye area. Remove after 15–20 minutes and wipe off excess moisture with paper tissues.

ASTRINGENT FACE MASKS

Any face mask which incorporates the use of an astringent will be helpful in treating oily skins.

A good astringent should always be used and not one which has a high spirit content as this can be too harsh on the skin. They should be used once a week.

MILK OF MAGNESIA

This can be painted onto the skin and allowed to dry. Removed with warm towels it is exceptionally beneficial for greasy acidic skins.

DRY FRECKLED SKIN

TREATMENT

Clean with cream after the skin has been warmed. A mixture of lanolin and glycerine is applied to the eyelids and immediately underneath the eyes but nowhere else. The remainder of the face is treated with a pack of oatmeal and warmed olive oil applied on strips of gauze. Lemon juice can be added if deeper bleaching is required but this can be drying. Hot towels are placed over the pack to prevent it from cooling.

Remove the cream from the eyes first most carefully with cotton wool soaked in hot water. Before removing the pack, press it carefully onto the face to leave an excess of olive oil. Massage the face with the oil and then cleanse face and apply gentle toner.

FADED WRINKLED SKIN

Faded skin with many wrinkles, sagging muscles and wasted tissue is treated with flabby tissue packs such as the following recipes.

Recipe: Equal parts of camphor and witch-hazel with sufficient oats to make a pack.

Method:

1. Cleanse the face and neck with warm almond oil and proceed as for full facial massage.
2. Apply the contracting pack between cut shapes of gauze and place on the face leaving out the eyes and lips.
3. Leave for 20 minutes.
4. Remove, and cleanse the face with oil.
5. Apply astringent or rose water as required.

Recipe: 4 tablespoons Epsom salts.
1 tablespoon powdered oatmeal or bran.
2 teaspoons powdered sulphur.

Method:

1. Prepare client.
2. Mix ingredients with boiling water to a paste and place between cut out gauze with spatula. Apply as hot as client can bear to neck and face.
3. Leave for 15 minutes; using gentle heat from lamp is necessary to keep the pack hot.
4. It can be repeated immediately, if the tissues are very flabby.
5. Remove the pack and give a brisk toning massage.
6. Wipe carefully with a toner.

Can be given once a week.

OLD SKIN WITH SAGGING CONTOURS

Sagging contours and old skins can be treated with a cucumber rejuvenating mask.

Recipe: White of an egg.
Tablespoon of cucumber juice.
Teaspoon of thick milk cream.
Method: Mix thoroughly then add 20 drops tincture of benzoin and 20 drops of rose water, whisking to a froth. Place between two layers of thin gauze and leave on for 30 minutes. Remove and clean excess away with warm towels. Apply rose water.

Special Face Packs and Masks

THE USE OF OLIVE OIL IN BEAUTY THERAPY

DRY SENSITIVE SKIN

Olive oil can be used for softening and soothing dry, sensitive, and delicate skins. It can be incorporated into face packs or used in facial massage. General body massage often incorporates the use of oil and it is used in treatment of broken and split nails. No beauty salon is complete without a supply of olive oil.

OLIVE OIL AND GROUND ALMONDS

Ingredients: Olive oil warmed, ground almonds, gauze.
Method: Cut double thickness gauze to fit the face areas. Mix the ground almonds and olive oil to a thick paste. Place the mixture between the gauze and apply to the face and neck. Place cold water pads over the eyes (*see* Figure 52). Apply heat lamp for 5 minutes, leave the mask for 20 minutes. Remove the mask and massage the face with

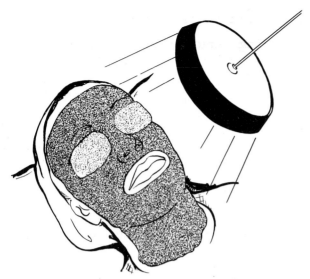

FIGURE 52   Face pack and heat lamp

gauze and oil for 15 minutes. Remove excess oil, after gentle stroking massage, with paper tissues. This treatment is excellent for puffy skin, especially under or over the eyes.

OLIVE OIL, OATMEAL OR BRAN

Method: Mix olive oil oatmeal or bran to a paste, apply to the face between cut out layers of gauze.

Use the heat lamp to warm the mask whilst on the face, for 10 minutes. Remove mask after 15 minutes, massage and remove excess oil with tissues and hot towels, followed by patting with rose water.

any oil left on it. Remove the excess oil with paper tissues and wipe over with rose water. Proceed if required with make-up or other treatments.

OLIVE OIL AND HONEY

Wrinkled, lifeless skin can be treated by the following method.
Ingredients: Equal parts of honey and olive oil are used with gauze.
Method: Cut gauze into simple shapes. Mix honey and warm olive oil until they form a smooth paste. Dip each strip of gauze into the mixture and apply to the face. Apply cold pads to the eyes. Leave the mask for 20 minutes. Remove the gauze, and give gentle upwards stroking manipulations with any excess on the face. Remove surplus with cream, and follow with rose water.

HOT OIL TREATMENTS

Method: Heat the oil as hot as the client can stand. Test that it does not burn on the skin inside the wrist. Cut several face shapes of gauze. Dip the gauze in the oil and apply to the face. Keep applying fresh pieces of

MILK FOR SENSITIVE AND TENDER SKINS

MILK PACK NO. 1

Recipe: almond meal ⎱ mixed to a
    milk ⎰ paste
Method:
1. Prepare the client.
2. Apply pack to face except eye areas, with a spatula.
3. Allow to dry (20 minutes).
4. Remove pack with hot towels.
5. Sponge the face with warm milk.
6. Cleanse with rose water and then moisturize.

Milk has a soothing and softening effect.

MILK PACK NO. 2

Have client prepared as for facial treatment. Apply generous quantity of milk to the face with tapping upward movements of the fingers.

If a dragging of the skin is felt when tapping apply more milk. Use a generous 50 grams of milk. Wipe face with rose water and moisturize.

THE USE OF HONEY IN BEAUTY THERAPY

HONEY

Honey has always been used in rejuvenating treatments. It can be used on any skin type and its purpose is to tone up the muscles therefore improving sagging contours. Quickly and efficiently the blood is brought to the surface. Impurities are lifted out of the skin and dead skin cells are taken away.
Method: Cleanse the face. Apply a thin film of liquid honey over the entire face and neck with a spatula, avoiding the eyes. Proceed to tap the skin firmly in an upward manner with the fingers until the honey thickens. This will take 3–4 minutes. Remove with hot towels unless the skin is very dry in which case use cleansing cream and tissues. This mask should only be given once every two or three weeks and not used on young skin.

PLATE 7B   Face pack for a combination skin

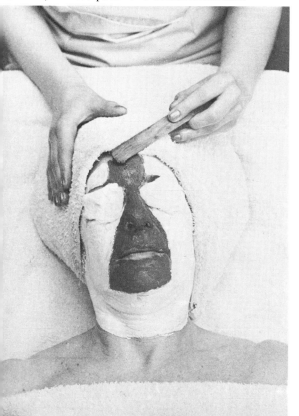

HONEY, LEMON JUICE AND OATMEAL

This pack is suitable for neglected skins, faded complexions, and sagging contours. Only repeated every three weeks, this mask would have adverse effects if used more frequently.
Method: Mix honey, lemon juice, (one lemon) and oatmeal to form a paste. Put between pads of gauze and apply to the face and neck. Leave this for half an hour and press into the skin before removing. This should leave a light film of honey on the face. Proceed as in the previous pack.

HONEY AND LEMON JUICE

This may be used on a client who has fine lines and wrinkles. Age and skin type is of no consideration and it can be used around the eyes. Care must always be taken not to allow any particles to splash into the eyes.
Method: Mix honey and lemon juice partially melted in a pan. Using a fine pastry brush spread the mixture over the entire neck and face. Leave for twenty minutes. Remove with cotton wool soaked in skin tonic for greasy skin, cleansing milk or cream for a dry skin. Use every three weeks.

SKIN CLEANSING PACKS

YEAST PACK

Used for deep cleansing the skin, beautifying, softening and generally improving the appearance of the skin.
The yeast can be mixed with:
water—normal skin.
astringent—greasy skin.
rose water—dry skin.
Only a few drops of the chosen liquid are used with the yeast otherwise it becomes too runny and does not stay on the skin.
Method: apply the yeast to the face, except the eye and lip areas. Leave for 20–25

minutes. Remove with hot towels, taking care to remove every trace.

Pat the skin with appropriate liquid.

MUD PACK (pre-mixed)

Prepared as for yeast pack. Used for an oily or greasy skin, and helps to brighten a sallow skin, it can be painted on with a brush.

GELATINE MASKS

This helps in deep cleansing, drawing out impurities from the skin, and causing it to sweat. It can be used on any skin type other than sensitive skins. The gelatine is cut into strips and run under hot water until slightly tacky when it is immediately placed in position on the face and left for 10 minutes. It is then peeled off easily.

MAGNESIUM FACE PACK

This mask is intended to:
1. Close the pores of the skin.
2. Soften the skin.
3. Smooth the skin.

Recipe: The magnesium is mixed with rose water, witch-hazel, or water according to the skin types.

Method: Add sufficient liquid to the magnesium to mix to a smooth paste. Apply to the face and neck area avoiding eye-area. Leave for 20–25 minutes. Remove the mask with a tepid towel followed by a cold towel. Apply an astringent accordingly. The mask does not need to be completely dry before removal and can be used frequently, e.g. twice a week.

NECK MASKS

These masks should be used with heat.

1. STIMULATING MASK

Recipe: 1 egg white.
$\frac{1}{4}$ teaspoon peppermint essence.
$\frac{1}{4}$ cup purified water.

Method: whip the egg white until stiff then add peppermint and water. Apply to neck area thoroughly and leave for 15 minutes, remove with damp warm towels and apply an astringent.

2. BLEACHING MASK FOR DISCOLOURED NECK

Recipe: 2 tablespoons Fuller's earth
1 teaspoon witch-hazel.
1 teaspoon of liquid from sour milk.
1 pinch of ground cloves.

Method: Mix these ingredients thoroughly and then add one teaspoonful of honey to the mixture (keep adding sour milk liquid if too thick). Leave on the neck for 25 minutes. Cleanse off with milk carefully or wash off with warm water.

3. CLEANSING MASK FOR NECK

Recipe: $\frac{1}{2}$ teaspoon powdered yeast.
1 teaspoon finely ground oatmeal.
Small quantity plain yoghourt.

Method: Mix to a paste with a little yoghourt. Apply to neck (and face, except the eye and lip areas, if desired) and leave for 15 minutes. Wash off thoroughly with warm towels.

4. NOURISHING MASK FOR NECK

Recipe: $\frac{1}{2}$ a ripe avocado pear.
1 teaspoon of honey.

Method: Mix well to a smooth paste. Apply to the neck and face, avoiding the eye area, and leave for 15–20 minutes. Remove with warm towels.

Skin Conditions and Treatment

WHITEHEADS

RECOGNITION AND CAUSE

Sebum which has accumulated in the mouth of the hair follicle and lies underneath the skin appearing as a white spot.

TREATMENT

Thoroughly cleanse the skin as in facial cleanse. With a sterile needle pierce the whitehead sideways, very gently press the sebum out using the sides of the fore-fingers, wrapped in a tissue. Apply an anti-septic or astringent afterwards. Sometimes high frequency and infrazone are used after piercing the whiteheads. Advise the client to pat the skin with tonic night and morning.

OPEN PORES

CAUSES

Extreme weather conditions.
Acne.
Oily skin.

TREATMENT

Face scrubbing with a complexion brush should be given, followed by a thorough rinsing with luke-warm water. Application of various packs and astringents follow (egg, yeast, mud, astringent packs).

HOME CARE

Liquid cleansers should be used followed by astringents and toners.

ACNE

This disorder of the skin is of extreme importance to the beauty therapy worker because it affects a large proportion of teenagers to a greater or lesser degree. In severe cases bad scarring occurs and the client may tend towards a greasy skin with blackhead formation. It is a condition which results in a blockage of the hair follicles and oil glands of the face, neck, chest, and back. The incidence of acne in the sexes is roughly similar. There are varying forms, the most common being called *acne vulgaris*.

APPEARANCE

Raised red papules and lumps occur on the skin which are sometimes filled with pus. The skin is greasy and shiny with enlarged pores. There is usually a large number of blackheads.

NATURAL HISTORY

The first signs and symptoms sometimes appear at the age of eight or nine years with blackhead formation and small papules developing on an increasingly greasy skin. Suddenly at the beginning of puberty the condition may erupt or at the age of fifteen and sixteen when there seems to be further body growth. Milder forms may clear by the age of twenty. More severe cases however, especially in men do not acquiesce until the late twenties arrive. Acne is most prevalent in greasy skins.

CAUSES

1. The idea is now current among derma-tologists that Acne Vulgaris is due to several factors occuring in conjunction with each other :-
   (a) Increased rate of sebum excretion.
   (b) Thickening of the keratin in the pilosebaceous duct or hair follicle leading to a narrowing of the lumen and the formation of open pores and blackheads.

There is very much more keratin in the sebaceous canals of people with acne than those with a greasy skin, and those suffering from severe acne have more keratin than those with mild acne.

(c) The presence of colonies of bacteria in the hair follicle. The normal bacteria found on the skin thrive in the hair follicle of the acne sufferer, and people with severe inflammatory acne have greater quantities of resident organisms than those who only have blackheads of comedoes.

(d) The changes in composition of the sebum due to these bacteria. Due to the increased rate of sebum excretion and the thickened follicles, the sebum cannot reach the surface of the skin, therefore the pores become blocked, resulting in the formation of a plug of sebum which turns black when exposed to the air, producing a blackhead. The normally harmless germs in the hair follicle then produce an enzyme which acts on the sebum creating free fatty acids. These cause the walls of the follicle to flake off, and the sebum then leaks through these weakened walls into the surrounding tissues where it sets up an irritation resulting in a papule or pimple.

(e) Formation of flammatory lesion. The irritation caused as above makes the blood respond by bringing white blood cells to the area to fight the pseudo infection. It is these white blood cells that cause the pus. Sometimes the degree of reaction may not come to the surface but may remain dammed up in the dermis to form a cyst.

(f) It has been proved that the skin itself acts as an endocrine gland. In 1971 Sansone and Reisener showed that the skin from severe acne sufferers is 20 times more active in converting the circulating androgen to the tissue androgen, Dihydrotesterone.

2. *Hereditary:* acne can be hereditary and react to hormonal changes which increase the activity of the sebaceous glands.

The hormones which influence the production of sebum and cell activity in this way are testosterone and progesterone, both male hormones.

3. *Anxiety, stress, tiredness, and emotional strain* can also worsen the condition or be a predisposing factor by upsetting the balance of the hormones in the body. An increase in fatty acids has been found in sebum during periods of stress.

4. *Diet:* chocolate and fats have a detrimental effect on the skin.

5. *Poor hygiene* can lead to secondary infections if the skin is not cleansed properly. Spots must not be picked and the hands of the operator and client should always be clean and washed especially before and after treatment. Scarring can result if the spots are interfered with.

6. *Further lesions* can occur by irritation from hair fringes and friction from clothes.

7. *Violent exercise* increases sweating and causes more blocking of the pores.

8. *Hot humid* climates should be avoided by acne sufferers.

9. *Ultra-Violet Light:* Natural sunlight is known to be beneficial. The spectrum of artificial light is narrower than that of natural sunlight which may explain the comparatively poor response in the treatment of acne to artificial ultra-violet light. The effects of ultra-violet light are as follows:

(a) The initial erythema and subsequent tanning has a camouflaging effect.

(b) Bacteriocidal effects penetrate the lower as well as the upper epidermis.

(c) It increases desquamation.

STAGES OF ACNE

1. *Blackhead:* is the result of the hair orifice being plugged with its over-proteinous secretions.

2. *Papule:* the raised red lump is caused by

the distension and inflammation of the sebaceous gland.

3. *Pustules:* the papule becomes filled with bacteria.
4. *Nodules:* deeper and more painful lesions form.
5. *Inflamed cysts:* in very bad cases of acne are the most conspicuous lesions and can almost resemble boils. These are most frequently found on the back of the neck and back. They are slow to heal and excessively painful.

N.B. It is advisable for clients suffering from acne to seek medical advice before treatment.

TREATMENT FOR ACNE VULGARIS

1. *The client* must be reassured that it is within the province of the beauty therapist to treat acne in its early and mild stages. An explanation of the condition should be made simply, reinforcing the fact that eventually this condition will clear up.
2. *Encourage* the client to wash her skin with soap and water and with the special cleansers available. Advise the client against eating chocolate and fats.
3. *Deep cleanse* the skin with a greaseless cleanser and a complexion brush to remove dirt from the face.
4. *High frequency treatment* using the direct method is of great benefit to acne skins. This would be given before a massage treatment, and a special cream may be used in conjunction with it.
5. *Facial massage* can follow a high frequency treatment using effleurage strokes but no tapotement. This will encourage the flow of lymph and blood to remove and absorb the impurities in the skin. Any excess cream can be removed with hot towels followed by the application of an astringent.
6. *Face steamer apparatus,* used after a

massage for 20–30 minutes, has the effect of opening the pores and drawing out the impurities, combining germicidal and slight desquamation effects also.
Blackhead extraction follows face steaming.
8. *Face pack* which would help to peel off the top layer of skin and close the pores, only after comedo extraction.
9. *Long term oral antibiotics* are now widely used for severe pustular acne. These are usually Tetracyclines and treatment lasts from 2–3 months. These drugs must be taken at least one hour before meals as their absorption is adversely affected by milk. Tetracycline reduces the amount of keratin in the hair follicle and reduces the amount of free fatty acids. Tetracyclines have little effect on blackheads. Benzol Peroxide is a powerful oxidizing agent which has bacteriocidal effects. It is effective in treating inflamed or pustular acne. Retinoic Acid is a Vitamin A jelly. It produces an initial irritation and an increase in lesions after which it causes peeling and thinning of the Stratum Corneum. It is effective in treating blackheads and early inflammatory acne.
10. *Ultra-violet light* to aid skin peeling and healing of the skin.
11. *Skin peeling.*

TREATMENT TO REMOVE COMEDOS AND FOR OILY SKINS

1. Prepare the client as for facial massage.
2. Prepare the steamer (making sure there is sufficient water in it and that the nozzle is turned away from the client, switching down when steaming).
3. Prepare the trolley.
4. Cleanse the client's face with suitable cleanser (liquid, or soapless and non-greasy) for skin type without massage, using either a sponge or complexion brush which have been sterilized. Apply hot towels to remove all traces of lather.

5. Steam the skin 20 centimetres away for 20–30 minutes (on a greasy, pale faded skin) to soften the blackheads.
6. Remove the steamer and blot the skin with paper tissues.
7. Remove the blackheads carefully pressing the extractor over the comedo without damaging the surrounding tissues. When the comedo has been loosened remove it from the surface of the skin with an antiseptic, dampened piece of cotton wool. Between eight and ten blackheads only may be removed in one session of up to 20 minutes duration. Leave any stubborn comedos for another time.
8. Pat each area as the comedo is extracted with antiseptic, never apply make-up after the above treatment for oily skins, until at least 24 hours later. Do not follow the above treatment with massage as this can inflame the tissues and make them sore and excessively oily again. A face pack can be used to close the pores choosing the correct one for the condition and skin type.

N.B. All equipment including cotton wool, gauze, should be sterile and used with with scrubbed hands.

<h2 style="text-align:center">CROW'S FEET</h2>

CAUSES

Expression lines, dry skin, and also due to ageing processes. Can be caused by screwing up the eyes in bright lights or when reading.

TREATMENT

Massage: Gentle movements such as circular finger kneadings and gentle tapping. A light cream only must be used and care must be taken not to drag the tissues.

Facial faradic but without visible contractions.

Face packs, such as egg, or a mild oil pack.

HOME CARE

Advise client to use moisturizer, light creams, and skin fresheners. Rest the eyes as much as possible. Eye exercises.

<h2 style="text-align:center">DOUBLE CHIN</h2>

TREATMENT

1. Skin cleanse.
2. Oil mask, concentrating mainly on the neck area.
3. Facial massage using tapotement movements in the chin area and knuckling.
4. Vacuum suction.

10 minutes total
{ 5. Facial vibrators.
6. Facial faradic, or interferential.

7. Face steamer to remove excess oil.
8. Soak a pad of cotton wool in astringent and tie firmly under the chin with a crêpe bandage.
9. Whilst this is on apply a face tightening pack.
10. Corrective and camouflage make-up.

Requires: Two treatments per week at least, for three weeks.

HOME CARE

1. Instruct client to use a nourishing cream on the neck every night, tapping it on with the fingers.
2. Tell her to use her own chin straps.
3. Throat and neck exercises must be practised regularly.
4. Looking in a mirror to check posture will help reduce double chin formation.
5. Reduce number of pillows.

<h2 style="text-align:center">DROPPED CONTOURS</h2>

RECOGNITION

Drooping sagging skin, double chins, bags under the eyes making it appear as though the flesh and muscles of the face have dropped.

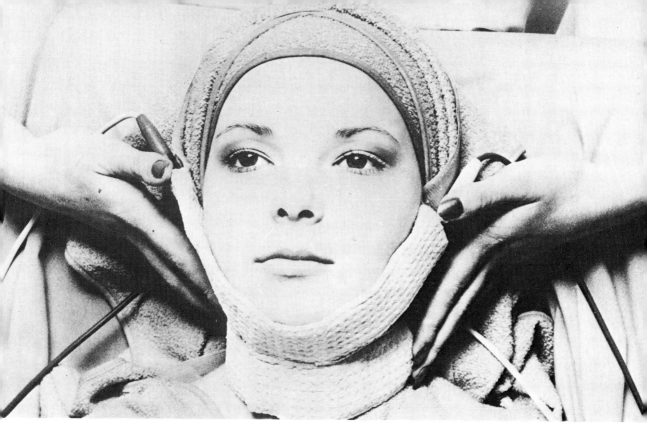

PLATE 7C   Double chin treatment with interferential current

CAUSES

Poor muscle tone, sudden weight loss, age, dragging treatment of the skin, harsh weather conditions, and obesity.

TREATMENT

If the condition is moderate, the following treatments should be given.
1. Facial faradic.
2. Massage.
3. Face packs.
4. Light vibrators.
5. Facial exercises.

HOME CARE

Liberal use of astringents. Gentle upwards massage against gravity, facial exercises.

SKIN EXHAUSTION

RECOGNITION

The skin appears flabby and lacking in body. Lips are pale and dull and eyes are lifeless.

CAUSES

1. Illness, or nervous tension.
2. Diet.
3. Lack of fresh air.
4. Lack of exercise.
5. Lack of sleep.
6. Age.
7. Drugs.
8. The wrong face pack.

The cause must be identified before treatment commences, and stopped if possible. Basically the aim of treatment will be to increase the circulation and stimulate it so that the skin cells will be nourished and waste products removed.

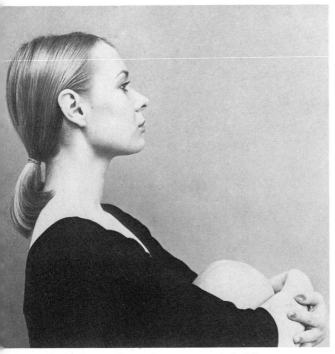

PLATE 7D   Correct posture static holding
for reducing double chins

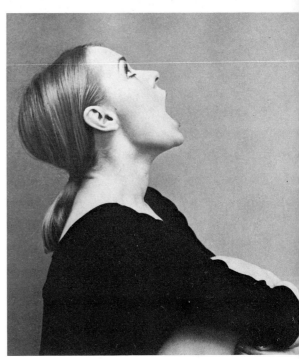

PLATE 7F   Neck backward stretching,
opening mouth, for neck muscles

PLATE 7E   Head forward bending,
strengthening neck muscles

PLATE 7G   Neck backward stretching,
mouth closing, for neck muscles

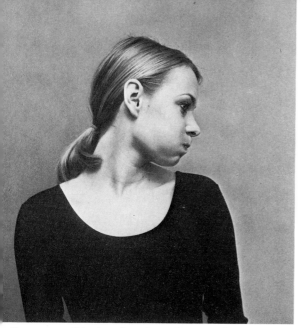

PLATE 7H   Head and neck circling, puffing out cheeks, for sterno-mastoid and facial muscles

TREATMENT

1. Massage.
2. High frequency.
3. Vacuum suction massage.
4. Electrical vibration.
5. Stimulating packs.
6. Steaming.

HOME CARE

Skin tapping with toners and massaging right cream into the skin.

TO IMPROVE CONTOURS AND REDUCE NECKLINE LINES

CHEST, NECK AND THROAT MASSAGE

1. Prepare client as for facial.
2. Wash hands.
3. Smooth necessary amount of cream or lotion over the throat neck and chest area.
4. Stroke with left hand along the left jawline from below the ear down to the side of the neck crossing over the opposite side of the chest out to the point of the shoulder. Draw the hand firmly upwards and in along the upper border of the trapezius muscle, towards the right ear. Still using the left hand, firmly stroke up the right side of the face across the forehead and down the left side of the face to the beginning.
5. Repeat this movement on the opposite side.
6. Repeat to each side twice more.
7. With both hands stroke firmly down the sides of the throat and neck from the jawline and over the sternum. Turn the hands and stroke across the chest outwards to the shoulders.
8. With the thumbs abducted and behind the trapezius, fingers and palms lightly in front, circularly knead this muscle from the shoulders to the cervical vertebrae and base of skull (*see* Figure 53).
9. Gently overlap the fingers and thumbs picking up the neck tissues and vibrate twelve times.
10. Still maintaining contact glide the hands to the front of the neck and make loose fists with them both.
11. Place the middle knuckles at the base of the throat and massage with knuckling movements in the following order.
    a. From the base of the throat outwards and up towards the ear and behind it on the hair line. Give several knuckling movements, following sterno-mastoid muscle (*see* Figure 54). Return to base of throat, still knuckling.
    b. From the base of the throat directly upwards to under the chin and then under the jawline out to the ear, and in continuation to the base of the skull. Return with light stroking, maintaining continuity.
    c. From the base of the throat up to the chin and over the jawline and mandible

111

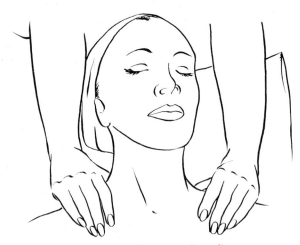

FIGURE 53   Trapezius kneading

towards the lobe of the ear, finishing at the base of the skull.

d. Repeat the above movement but continue up over the expression lines round the nostrils, and then across the cheeks to the ear, up over the temples and muscles on the forehead.

e. Knuckle circling round the eyes from the temples towards the bridge of the nose, over the brow bone and back to the temples and ears.

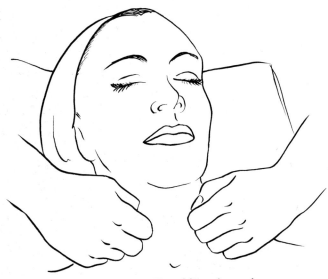

FIGURE 54   Knuckling the neck

f. Repeat 4 and 5 stroking manipulations to complete the treatment.

N.B. Additional knuckling can be given across the chest if required for platysma and the pectoral muscles. This should be done first from the sternum (and base of throat) across the upper chest out towards the shoulders and returning in a triangular manner to the base of the throat ready to commence from (a) as above.

Do not knuckle too deeply. Lift the muscles against the pull of gravity.

12. Wipe away excess grease with hot towels.
13. Tone with astringent or toner and follow with exercises.

FACIAL EXERCISES

CHIN, NECK, AND JAWLINE CONTOUR

1. The head and neck should be rotated first in one direction and then in the other. At the same time the client must huff and puff out the cheeks in a hard blowing action. (Circle only once to the left and once to the right to prevent dizziness. Allow client to rest before two more repeats.)
2. Ask client to look straight ahead and then to pull down the outside corners of her mouth as far as possible in an expression of horror. All the skin across the front of the throat out to the points of the shoulders should tighten and contract. (Platysma muscle over the jawline is toned up including loose skin.) Repeat 10 times.
3. Make double chins disappear by asking the client to stick out her tongue as far as possible. Repeat 10 times.
4. Client must be placed leaning backwards with head supported. Ask her to raise only her head to mid position. Watch for sterno-mastoid muscle to stand out and

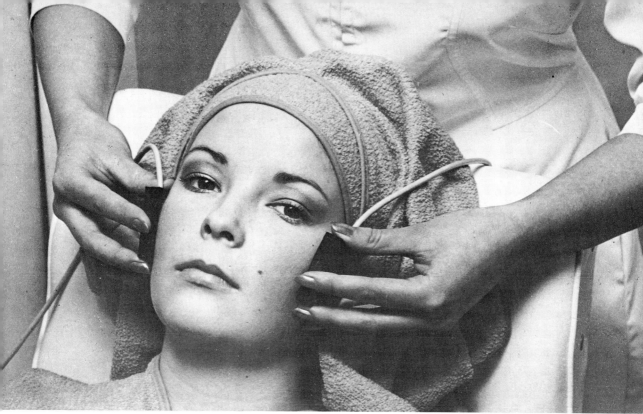

PLATE 7I   Improving the tone of the facial muscles

PLATE 7J   Lymphatic massage

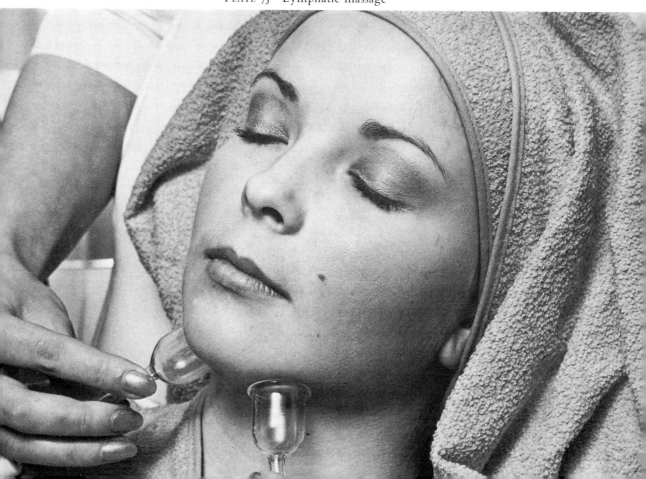

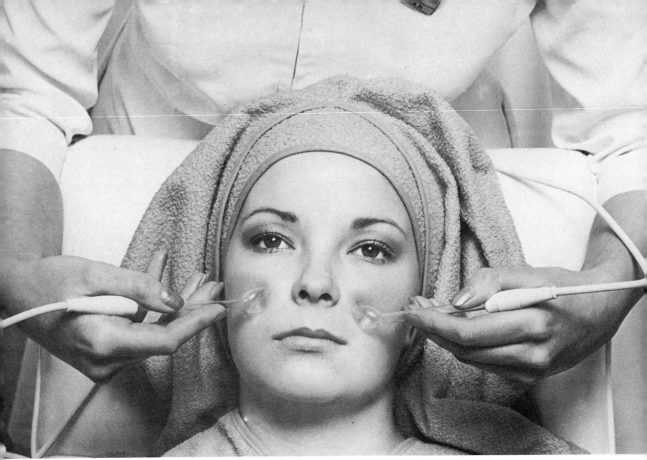

PLATE 7K   Lymphatic massage producing controlled percussion movements

tighten up neck, throat, and chin contours. Repeat 10 times.

5. Relax forehead and furrow lines between the eyes, by asking the client to raise her eyebrows in surprise and tighten the scalp. At the same time she should tilt the head backwards. As she relaxes the muscles, she should straighten her head and look down at the floor, returning to the mid position again in one smooth movement, feeling the tension in the face flowing away.

6. Correct the client's posture, teaching her to stand with head erect and back. Shoulders must be relaxed and down. Tummy pulled in with feet firmly gripping the floor. This does a vast amount of good in reducing sagging contours in this region, and helps to reduce tension in the face, which is often responsible for unnecessary lines and creases.

Explain to the client that the exercises should be done twice daily at home. Write them out for her.

She must not expect any result in less than four weeks. At first she may experience a little muscle stiffness which will gradually wear off, especially if she has massage treatments.

Skin Bleaching

REASONS FOR SKIN BLEACHING

1. Faded tan.
2. Sallow complexion.
3. Sluggish complexion (neck area in older clients).

4. Freckles.
5. Dark hair.
6. Discolouration under and above eyelids.
7. Discolouration above the lip due to nicotine.
8. Pill pigmentation (contraceptive pill).
9. Elbow and knee discolouration and redness.
10. To remove nicotine stains from fingers.

N.B. Bleaching of the skin has little effect. Great care must be taken when bleaching the skin especially around the eye area. The client's skin must be assessed when she enters the salon to determine the strength of bleach to be employed.

METHOD

Cleanse the area thoroughly, removing all excessive grease with either a toner or surgical spirit. Allow this to dry. Apply the bleach to the area and leave for the required length of time. Remove with a damp sponge and apply moisturizer to the area.

RECIPES

1. $\frac{2}{3}$ Egg white $+$ $\frac{1}{3}$ peroxide (strength from 5 volume to 20 volume according to area and skin).
   Make up a small amount and apply to area with a brush leaving for 10–20 minutes. Wash off with warm water, dry area thoroughly and moisturize.
2. Equal parts lemon juice, 20 volume peroxide, and witch-hazel mixed together can also be used to bleach fine hair. Leave for 15–20 minutes, washing off with warm water. As it is drying to the skin, use a moisturizer afterwards.
3. Equal parts lemon juice, glycerine, and rose water combined. This is very mild and can be used around the eye area. Care must be taken not to allow any to stray into the eye. Leave on for 10 minutes and remove carefully.

4. 20 volume peroxide (20 parts) ammonia (1 part) (cosmetic ammonia is 28 per cent solution of ammonia gas dissolved in water) mixed to a paste with Fuller's earth or magnesium carbonate to thicken. This is a strong bleach and can be used on hair. It should be removed after 5 minutes with water and a moisturizer applied.

There are also some excellent ready prepared preparations on the market by Rose Laird and Helena Rubenstein.

CONTRA indications for bleaching

1. Broken skin.
2. Skin infections.
3. Sensitive skins.
4. Dry flaking skins.

High Frequency

This is a rapidly alternating current many thousands of times per second. It is applied by means of glass electrodes of various shapes in keeping with the area treated. The electrodes fit into a ebonite handle which in turn is connected to the apparatus which receives its electricity from the mains supply. The glass electrodes are partial vacuums which allow the current to flow through them. On the apparatus there is an on and off switch with an intensity control switch to decrease or increase the amount of current. Inside the apparatus the component parts making up the electrical circuit are housed. When the current is switched on there is a hissing sound and a violet light floods the glass electrode. It is important to warn the client about the noise as it can be alarming if unexpected. A sparking effect may occur if the electrode is near the clients skin when the apparatus is switched on. Due to the formation of ozone in the air good ventilation is essential when the machine is in use.

The comb: This is used to stimulate the scalp and is helpful in the removal of dandruff. Alopecia is also treated with the use of the comb and high frequency. The comb electrode resembles a hollow glass rake, one end of which fits into the receiving electrical connection on the machine.

The bulb electrode consists of a glass rod, one end of which expands into a bulb. It is used directly on the face and body.

The fulgurator consists of a glass rod, the end of which shapes into a needle. This is used to spark spots or for treatment of naevus.

The metal electrode and saturator is a hollow metal tube which the client holds when a manual massage treatment by the beauty therapist is performed.

1. High frequency has psychological effects.
2. It has a germicidal effect, due to the ozone formation from the sparks.
3. Produces a mild erythema on the skin when used in firm contact and a stronger one when further away from the skin.
4. Nerve endings are stimulated by its sparking effect.
5. The lymphatic and venous blood circulation are improved.
6. Aids desquamation by producing slight skin peeling.
7. If used with massage can relieve muscular fatigue and pain.
8. The pores of the skin dilate and impurities are released.
9. Because there is no polarity or chemical

PLATE 7L   High-frequency treatment with a moisturizer

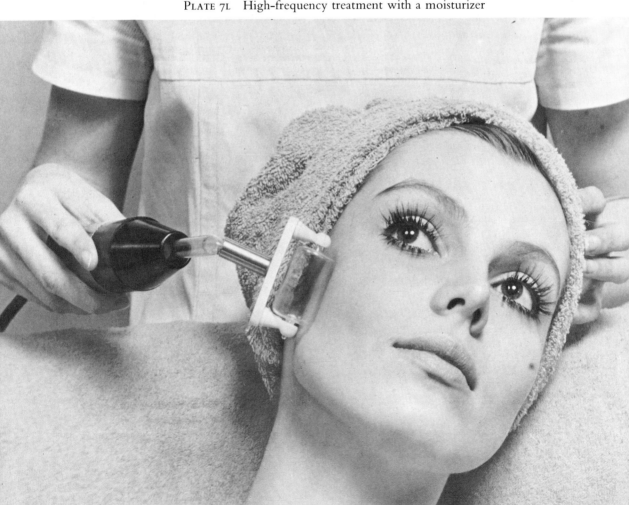

action with this current, chemicals cannot be driven into the skin. There are no harmful effects on the nerves or muscles.

USES FOR HIGH FREQUENCY

1. Skin exhaustion or sluggish circulation.
2. Thread veins or broken capillaries.
3. Helps spots and pimples (oily skin).
4. Dry scaly skin.
5. Tired feet.

CONTRA-INDICATIONS

1. Headaches and migraine.
2. Inflamed areas, puffiness, and swelling of the skin.
3. Pregnancy.
4. High blood pressure.
5. Any heart condition.
6. Any skin diseases or undiagnosed rashes.
7. Cuts and severe bruising.
8. New scar tissue.
9. Sensitive areas and skins, and fear of the treatment.
10. Any medical condition.

PRECAUTIONS NECESSARY

1. Never use high frequency when standing on a wet surface, or in contact with water, near gas or water pipes, or wash basins.
2. Never use metal lagged chairs or allow the client to come into contact with metal on the couch.
3. Ask the client to remove all jewellery and the beauty therapy operator should do likewise.
4. Never use the H.F. current excessively, or beyond the limit of the client's tolerance. Time and strength should be accurately gauged.
5. The electrodes must not be pulled but gently pushed along the surface of the dry skin.

6. Sterilization and cleaning of the electrodes after use must be carried out.
7. Correct voltage and fuse in the plug are essential.
8. General safety precautions when using electric currents and equipment.

METHOD OF USE OF HIGH FREQUENCY

There are two methods used for high frequency in beauty therapy.

1. GLASS APPLICATORS (Direct high frequency)

This method uses the glass applicators on the skin.

1. Prepare the client comfortably on the couch.
2. Proceed to cleanse and tone the skin.
3. Blot dry the face with tissues.
4. Place the facial electrode in the handle (bulb or bulb intensifier).
5. Check the controls are at zero.
6. The beauty therapist must test the H.F. on her own arm first to reassure the client. Switch off the current again.
7. Place the electrode on the client's face and increase the intensity to the point where the client feels a mild tingling sensation (*see* Figure 55).

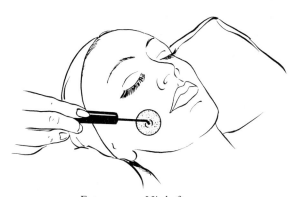

FIGURE 55   High frequency

Move the electrode smoothly and slowly over the face. Its effect should be a mild warmth and erythema reaction for soothing and relaxing. If a more stimulating effect is required, contact with the skin should be light. Circulate the electrode from the neck upwards then from the chin to the lower ear. From the corner of the mouth next towards the middle of the ear level, and from the nostrils to the temples. Remain in contact throughout the treatment. When treating the forehead reduce the intensity of the current for comfort.

If there are any pimples or spots they can be sparked by raising the electrode 1·5 centimetres off the skin, sparking the area between two and three seconds each. On completion of the treatment lower the intensity and then switch off the machine. Remove the electrode from the face.

2. SATURATOR ELECTRODE (Indirect high frequency)

1. Prepare the client as for the direct method.
2. Make sure the skin is dry.
3. Place the saturator electrode in the handle and ask the client to hold it.
4. Place one hand on the face and switch on the current with the other increasing the strength until the client can feel a pleasant tingling sensation.
5. Place the other hand on the face and apply massage omitting any percussion. The hands must remain in contact.
6. When the massage treatment has been completed, keep one hand firmly in contact and turn down the intensity before switching off the machine.
7. Remove the other hand.

N.B. Twice-weekly treatments of up to 10 minutes are advocated for six weeks.

118

High Frequency Treatments in Beauty Therapy

ACNE

Cleanse the face with a greaseless cleanser. Make sure the skin is dry. Use the direct method of H.F. and spark the spots. Apply astringent, and medicated make-up if required.

High frequency increases sebum secretion, so that a prolonged treatment would have adverse effects in the treatment of acne. Some beauty salons use special acne creams with high frequency.

SCALP TREATMENT

INDICATIONS FOR USE

1. Where growth stimulation is required.
2. Where there is a loss of hair, but no visible scalp disorder.
3. Post-natal hair loss.
4. Impending baldness (it will alleviate baldness in senility for perhaps a few months).
5. Alopecia Areata—spot baldness, may be psychological.
6. Tonic when the hair is out of condition.

INDICATIONS AGAINST USE

1. Inflammation.
2. Oedema (puffiness or swelling).
3. Severe headaches (migraine).
4. If there are nervous symptoms.
5. Compound or advanced dandruff.
6. Excess sweating on the scalp and excess greasiness.
7. Where there is any infection.

PRECAUTIONS

1. Hair should be dry, clean, and also free from spiritous solution or sulphur.

2. Never use high frequency when standing on a wet surface or in contact with water, near gas or water pipes or on a metal legged chair.
3. Never use a high frequency current excessively either in strength or in timing.
4. The electrodes must be sterilized after use.
5. Do not give H.F. treatment when wearing jewellery (this also applies to the client as well).
6. Never pull the electrodes through the hair. They must be pushed.
7. Thoroughly brush the hair prior to treatment to ensure there are no tangles.

THE TREATMENT

1. Client preparation and discussion, explaining treatment.
2. Comb out hair tangles.
3. Scalp examination.
4. Insert rake electrode into the holder. Switch on, adjust volume. Place finger on electrode then place firmly on scalp, and work from back of head to front in sweeping upward movements for 2 to 3 minutes. Switch off.
5. Insert bulb electrode on weak growth areas in small rotary movements for 2 to 3 minutes.
6. Place saturator in client's hand, place free hand on scalp, then switch on and proceed to massage with both hands for 2 to 3 minutes. Switch off with one hand on scalp before removing saturator.

N.B. All treatments are limited up to, but never beyond, point of client's tolerance.
Normal use is direct method.
Saturator is indirect method.
Give 6 treatments on average, twice weekly.

THREAD VEINS (or broken veins)

Caused by poor circulation, extreme weather conditions, or a congestion of veins. Cleanse the face and massage lightly over the affected areas using either method. 5 minute periods at a time is sufficient. The course of high frequency treatments once or twice per week for six weeks should improve the condition. Use a make-up of one tone darker than the natural skin and a powder with green tones if the colour is very high.
Treatments of high frequency will benefit the following conditions:
1. Skin exhaustion or sluggish circulation.
2. Spots and pimples.
3. Dry scaly skin.
4. Tired feet.
5. Alopecia.
N.B. Never use high frequency when sulphur products have been used on the face. It is always advisable to apply any medicated or cosmetic preparation to the skin after the treatment, when it will be more receptive.

8. *Removing Unwanted Hair*

What is Superfluous Hair?

Superfluous hair is an excessive amount of hair, more than that which is wanted or needed. Certain areas in the female body which are normally regarded as hairless may develop the formation of hair, such as the breasts, abdomen, legs, and face. This hair has been termed superfluous and is as a rule unwelcome and unwanted. The abnormal growth of hair should not be regarded as a major malfunctioning, but nevertheless develops an unhappy cosmetic problem for most of those who suffer with it. Sometimes this hair may be nothing more than a light down but it may also grow to a heavy disfiguring degree. There is a condition which is called 'hirsutism' which is regarded as a disease due to a tumour affecting the adrenal or ovary glands and for which the only answer is surgery.

Fortunately today many women are able to talk about this problem in much the same way that they will discuss a manicure or a 'hairdo'. But at one time the subject was strictly taboo for it was considered to be shameful and disgusting. Because of this frankness, much of the mental and psychological damage is alleviated. There are still a minority of women however, who suffer so acutely that they completely withdraw from society, feeling bitterly ashamed to be seen with what is commonly thought to be a masculine trait. No honest operator can give a guarantee that any hair removal method is permanent but they can reduce the growth and keep it under control. So many factors are unknown about the growth of the hair itself that such a guarantee is impossible. However, the methods available today for the removal of unwanted hair are excellent and should result in the client's total reassurance. When the therapist has inspired sufficient confidence, the client will hardly ever think about the problem.

Not all sects and races consider body hair to be superfluous in women. Several countries such as France and Italy do not find the sight of hair offensive and hair, especially under the arms and legs is allowed to grow naturally and is not tampered with. The men prefer their women this way. Despite some fierce medical opinion against its removal, hundreds of thousands of women still seek help and advice for this very end (*see* Figure 56). From time immemorial women have been pumacing, rubbing, shaving, and plucking out these superfluous hairs which seemingly offend their femininity.

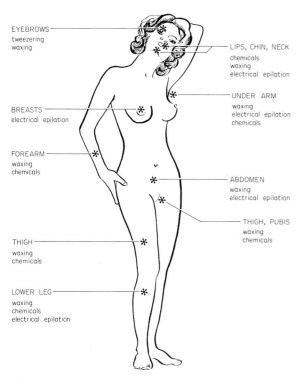

EYEBROWS
tweezering
waxing

LIPS, CHIN, NECK
chemicals
waxing
electrical epilation

UNDER ARM
waxing
electrical epilation
chemicals

BREASTS
electrical epilation

FOREARM
waxing
chemicals

ABDOMEN
waxing
electrical epilation

THIGH, PUBIS
waxing
chemicals

THIGH
waxing
chemicals

LOWER LEG
waxing
chemicals
electrical epilation

FIGURE 56   Areas for removal of superfluous hair

Causes of Superfluous Hair

1. Puberty.
2. Mid-twenties.
3. Menopause.
4. Old age.
5. Exposure to tropical sunlight.
6. Heredity.
7. Shock.
8. Glandular disturbances.
9. Hormonal unbalance.
10. Drugs.
11. Interference with natural down, such as shaving which causes it to thicken and strengthen.

All the above causes relate mainly to endocrine disorders and to excessive secretion of male hormones or insufficient female hormone secretions.

Beauty Therapy Methods for Removal

1. Galvanism.
2. Diathermy.
3. Waxing.
4. Bleaching.
5. Tweezers.
6. Chemicals.

CONTRA-INDICATIONS FOR REMOVAL

1. Swelling (oedema of legs).
2. Tender skin and extra-sensitive skin.
3. Skin diseases.
4. Varicose veins.
5. Unrecognized conditions.
6. Poor circulation.

CLIENT CONSULTATION

Before undergoing treatment for the removal of hair on the face or body it is wise to advise the client to visit her doctor. A thorough examination and consultation with the client is of vital importance before commencing treatment. The beauty therapist should adopt a positive but sympathetic attitude. It is essential to establish certain facts first before ascertaining the degree of help that can be expected from depilation whatever the method. The skin and hair growth should be examined under an illuminated magnifying glass and its condition noted. When the method of removal has been chosen, its technique should be explained. A demonstration of the electric treatment could be shown on the operator's arm, or even tested on the client.

RELEVANT QUESTIONS FOR ALL METHODS

1. How long has the client had the growth?
2. What method of interference if any

121

(i.e. tweezers, razor, depilatory creams) has the client used previously?

3. How often?
4. When was the last time?
5. Any previous electrical treatment?
   (*a*) Where?
   (*b*) How often?
   (*c*) When was the last time?
   (*d*) Was it successful?
6. Method of electrical treatment (observe any scarring).
7. Establish possible cause of growth.
8. Note skin type.

One of the most relevant answers required for electrical treatment will be as to whether the client has previously interfered with the hairs prior to seeking professional advice. If she has tweezered the hairs, permanency of removal is more difficult. This is because the hair root becomes distorted and even twisted and accuracy of direct penetration to its root by the needle is hampered. The hair also thickens from the root which may have split into two. Despite such interference which will hamper the electrical treatments, better and more permanent results can still be accomplished with careful and expert treatment from electrical removal than from any other, especially important to those clients who have facial hair, rather than for those who require legs to be depilated. Electrical depilation on the legs is successful but takes a tediously long time. The effort, expense, and result which cannot be a guaranteed foregone conclusion is not one which is highly recommended by the beauty therapist. Leg waxing is far more satisfactory for the client.

GALVANIC ELECTROLYSIS

This method of hair removal employs the use of direct constant current. It works on the principle of the destruction of cells by a caustic substance known as lye, which forms at the negative electrode. A chemical reaction is produced by this substance which destroys the root of the hair. Malpractice by connecting the needle to the positive pole of the equipment will result in bad scarring, which appears as a carbon deposit under the skin, like a tattoo which is irreversible. Usually galvanic electrolysis is employed by the physiotherapist, medical practitioners, and other specially trained operators. It can be dangerous, painful and produce bad scarring which will pit the skin permanently if used by the inexperienced. Progress is slower with this technique of treatment although it only results in a 10–20 percent regrowth compared with a 70 percent regrowth in diathermy. A maximum of 3 milliamps of current is given, although lower intensities of between 0.5 and 1.0 milliamps are usually sufficient, for a maximum of 16 seconds.

DIATHERMY

This method of hair removal is sometimes called high frequency epilation as a high frequency short wave current is used. The current alternates so rapidly that electrolytic burns cannot form when the needle is inserted. There are no negative or positive electrodes. However a very high current density is employed for a short time, so that the hair root is destroyed by heat. Small scars should not appear but occasionally form due to the burning, but these are less noticeable than those caused by electrolysis. Using this method of treatment, a greater number of hairs can be removed in one sitting. It is also a more tolerable form of treatment for the client and safe in experienced hands. Nevertheless the technique requires the skill and confidence of an experienced operator to be successful. This method of hair removal is frequently used by the beauty therapist and general beauty practitioner.

The apparatus can be battery operated or

used on the mains supply. There are several manufacturers and schools which give their own training. Some apparatus is controlled by a foot pedal leaving both hands free to concentrate on the hair being removed. Others incorporate a press button on the needle holder.

NEEDLES

Steel and platinum needles are used and the fine gauge required depends upon the skin and hair texture of the individual being treated. Platinum needles are used in cases of allergies. All equipment must be thoroughly sterilized and kept sterile for use for every client.

AREAS TO TREAT

Upper and lower lip.
Chin.
Sides of face.
Neck.
Sternum.
Back.
Breasts (but not nipples).
Abdomen.
Arms.
Legs.
Hairlines round scalp with discretion.

AREAS NOT TO TREAT

Eyebrows.
Nostrils.
Ears.
Underarms.
Pubic hair.

PEOPLE NOT TO TREAT

Under 16's.
Bad heart cases.
Diabetics.
Epileptics.
Aged.
Very nervous.
Acnefied skins.

TROLLEY LAYOUT WITH DIATHERMY

1. Surgical spirit.
2. Weak solution of disinfectant, or astringent, TCP.
3. Cleansing milk.
4. Healing lotion or cream.
5. Cotton wool.
6. Tissues.
7. Tweezers.
8. Scissors.
9. Needles.
10. Spare lead.

FACIAL EPILATION

METHOD

1. Prepare client comfortably, supporting her head and back and lying her on a prepared couch.
2. Switch on magnifying glass light flood-lighting the area to be treated.
3. Thoroughly cleanse the area with surgical spirit, or wipe over with witchhazel and dry. Wipe over with antiseptic or TCP.
4. Explain the sensation of the current to be experienced to the client. It is that of a hot pin prick.
5. Place illuminated magnifying glass in position apply sterile needle to hair follicle and gently insert down into the follicle.
6. Take care not to force the needle against any resistance encountered, following the direction of the growth of the hair accurately.
7. When completely satisfied that the needle has penetrated to the root of the hair, and not encountered its shaft, switch on the current (apply all electrical safety precautions first).

8. Turn the intensity control to about number 3. Press the button on the needle holder for up to 2 seconds (or the foot pedal). Release immediately after required length of time. (Most modern epilation units have a thermostat which controls precisely the amount of current to flow to the part so that an overdose of heat can rarely be administered.)

9. Withdraw the needle.

10. Remove the hair with the sterile tweezers, wipe them on a piece of cotton wool and place it in the bowl.

11. Repeat the process. As many as seventy hairs may be removed in one sitting, which should not exceed 20 minutes. Much depends upon the client's tolerance and ability to relax as well as the skill of the operator.

12. After the treatment apply a healing lotion, or cream.

REACTIONS TO NOTE

1. *Normal reaction:* reddening of the skin plus a pinhead spot.

2. *Acidic reaction:* excessive reddening of the skin plus a whitehead formation.

3. *Septic reaction:* very red skin extremely sensitive, with spots.

4. *Pigmentation:* may occur due to a chemical reaction in the skin caused by the excessive heating of the tissues.

5. *Scarring:* may occur if too long a current is passed.

6. *Secondary growth:* may occur if the hair root is not destroyed completely. This is usually much finer hair and can be controlled quickly and more easily. The life cycle of new hair will show after three weeks.

7. *Hypersensitivity:* much tenderness of the area.

8. *Allergic reaction:* swelling of the area and a rash.

AFTER-CARE OF THE SKIN

Advise all clients to refrain from wearing make-up and night creams for 48 hours. A healing lotion or cream can be used every 4 hours.

Acid reactions require hot bathing and healing lotions as often as needed.

Spotty reactions require bathing with TCP and water as hot as the skin can bear, with a healing lotion used afterwards. For the chin or neck a zinc ointment would be beneficial. For the lip a light antiseptic ointment such as Savlon would be helpful.

Instruct the client not to interfere with any new growth, although she may cut the hairs. N.B. This method of treatment can be followed and applied to other areas of the body in the same manner. The current intensity is increased according to client's tolerance, coarseness of hair, toughness and sensitivity of the skin.

Treatments may be repeated every 2 weeks and gradually reduced to monthly visits as the hair diminishes. Some clients need weekly sessions which gradually decrease.

WAXING

HOT WAXING

This method removes the entire hair shaft out of the follicle although the effect is not permanent as the root has not been destroyed, and the hair grows again. With the exception of electrolysis, which is most impractical owing to the number of hairs on the limbs, this method is popularly used in the beauty salons. It can be used on the legs, arms, underarms, lips, and other parts quickly, efficiently, and successfully. The skin remains smooth and in good condition. Rarely do allergies occur. Again it is a service welcomed and given often in the hairdressing salon.

Depilatory wax is made up of beeswax

and resin. Although the two can be purchased separately and mixed in the salon it is wiser to buy the ready mixed blocks, ensuring the correct proportions.

A thermostatically controlled heater is by far the best method of heating the wax. This ensures slow and even heating and when it has reached the required temperature for application it remains static, keeping the wax ready for use at all times.

GENERAL RULES TO FOLLOW FOR ALL TREATMENTS

1. Wash the hands.
2. Cleanse and prepare the area (test sensation).
3. Dry the area.
4. Powder against the growth.
5. Test wax first.
6. Apply against–with–against the growth.
7. Curl up edge of the wax.
8. Press down.
9. Rip off with one stroke.
10. Massage area immediately with firm pressure.

FULL LEG WAXING

Length of hair should be at least half a centimetre in length for the wax to grip.

CONTRA-INDICATIONS

1. Any skin disease.
2. Varicose veins.
3. Extra-sensitive skins which may result in an inflammation or bruising.
4. Aged skin or skin which is too thin or loose. If it is stretched and delicate it will be unable to cope with the stress of further stretching which occurs as the wax is pulled off. It could cause the skin to tear and bleed and even damage the walls of the underlying blood vessels.

PRECAUTIONS NECESSARY

1. Test the skin sensation for hot and cold.
2. Test the wax on the operator first before application. If it is too hot, burning and bruising can occur.
3. Do not allow the wax to harden on the area being treated as it becomes difficult and painful to remove. Re-apply fresh wax over areas which have become brittle, before removal.
4. Do not apply cream before waxing as this prevents adherence of the wax.
5. Keep the edges of the wax strips thick.
6. Keep the wax equipment away from the client.
7. Wear protective clothing such as an overall especially for this purpose.
8. Use the appropriate wax for each area e.g. lip wax only on the lips or chin.
9. Overlap the treated areas at each end to ensure that no area of hair growth is missed.
10. Thoroughly clean wax.
11. Follow the manufacturers instructions on different products of wax.

Four to six weeks is recommended between treatments.

METHOD

1. Prepare the wax by heating to required temperature.
2. Prepare the trolley laying it with cotton wool, soap and water solution, waste bowl, cream, powder, antiseptic.
3. Prepare couch by covering with plastic sheet and greaseproof paper.
4. Prepare the client who should be relaxed on the couch. All clothes should be removed from the area or protected with towels. An explanation of the waxing procedure should be given to the client.
5. Wash the legs with the soap solution and allow it to dry.

6. Wipe them over with diluted solution of disinfectant and allow it to dry.

7. Dust the legs with dry powder against the hair growth so that the hairs will stand up and grip the wax.

8. Test the wax on the front of the wrist using a 4 centimetre width brush, to make sure that it is not too hot.

9. Apply the wax in two 15-millimetre strips on the anterior surface of the lower leg from the ankle to the knee.
   (a) first brush stroke, against the hair growth.
   (b) second brush stroke, with the hair growth.
   (c) third brush stroke, against the growth. Keep the edges of the wax strips thick, do not allow them to thin out.

10. *Repeat* the two strips with three brush strokes each on the other leg in the same manner whilst waiting for the wax to dry out.

11. Press all the wax down with the knuckles preventing it from hardening and setting. This also helps it to grip the hairs. (*See* Figure 57.)

FIGURE 57   Leg waxing

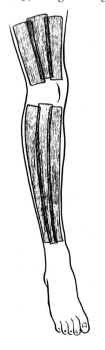

12. Remove the first strips by lifting or flicking up the bottom edges of the wax strips and ripping it off quickly in one complete strip against the growth of the hair. Immediately the wax is removed press treated area with the hand and firmly stroke it along the dewaxed area. This reduces the discomfort if any, by acting as a counter-irritant, to the sensitivity of having the superficial skin cells and hair being removed.

13. Remove the wax from the other leg in the same manner.

14. Apply the wax to new areas at the required temperature on the lateral and medial aspects of both lower legs. Be careful to apply the wax against the direction of growth which may vary. Some hair growth is finer than others and may lie in the same direction. Those hairs which grow in different directions and is coarser may take longer to treat.

15. When all sides of the anterior aspect of the lower leg have been treated, proceed to treating the hairs round the knee and thigh, in a similar manner. First treat the central aspect and then the medial and lateral aspects of the thigh, on both legs.

16. When the whole of this surface is completely finished gently apply some massage cream to the skin to ease any tightness in the skin which may be experienced. It also helps to prevent any loose bits of wax adhering to it. Replace the sheet of greaseproof paper with a clean sheet under the freshly waxed legs to avoid the excess wax clinging to them.

17. Wax the posterior aspects of the legs in a similar manner to the anterior, starting from the back of the ankle to the back of the knee joint in long strips. Proceed to the thighs and when all wax has been removed apply massage cream.

18. If required, powder the legs before the client dresses.

Stubborn hairs may require a second waxing. It may not be advisable to re-wax the back of the knee joint or inner side of the calf, as these areas are tender. Sometimes the reason that some hairs resist removal is because the wax may not be hot enough so that when it contracts on cooling they are not gripped firmly by the wax. Hairs which do not adhere to the wax can very often be easily lifted out with tweezers or quite quickly with the fingers. The client should not be allowed to leave with any hairs which should have been removed. However, there are some stubborn hairs which seem to elude the most careful and skilful beauty therapist. These generally lie just below the surface of the skin, are usually quite loose and wash off in the bath.

Time for a complete leg wax by an experienced operator should take 45 minutes. *Comfort* during the dewaxing process is ensured by using wax which is not new. Any client who has been treated with new wax will experience great discomfort. New wax should be added to the old wax, or heated through several times before use on the client. After it has been heated and used several times it thickens. Thin wax is uncomfortable and can even be painful when applied, for it loses its heat quickly and becomes brittle. Normally discomfort and pain are only caused through poor technique. *Cleansing* the wax is most important after treatment. It should be thoroughly heated to a high temperature and then sieved through a fine mesh sieve so that the hairs are strained out of the wax. Placing the brushes in boiling water will help to remove the wax after which they should be wiped and stored neatly away. All drips of wax should be cleaned off the equipment and adequate protection for the sheets and blankets is essential. The equipment must be kept clean and in good working order with all the electrical parts adequately maintained. When not being used the heating element must be turned to zero before being unplugged, if using a thermostatically controlled wax heater.

AFTER-EFFECTS OF WAXING

1. The skin may be a little sensitive to hot and cold as the top layer has been removed with the hairs. Care should be taken by the client at first when bathing.
2. The use of depilatories or shaving the legs will counteract the benefits of waxing. It is often said that constant waxing of an area will make the hair growth finer and sparser. The fineness is because, as the hair has been removed from its root, it will regrow with a fine tapering point unlike the stubbly growth which results from shaving. As for the sparseness there are always a few hairs which quite normally will not reproduce themselves when a large area has been epilated. However as the non-reproduction of hair follicles increases with age this would have happened in any case. It must be remembered that waxing is in effect mass plucking of an area and as such the action of it may distort the follicles making electrolysis at a later date more difficult.

OTHER AREAS FOR TREATMENT

Follow the procedure and method used for leg waxing in the following treatments.

Bikini wax: the same technique is applied as for leg waxing but the client should wear a pair of brief plastic or disposable pants which will indicate the line of removal.
Precaution: it is not advisable to repeat the waxing in the groin and femoral triangle, if

the hair is not removed the first time, as the skin is very tender in this region.
Treatment: every six weeks.

Abdominal wax: apply one strip of wax if possible over the area required. Usually it extends from the centre of the pubic line to the navel.
Treatment: six to eight weeks.

Axillary wax: the skin in the axilla is extremely delicate and a danger of infection may occur here causing the glands to swell. Small strips are used starting at the outer edges of the armpit, working inwards to the central region. The skin must be kept taut. Treatment should never be given in cases of mastitis.
Treatment: six to eight weeks.

Lip wax: use small strips of wax and follow the procedure as for leg waxing. The skin must be kept very taut by stretching it and pulling the wax back along the skin, quickly placing the hand over the area with firm pressure. The area must be thoroughly cleansed before treatment.

FIGURE 58   Lip waxing

Chin waxing: small strips must be used again over the chin region. Remove all wax when finished and do not re-wax the lips or chin straight away.
Treatment: four to six weeks for lip and chin wax; sometimes it is necessary to give fortnightly treatments.

Eyebrow wax: use small strips of wax and apply beneath the eyebrow, as shown in Figure 59. The procedure is the same as for other wax facial treatments.

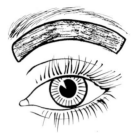

FIGURE 59   Eyebrow waxing

Arm wax: if possible persuade the client to bleach this region as the new growth of hair looks ugly and really shows. For those clients who insist follow the same procedure as for leg waxing.

BLEACH

20 volumes of peroxide, cosmetic ammonia, Fuller's earth.
Mix the Fuller's earth to a stiff paste with *five* parts peroxide and one part ammonia.
Apply to area with a pad of wet cotton wool and allow to dry and crumble.
Remove thoroughly with wet cotton wool and apply a skin food, massage, or hand cream. Bleach as often as required until the degree of fairness is obtained.

TWEEZERS

This method is most favoured by the beauty therapist for eyebrow shaping, and can be used on the other areas. It is simple, quick, and effective. If performed correctly it is also painless, but not permanent. Fine hairs will grow stronger and coarser after plucking so that it is not really recommended for use on other facial or body hair. Tweezers must always have been sterilized before use and immediately prior to use, wiped over with surgical spirit, or pure alcohol. There are three kinds:

1. *Automatic tweezers:* usually have a spring loaded catch between the two arms which, immediately the grip is released, spring open again after plucking out the hair. They have oblique ends as a rule.
2. *Electric tweezers.*
3. *Hand manipulated tweezers:* may have oblique, straight, or rounded ends. When selecting the tweezers it is a matter of personal choice as to which type is preferred for use. It is important, however, to see that the tweezer grips the hair firmly and accurately.

PREPARATION AND TREATMENT OF THE CLIENT

The client is prepared as for a facial massage. Her hair is protected and caught back off her face if facial hair is being removed. If the hair is on the body, the part to be treated is exposed only, but it is in the client's interest to remove her clothing so that it will not be crumpled whilst lying down. The skin must be clean and dry. It can be wiped over with alcohol or surgical spirit before treatment. Some therapists prefer to use an antiseptic as a safety precaution. The skin under the hand must be held taut before the hair is plucked out in the direction in which it grows. A skin tonic may be used after the treatment to close the pores.

N.B. All hair removal, with the exception of waxing, should be performed with the aid of an illuminated magnifying glass.

CHEMICAL DEPILATORIES

May also be used in the beauty salon. These would be an excellent alternative treatment to give in cases of varicose veins when leg waxing would be contra-indicated. It is important to test to see that no allergic condition is present when using chemical depilatories. The areas are cleansed and dried. The depilatory is smoothed on with a spatula and left for 7 minutes, depending upon the hair. It is then gently removed with a wooden spatula, taking care not to scrape the skin. The areas are rinsed with cold water and patted dry. Soap or detergents should not be used for several hours afterwards.

COLD WAX

Is yet another method favoured for use by some salons. Here the same procedure follows as for hot wax, but the wax is removed by pressing gauze strips into it and pulling off the skin. It is simple and safe.

9. *More Beauty Treatments*

Dry Heat

THE SAUNA

The sauna is thought of as being dry heat, although it is not completely dry because there is a very low humidity caused when water is added to the coals. Sauna baths are essentially pine-wooded rooms in which benches of varying heights are available on which to lie or sit. There may be several rooms of graded temperatures for the client's use, as the temperatures can exceed 40° Centigrade. The higher the client sits in the room the hotter it is. If the air feels too dry, water can be ladled on to the coals or special stones which heat the room to provide a little humidity, and more heat.

During the course of the sauna bath, the client may keep going out for cold showers or a cold plunge into a tepid pool. For those who are really hardy some sauna establishments add blocks of ice to the pool. In Norway and Denmark a plunge into the snow or an icy lake is the rule after a sauna. The contrast of temperature is not immediately experienced so there is no shock to the system. Swedish massage followed by relaxation and even sleep, complete the sauna bath routine.

DRY HEAT BATHS

Dry heat baths are often employed on health farms and hydros. These take many forms from radiant heat tunnels, to blankets, electrically heated. The client is covered up to the neck and the heat gradually becomes hotter and hotter. Again after the prescribed time which should range from 15 minutes the first time to a maximum of 30 minutes, the client is cooled with a cold shower and then a massage follows.

Steam Heat

Steam is a wet heat with a very high humidity.

TURKISH BATHS

These involve the strongest use of steam. There are several rooms each one of which varies in heat, i.e. some hotter than others. In the baths are slatted benches on which the clients can lie or sit. They are laddered in height and if preferred the client can climb higher where it will be hotter. Usually the client sits in the cooler rooms before entering

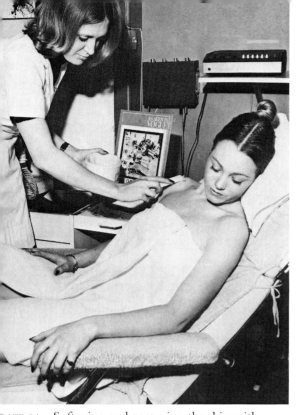

PLATE 9A Softening and preparing the skin with a rose and jasmine cream prior to the sauna

PLATE 9C Sprinkling the perfumed water on to the coals

PLATE 9B Adding an essential oil to the water inside the sauna

PLATE 9D A refreshing herbal body lotion being sprayed on the skin after the sauna and shower

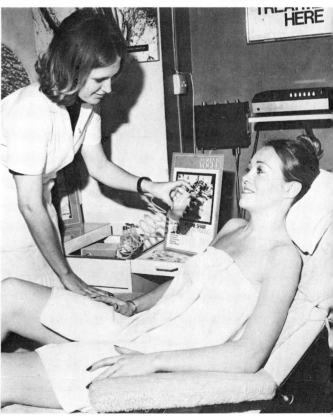

the hottest in order to gradually acclimatize her body to the high temperatures, and then the procedure can be reversed. Many clients prefer to plunge into a cold or tepid bath after the turkish bath or scrub themselves down under a cooling shower, before having a massage. Turkish baths are relaxing, they soften the body tissues and are helpful for those who are weight reducing, and they stimulate the blood, sweat, and sebum. It is essential to have facilities available for the clients to relax and even sleep in whilst cooling off, after any form of heat treatment especially general body treatments.

STEAM BATHS

A steam bath is more popularly used in the beauty salon and is often in the form of a fibre glass cabinet inside which there is a wooden slatted adjustable seat and a hole for the client's head to protrude.

On the floor of the cabinet and underneath the seat is a metal water box which contains an electric element. The element heats the water producing steam, rather like an electric kettle. All the controls are on the outside of the cabinet. These control the heating element and register the temperature of the bath.

CONTRA-INDICATIONS

Contra-indications for all general heat treatments are:
1. Headaches, dizziness and nausea.
2. Heart diseases or blood pressure variations.
3. Any skin disease.
4. Medical conditions (including circulatory diseases and diabetes).
5. Claustrophobia or nervous complaints.
6. Pregnancy.
7. Verrucas and athletes foot.

8. High temperatures. Ideally the temperature of the client should be taken before and after the treatment.

EFFECTS OF STEAM BATHS

1. Opens the pores and stimulates sudiferous and sebaceous glands, removes impurities, and softens the skin.
2. Causes hyperaemia.
3. Eliminates fluid through sweating.
4. Softens body tissue making it more receptive to massage.
5. It is very relaxing.
6. Clients enjoy this treatment, (psychological effects good).

A steam bath can be used as a preliminary treatment for the following:
1. Manual massage.
2. Slimming treatments using electrical equipment.
3. Skin conditioning treatments.
4. And after exercises.

METHOD OF USE

1. Prepare client asking her to undress completely.
2. Place a towel on the floor and seat of the steam bath, check that the water box is full.
3. Switch on the machine and turn up the heater control.
4. Ask client to sit in the steam bath, when it is steaming.
5. Warn the client that the heat must not be more than she can comfortably stand.
6. Tuck a towel round her neck and the opening of the bath.
7. Keep the client in sight asking periodically if she is comfortable. For the first treatment leave her only for 10 minutes. The subsequent treatments can be increased up to 25 minutes. The client's

reaction must be watched at all times.

8. Switch off, open cabinet, and hand client a bath robe, or towel.
9. Show her to the couch and allow her to rest until completely cool before leaving the salon.

N.B. Prolonged steamings can cause weakness and faintness.

After use the steam bath must be cleaned and wiped with a disinfectant or an antiseptic immediately. Fresh towels are always used for each client.

Duration of treatment: twice weekly for 6–8 weeks than a period of rest before recommencement.

Wax Baths

Paraffin wax is used when giving wax baths either to the body or hands and feet. There are several methods which can be employed. Basically the wax is heated to melting point and to a temperature which can be comfortably tolerated by the client. There are excellent pieces of apparatus on the market all of which make the administering of this pleasant treatment more efficient. Different sized metal baths in which the wax is melted and electrically stirred, sit inside an outer casing which contains a heating element and water. A control switch is found on the side of the equipment together with a thermostat for regulating the heat. When the wax is heated to the desired temperature and all the wax has been melted the treatment can begin.

CONTRA-INDICATIONS

1. Skin diseases and open cuts and wounds.
2. Medical conditions, although arthritic conditions are greatly benefited by wax baths (permission from doctor).

USES IN BEAUTY THERAPY

1. *Deep Cleansing* caused by excess sweating so ridding the skin of impurities and toxic products.
2. *Weight reduction* by excretion of fluid via the skin. Used for slimming treatments in health farms and beauty salons.
3. *Relaxation* is induced by its warm and soothing effect on the nerve endings of the body.
4. *Suppleness and softness* of the skin are improved because of the increased circulation, easing hard calloused skin.
5. *Pre-beauty* treatment, e.g. manicure, massage.
6. *Eases aches* and pains, refreshes tired feet and parts.

TECHNIQUE

For all treatments with wax it is essential to have ready greaseproof paper, small and large blankets and some polystyrene sheeting. The parts are dipped into or covered with the wax. It is allowed to dull and four more coats are applied. Hands and feet are wrapped in a protective covering and then a blanket for 20 minutes. Body waxing treatments are used in conjunction with slimming treatments. Here the client is painted with the wax and covered for 30 minutes.

FACE WAX

Paraffin wax is used and painted on to the face with a fine brush of width 2 centimetres. This may be given during facial treatments as a wax mask. It is easily applied and simply removed, allowing the skin to excrete waste products, dirt, and grime which are deeply embedded. After removal, the pores must be closed again with skin tonic or an astringent.

Faradism

The faradic current is an interrupted, surged current used in beauty therapy, to produce muscle contractions by electrical stimulation. The surging, or gradual contracting of the muscle, the length of the contraction period of the muscle and its relaxation period, can be regulated together with the current intensity, by the beauty therapist. Control switches and dials are fitted to the outside casing of all the available equipment, connecting to the component parts inside making up the apparatus. These must be carefully studied and understood before use. Regulation and adjustment of the patterns and currents depends upon the client's tolerance. Basically, it is the muscle contraction which is of prime importance in this treatment. In healthy muscles with unimpaired nerve supply, best and most efficient contractions are achieved by the faradic currents, although in some equipment the galvanic current has been superimposed.

DANGERS

There are no electrical dangers as such when using the faradic current on its own, or in a pure faradic piece of equipment. Only the normal electrical precautions should be taken. Discomfort causing shock, could occur with poor technique. When the sinusiodal and galvanic currents are incorporated in the same apparatus as the faradic current, extra care is necessary. The manufacturers' instructions should be studied carefully and followed implicitly. Usually the manufacturers will arrange for a demonstration of the machine to be seen. Care must always be taken to see that all control switches are at zero, and if a current selector switch is in operation, that it is at the right position before turning on the main inflow of current. Other general electrical precautions should be closely adhered to. Always turn the currents down slowly before switching off or removing the pads from the part. Turn the intensity up slowly also when increasing the current. As with all treatments, especially electrical, test the current first, explaining sensation and any noise to the client to prevent unnecessary fears.

EFFECTS AND USES

Faradism produces a pins and needles sensation in the skin which gives rise to contractions in the muscles. Its main use is in stimulating muscle contractions, and is the most tolerated of all currents for this purpose. *Skin exhaustion* and tiredness is lessened with a tonic treatment of faradic current using the labile method.

Swollen ankles can be reduced (providing there is no medical cause).

Arches of the feet can be restored and maintained with faradism.

Flabby tissues: contractions of main muscle groups over fatty areas help to reduce the girth. If sandbags or weights are placed over the parts more energy is used and a greater reduction may be achieved. The muscles having been exercised and toned up, become firmer and slimmer. The outline and shape of the body is improved. Taking up its flab and slackness with toned muscles, the tissues of the skin appear firmer. This is also due to the increased circulation to the flabby tissues.

Sluggish loose skin: Stimulation of the skin and sensory nerve endings in the skin help to tone it up and make it appear tauter and firmer. Sagging contours such as in the face

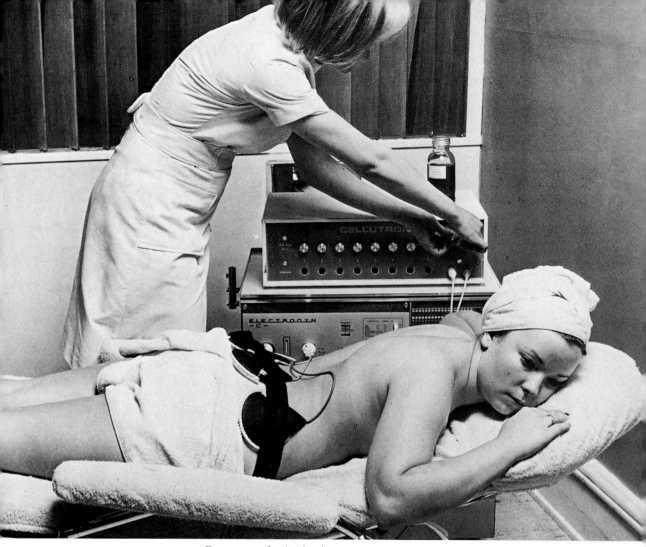

PLATE 9E   An ionization treatment

are improved by toning up the underlying muscles and firming its lines by filling out the skin. The benefits of an improved blood circulation to the skin help its appearance. Faradism provides a stimulating treatment. *Muscle fatigue* is relieved by faradism especially in the feet and back when an increased blood supply helps to carry away waste products and bring fresh nutrients to the part. The muscles are toned up with the contractions and temporarily revived and refreshed, having been given new strength. Aches, pains and stiffness can be alleviated by the use of the above current. *Tissue fluids* are reduced by the use of

faradism and the area will appear to have lost weight and look slimmer. This is helpful when clients are dieting and using other slimming techniques.

Cellulite: This term is not recognised by the British Medical Association but it is used to refer to deposits of fat and fluid which cause a pitted and lumpy appearance to the area. It is commonly found around the thighs and the abdomen.

ELECTRODES

The electrodes are usually made out of malleable metal such as carbon or tin and

135

are the means by which the current is introduced to the tissues. There must be at least two. One electrode may be placed on a part and not moved again during the treatment. This one is called the indifferent electrode. The other moveable electrode or electrodes, usually smaller than the indifferent, may be used on different areas and muscles. This is called the active electrode. There may be several electrodes of the same size all being used at once over many areas. Each manufacturer of cosmetic equipment has his own design or electrode to suit the type of apparatus, and the convenience of use.

Many of the machines now used can be adapted for different treatments but various sized electrodes are required for face and body.

TYPICAL ELECTRODES OF THE BASIC FARADIC MACHINE

A disc electrode with a wooden handle is employed when individual muscles are required to be stimulated, or for labile treatments. These active electrodes are of different diameters and can be fitted into the handle to suit the area to be treated.

Roller electrodes can be used for labile treatments on the back or face where facilitation of smooth movement is desirable. These electrodes should be covered with about two or three thicknesses of lint. From the base of the handle of this electrode is a terminal for the attachment of a lead to the apparatus.

Flat plate shaped electrodes are used as the

PLATE 9F   Electro-kinetic massage

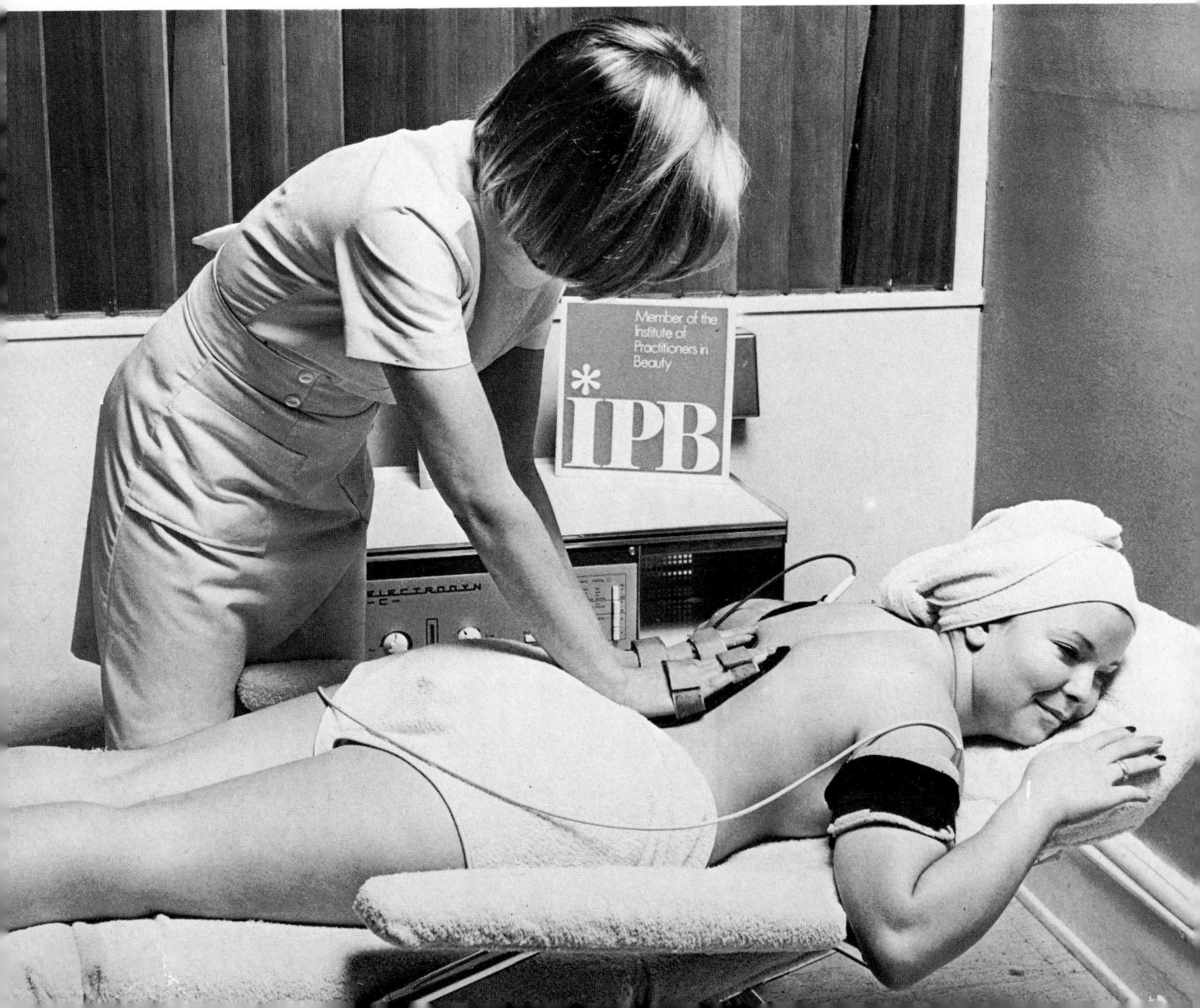

indifferent electrodes, or when whole muscle groups are being stimulated. Lint coverings soaked in salt solution are placed between the metal and the skin and firmly strapped into place for good contact. The streamlined cosmetic electrodes are very often built into larger circular plastic holders, which are also strapped into place by elasticated rubber bands. Several of these flat discs can be used at once easily, but are difficult to adapt for alternative treatments.

TECHNIQUE

Split Padding: This is where two muscles are stimulated by putting one pad of a pair of electrodes on the motor point of a muscle and the other pad on the motor point of the same muscle on the opposite side of the body.

Duplicate Padding: One pad of a pair of electrodes is placed on the muscle fibres near the origin of the muscle and the other pad on the muscle tissue nearest to the insertion. This is considered to be more effective than split padding and is therefore preferred if room permits.

Muscle stimulation: when a group of muscles is stimulated, the indifferent electrode is placed over the nerve trunk from which the nerve to those muscles comes. It may also be placed, if more convenient, on some other area away from the motor points of other muscles.

Each muscle is then stimulated individually of that muscle group, by placing the active electrode over the motor point of that muscle. If the muscle group is required to be stimulated as a whole, one electrode can be placed over the muscles near to their insertion, and the other over the nerve trunk, e.g. the quadriceps can be stimulated by placing one pad over the femoral triangle and one above the knee near to their insertion point.

Figures 60 to 64 inclusive show the motor

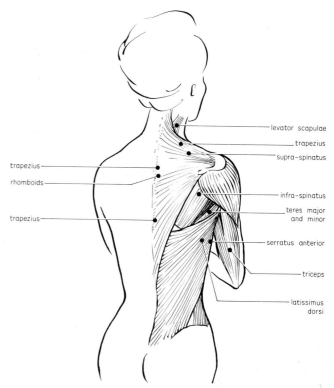

FIGURE 60   Motor points of the back

points of the various parts of the body.

Contraction of individual single muscles involves the use of very small electrodes in order to isolate that muscle, so preventing spread of the current to other muscles. These are placed over its area of origin and on its motor point. Good firm contact must be maintained to ensure the passage of current. This is obtained by sufficient moisturizing of the skin and pad with one per cent salt water, and firm strapping. In cases of obesity several main muscle groups are stimulated in the trunk and limbs simultaneously by using any of the described methods. The technique of muscle stimulation is one of the most sought after treatments in the beauty salon today.

LABILE FARADISM

Mild faradic currents are used in this method where the skin of the client is moistened with

137

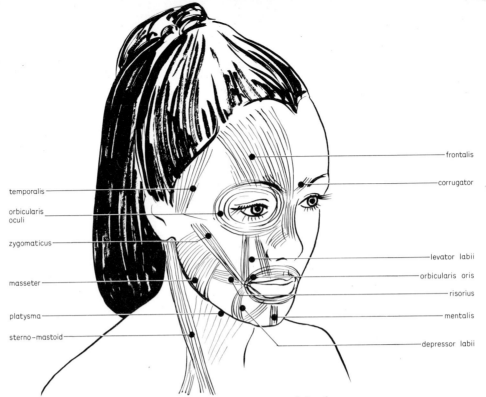

FIGURE 61   Motor points of the face

FIGURE 62   Motor points of (a) the front and (b) the back of the arm

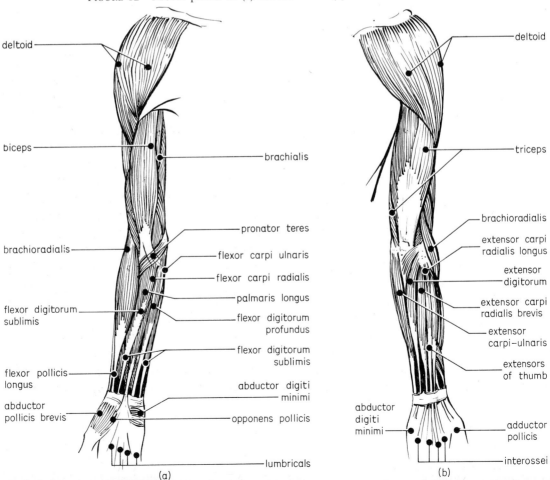

Figure 61 labels:

temporalis
orbicularis oculi
zygomaticus
masseter
platysma
sterno-mastoid

frontalis
corrugator
levator labii
orbicularis oris
risorius
mentalis
depressor labii

Figure 62 labels:

(a)
deltoid
biceps
brachioradialis
flexor digitorum sublimis
flexor pollicis longus
abductor pollicis brevis

brachialis
pronator teres
flexor carpi ulnaris
flexor carpi radialis
palmaris longus
flexor digitorum profundus
flexor digitorum sublimis
abductor digiti minimi
opponens pollicis
lumbricals

(b)
deltoid
triceps
brachioradialis
extensor carpi radialis longus
extensor digitorum
extensor carpi radialis brevis
extensor carpi–ulnaris
extensors of thumb
adductor pollicis
interossei
abductor digiti minimi

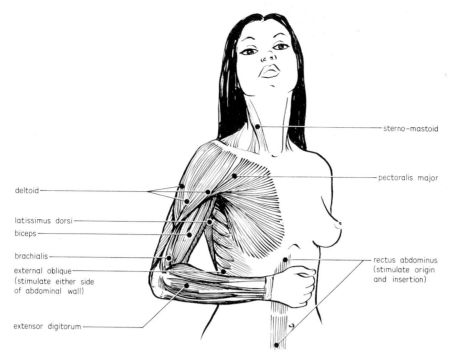

FIGURE 63 Motor points of the front of the arm and chest

salt solution and a large padded well-soaked indifferent electrode is placed over a convenient part. The active electrode can be either a small disc or a roller electrode which glides smoothly over the areas to be treated. N.B. The current is not surged for labile faradism.

FARADIC FOOT BATHS

A popular and beneficial form of treatment for tired and aching feet, refreshing and stimulating them. The surged faradic current is used, again using both electrodes equally. Both feet are immersed in a shallow amount of saline solution, in a plastic foot bath or bowl. The electrodes are placed in front of and behind the feet in order to stimulate the muscles in the longitudinal arches. They may also be placed transversely across the bath with the toes and heels of the feet resting on them. To stimulate the transverse arches of the feet, electrodes can be placed either side of the feet. Each foot and arch may be treated separately or all together. With all methods the water must only cover the toes, and be kept warm.

FARADISM UNDER PRESSURE

This technique, like the use of fluid reducing with hot and cold bandaging using 'secret' chemicals, is a simple and effective method of 'slimming' an area down in one treatment. It works on the same kind of principle that a pump does, except that the muscles when contracting and relaxing help to push away the fluid against an outside pressure. The outside pressure is supplied by rubber crêpe bandages wrapped around the limb, or area (hips and abdomen). One large electrode is placed around the ankle and the other can be placed over the quadriceps. These are firmly bandaged into place starting from the toes and covering the whole limb. The limbs are then placed into elevation and the muscles made to contract. After treatment all bandaged areas will be considerably thinner. However, unless the client is on a strict weight reducing diet

139

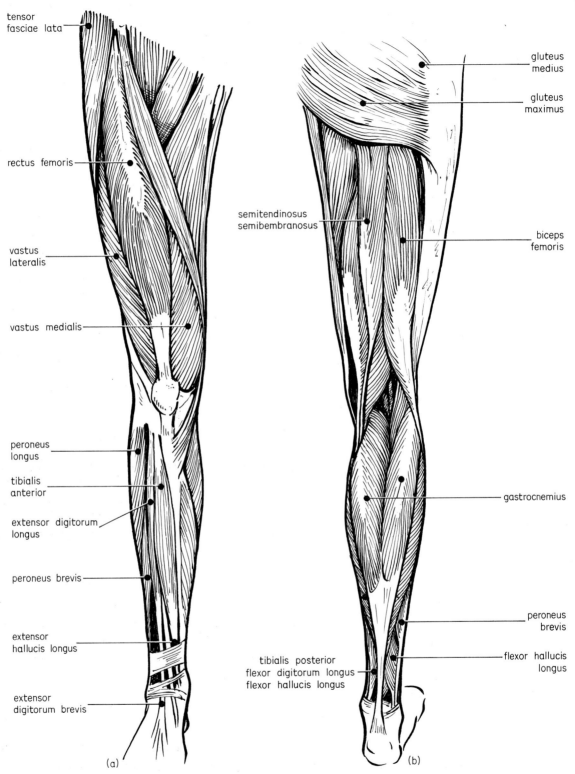

tensor
fasciae lata

rectus femoris

vastus
lateralis

vastus medialis

peroneus
longus

tibialis
anterior

extensor digitorum
longus

peroneus brevis

extensor
hallucis longus

extensor
digitorum brevis

(a)

gluteus
medius

gluteus
maximus

semitendinosus
semibembranosus

biceps
femoris

gastrocnemius

peroneus
brevis

flexor hallucis
longus

tibialis posterior
flexor digitorum longus
flexor hallucis longus

(b)

FIGURE 64   Motor points of (*a*) the front and (*b*) the back of the leg

plus restriction of fluid intake, the limbs will soon return to their former size. Weight loss is also claimed by this method, but it is usually the tissue fluids which are reduced, rather than fatty adipose tissue in one treatment.

GENERAL PROCEDURE FOR FARADIC TREATMENTS

1. Prepare the client comfortably in the position required for treatment, removing all jewellery and clothing from the areas to be treated. Cover any other clothing with towels, or protective sheeting. The client must be warm and relaxed.
2. Check the trolley layout making sure that all necessary equipment is ready for use.
3. Test the current by holding both electrodes or by placing the hand in the bath and turn up the current. This reassures the client and also makes sure that the machine is in working order.
4. Test the client's skin sensation, making sure it is normal over the areas being treated.
5. Explain the sensation of the current to be applied thoroughly to the client; asking her to say immediately she begins to feel it.
6. Soak the area or parts to be treated thoroughly with the salt solution. Also soak the discs and electrodes thoroughly and any lint pads to be used. (The water must be warm.)
7. Check that all the switches and controls are off and at zero.
8. Place the electrodes in position and secure firmly with elasticated or rubber straps.
9. Turn the switch to the required current, and slowly increase the intensity until the client can just feel it. Allow her to become accustomed to the sensation. Adjust the surge control for contractions.
10. When muscle stimulation is required aim at obtaining a good contraction, one which can be felt and seen, by slowly increasing the intensity. If the client cannot tolerate the current no matter how it has been modified there is no point in continuing with the treatment.
11. Make sure that the rest period of the muscle is sufficient, otherwise, coupled with long sustained contractions, incomplete relaxation can result in cramp and temporary anaesthesia. Strong contractions with short rest periods are required for slimming. Consideration of the client's age is important.
12. When the treatment is finished, turn the current down slowly.
13. Allow the client to cool off before leaving the salon.
14. Wash all equipment with antiseptic.

DURATION OF TREATMENT

Fatigue does not occur with normal healthy muscles, even those which are flabby and toneless. The treatment can be given for almost any length of time but it is usual to start with 10 minutes duration working up to 40 minutes as a maximum.

FREQUENCY OF TREATMENT

Daily treatments produce the best results, but not less than twice weekly treatments should be advised unless on a maintenance course.

NUMBER OF TREATMENTS

Thirty treatments should show excellent results especially if daily treatments or three times weekly are undertaken.

CONTRA-INDICATIONS

General contra-indications as for all beauty therapy treatments should be considered.

MOTOR POINT

The contraction of a muscle is caused by stimulation of its nerve supply. A muscle has one point over which its maximum contraction can be obtained. This is known as its motor point.

Usually it is the point at which the nerve enters the muscle or in its fleshy belly. Some muscles have several motor points as they have different sets of fibres, and may be supplied with more than one nerve.

GENERAL PADDING OF INDIFFERENT, FOR MUSCLE STIMULATION

1. For the upper half of the body and arms the pad should be placed over the nerve roots between the scapulae, on the lower cervical vertebrae.
2. For the lower half of the body and legs it can be placed over the lumbar vertebrae.
3. For the back, the client can lie on the pad (face down) placed between the separation of the rib cage.

FARADIC FACIAL TREATMENT

Faradism to tone and exercise muscles can be used two ways on the face. Either by using two electrodes together in a one-piece electrode or by stimulation of the motor points. The latter is less comfortable than the former method. Strong contractions are ill advised especially around the eye area as the muscles of the eye itself may be affected. A slight tingling sensation is all that should be felt in this delicate area.

TREATMENT WITH BOTH ELECTRODES TOGETHER

1. Prepare the client in a comfortable position.
2. Cleanse the area.
3. Tone the area well with an astringent or skin tonic, and blot dry with paper tissue.
4. Connect the machine and cover the electrodes with a piece of lint or cotton wool soaked in a one per cent salt solution.
5. Test the current and then explain its sensation to the client.
6. Place the electrode on the neck over the sterno-mastoid muscle.
7. Increase the intensity of the current slowly until the client can feel the prickling and slight contraction.
8. Stroke the electrode up the muscle on either side of the neck and check that the surge is comfortable.
9. Stroke with rotary movements under the chin.
10. Circulate the electrodes smoothly over the jawline to the lower ear, to the corner of the mouth, up to the middle ear level, to the corner of the nose, and up to the temple.
11. Repeat to the other side.
12. The treatment should take about 10 minutes and may be followed by a manual or individual muscle stimulation.

Infra-Red Radiation

The rays at the red end of the visible spectrum and beyond give rise to infra-red rays. When these rays are absorbed into the skin they produce heat which spreads into nearby tissues by conduction. This heat may also be carried around the body and raise the body temperature slightly.

In the electro-magnetic spectrum the rays extend from 4,000,000 to 7,700 Ångströms (400,000 to 770 nanometres). Short infra-red rays penetrate deeper into the skin than those of a longer wave length which are absorbed into the superficial epidermis. Infra-red rays are given off from any hot body to cooler bodies and so there are many sources to be found, e.g. the sun, electric radiators, coal fires, hot water pipes and so on. In beauty therapy the lamps commonly used to supply infra-red rays are those which consist of:

(a) a special filament of coiled wire on porcelain which is heated to just below red heat,

(b) flat metal plates heated behind with wires,

or (c) an incandescent lamp which consists of an airless glass bulb inside which is tungsten filament. This is sometimes called radiant heat.

All these several lamp bulbs can be used on one piece of apparatus called a radiant heat bath. This is used for general radiation. All these lamps have reflectors behind them which reflect the rays forward. The infra-red and visible rays from the incandescent lamp are those which penetrate the skin more than the other two lamps. However, an even better source of penetrating heat rays comes from the incandescent lamp which is filtered by a red glass filter. These rays are the shortest infra-red rays and are in the region of 10,000 Ångströms (1,000 nanometres).

TECHNIQUE FOR USE IN THE BEAUTY SALON

1. The skin sensation to hot and cold must be tested before irradiation to avoid burning.

2. When the client is facing the lamp the eyes should be protected.

3. The pure infra-red lamp should be turned on 5 minutes before use to allow the element to heat thoroughly.

4. Only a comfortable warmth must be experienced and the client must report any overheating.

5. The exact distance from the client should be measured and recorded for future treatment. The lamp should not be placed nearer than 46 centimetres and it can always be brought up to that distance.

6. An erythema is that amount of pinking and warmth which is produced in 10 minutes. It should fade within an hour.

7. After 10 minutes the intensity can be increased.

8. The maximum absorption and penetration of rays occurs when the face of the lamp is placed parallel to the part being treated.

9. Half an hour's exposure is the maximum length of treatment to apply on any part of the body and in general treatments. Local radiation on the face should not exceed 10 minutes.

EFFECTS

1. It has a sedative effect on sensory nerve endings and relieves pain, aches, and muscle tension and spasm. Therapeutic after exercising.

2. Short rays penetrate deeply into the skin and may reach the superficial fascia helping to soften the fat prior to massage or other slimming treatments.

3. Body temperature may be raised during irradiation in heat baths resulting in loss of fluid from sweating. This should be replaced by the client with a glass of water unless not desired as in weight reduction.

4. Secretion of sweat helps to eliminate

waste products and toxins from the body. Increased sebum secretion lubricates the skin.

5. Temporary increase in tissue fluids helps to absorb and remove broken down cells, and replenish the parts with nutritional components from the fresh oxygenated blood.

6. Useful in treating spotty skins or acne.

7. Superficial swellings such as when the tissues retain fluid, are reduced by gentle irradiation. Helpful in weight reducing schemes.

8. Cold limbs and clients can be warmed quickly.

9. The improvement in circulation from irradiation assists healing and stimulates the growth cells of the skin.

10. Infra-red or radiant heat radiation promotes relaxation and creates a sense of warmth and well-being. It is an ideal treatment prior to massage, warming the skin, relaxing the client and making her more receptive to treatment.

11. Can be used to dry out face packs and help to rid the skin of impurities by increased sweating.

12. Increased blood flow to the skin helps in the absorption of cream or oil, or other cosmetic products.

13. Infra-red treatments can be used whilst massaging to promote relaxation, soften the body tissues and ease tension.

14. It can also be used to keep a client warm whilst having faradic treatment.

PRECAUTIONS

1. Test skin sensation for hot and cold before treatment.

2. Cover the eyes with a shade or pads soaked in witch-hazel, boracic lotion or skin tonic providing there is no surgical spirit content, to prevent conjunctivitis.

3. Place reflector at right angles to the skin and never use directly over the part as this is dangerous.

4. Do not exceed exposure of more than 10 minutes on the face, 5 minutes for a sensitive skin.

5. Always keep asking the client if she is comfortable.

6. Wash all areas if any linament or medicated ointments have been applied, prior to exposure.

7. Allow the client to cool down sufficiently before leaving the salon.

8. Faintness may occur with general radiation or when used on the face.

9. Headaches may occur when the heat does not produce sweating.

10. Do not allow the client to touch the lamp.

11. Burning may occur if too hot.

CONTRA-INDICATIONS

1. Infra-red should not be applied to areas where bleeding may occur, such as varicose veins or to the abdomen during menstruation.

2. In cases of high fever.

3. Acute inflammation.

4. To the abdomen in pregnancy.

5. Any arterial disease such as poor circulation.

6. Loss of skin sensation.

7. Skin diseases except acne.

8. General diseases and medical conditions.

Ultra-Violet Light

The ultra-violet rays are high frequency waves producing little heat but a strong reaction in the skin. They may contain some infra-red rays which warm the skin and even cause it to feel hot. The most valuable of all the violet rays in the spectrum are those between 3,300 and 2,900 Ångströms (330 to 290 nanometres). These produce the tanning and erythema effect in the skin and also cause it to form vitamin D.

Ultra-violet lamps are used extensively throughout all forms of beauty therapy and particularly the UVA types of sun-bed are becoming very popular in the promotion of a year round bronzed, healthy appearance. The standard type of ultra-violet lamp producing ultra-violet B rays are now primarily used to aid and stimulate healing of the skin. In cases of acne they are sometimes used to assist healing and drying up of the lesions, and for skin peeling, or when mild desquamation is required for other cosmetic purposes. For any treatment with these lamps it is essential to test the lamp first on the client's skin to asses the reaction and therefore the correct dosage to be given.

There are four degrees of erythema (pinking reaction) which occur in the skin with ultra-violet radiation. The beauty therapist uses only the first and second degree.

ERYTHEMA

When ultra-violet rays are absorbed by the skin there is a destruction of cells. A substance called the 'H' substance is released amongst other products during this reaction which causes a dilation of the blood vessels. With stronger doses there is an inflammatory reaction of the skin and still stronger exposures lead to an exudation of fluid into the part, followed by swelling in the skin. The fluid then separates the granular layer of cells from the translucent layer and a blister occurs.

Because of a reflex action the deep circulation is improved with the stronger doses. The blister doses, however, may only be used for very small areas and usually only under medical supervision.

ERYTHEMA DEGREES

Unlike infra-red radiation there is no immediate reddening to be seen on the skin. Four to six hours later should mark the appearance of the erythema.

1ST DEGREE (E_1)

Only a slight reddening or pinking of the skin should occur. This should fade within 24 hours without irritation or peeling. With some lamps and solariums a tanned, bronzed appearance.

2ND DEGREE (E_2)

A more marked reddening of the skin occurs which is slightly irritating and is followed by a fine skin peeling when the erythema fades in 48 hours.

3RD DEGREE (E_3)

The skin swells, it becomes intensely hot and red with a severe irritation. The erythema begins to fade after 7 days when much peeling occurs.

4TH DEGREE (E_4)

Blisters occur on the skin and the course is similar to an E_3.

EFFECTS OF ULTRA-VIOLET RAYS

PEELING

When the erythema subsides, peeling occurs. This is a shedding of the superficial dead cells of skin which were destroyed by the action of the ultra-violet rays.

145

STIMULATION OF THE GROWTH LAYER

The growth cells of the epidermis are stimulated which leads to a thickening of the skin and pushes up healthy tissue cells. Together with pigmentation the protective function of the skin is increased. Stronger doses of ultra-violet rays are required to produce an erythema. The pigmentation of the skin lasts longer than the protective powers for it is the thickening of the skin which provides protection against the rays producing the erythema. Pigmentation is thought to protect against the visible and burning infra-red rays of the sunlight.

PIGMENTATION

Depending upon the intensity of the erythema and the number of irradiations, so the degree of pigmentation occurs. A chemical action takes place in the deep layers of the epidermis stimulating and forming melanin. Some ultra-violet lamps particularly those of the mercury vapour type, produce a greyer colour rather than the brown colour of natural sunlight.

INCREASED RESISTANCE

Because the blood supply to the skin has been increased, any infections present can be fought more speedily. Surface bacteria are also killed by the rays helping to prevent spreading of infections. Irradiation by ultra-violet light rays cause reticulo-endothelial cells in the deep epidermis to act more efficiently and ingest more bacteria. In this way resistance to infection is increased.

IMPROVEMENT OF NUTRITION

All the functions of the skin are stimulated with the increased flow of blood produced from the erythema and therefore its condition improves.

VITAMIN D FORMATION

Ergosterol is a chemical impurity found in the cholesterol contained in the sebum. Ultra-violet rays produce a chemical reaction with the Ergosterol in the skin to form Ergo-calciferol (vitamin D_2) A similar reaction occurs with 7-dehydrocholesterol, which is also found in the skin, to form cholecal-calciferol (vitamin D_3). Vitamin D is necessary for the correct absorption of calcium and phosphorus into the blood stream. It is transported to the liver for storage although some may be stored under the skin.

COUNTER IRRITANT

E_3 and E_4 have a counter-irritant effect and relieve pain.

TONIC EFFECT

Generally the after effects of sunlight irradiation are those of exhilaration. Sleep and appetite are both usually improved. Nervousness and tiredness are decreased. Most people feel and look much better when they are brown and bronzed from the sun.

USES IN BEAUTY THERAPY

1. Acne treatments benefit from ultra-violet treatments. These would be E_2 degree doses. Skin peeling as well as healing and bacterial effects would take place. Skin peeling clears the orifices of the hair follicles.
2. A general course of treatment would produce a tanned appearance (depending on the lamp).
3. Elimination of waste products is in-

creased and skin cleansing is aided (either a general course or an E₂).

4. Circulation can be stimulated which would increase the nutrition to the skin as well as the flow of lymph and blood (general course).

5. Increased resistance to disease by increasing iron and vitamin D content (general course).

6. The absorptive powers of the skin are increased when the circulation is improved so that the beneficial oils and creams could be applied (either a general course or an E₂).

7. Skin peeling for other cosmetic purposes (E₂).

8. Increased resistance to skin infection, assisting in the prevention or spread of spotty skin infections (general irradiation).

9. General tonic treatments for other than medical conditions.

10. Improving appetite due to tonic effect.

CONTRA-INDICATIONS

1. Any medical condition which has not received the consent of the doctor such as heart diseases, kidney diseases, tuberculosis, glandular diseases (thyroid).

2. Allergic and hypersensitive skins.

3. High temperatures.

4. When symptoms develop which show unfavourable reactions such as headaches, nausea, depression, loss of weight, increased nervousness, and insomnia.

5. Never to be administered on the same day as an infrazone treatment.

6. All skin diseases except acne vulgaris.

7. When drugs are regularly taken by the client, check with the doctor before a course of treatment is given.

8. After electrolysis or waxing because uneven pigmentation may result.

PRECAUTIONS FOR USE

1. Follow instructions apertaining to the individual lamp carefully.

2. Skin test for correct and accurate treatments.

3. Goggles must always be worn by both the client and the operator. Ultraviolet rays can cause permanent blindness. Remove contact lenses.

4. Generally the lamp is used at a distance of one metre away from the client, commencing at $1-1\frac{1}{2}$ minutes and increasing to a maximum of 15 minutes back and front.

5. A timer must be used with accuracy.

6. Increase each dose by one minute and treat every other day for an E₁.

7. Six to eight weeks is sufficient duration for one course of treatment. Allow the same length of time to elapse before recommencing the course.

8. Do not increase the dose if a client has not been irradiated for 10 days. After three weeks absence, resume the starting dose.

9. The skin must be free of make-up, perfume and suntan preparations of any kind.

10. Shorter courses are advisable for fair skins. Fair and red haired people are more sensitive to ultra-violet than those who have olive skins and dark hair.

11. E₂ degree doses must never exceed covering more than $\frac{1}{6}-\frac{1}{8}$ of the total skin's surface at one treatment.

12. Infra-red or radiant heat before ultra-violet treatment increases the skin's sensitivity; during treatment no added reaction; after treatment, counteracts the effects of ultra-violet overdoses.

13. Turn the lamp on for at least 3 minutes to stabilize before treatment. Do not switch off if required for further treatments. The bulb must cool down if once

having been turned off, before it will strike again.

14. Cold skins are less sensitive than warm or hot skins, therefore if warmed before treatment, the reaction may be stronger.

N.B. General irradiation doses aim at producing a first degree erythema reaction.

An E_2 is produced by multiplying the time for the first degree erythema by 2·5.

Repetition of an E_1—add 25 per cent of the previous time up to 4 minutes, then increase by 1 minute at a time.

Repetition of an E_2—add 50 per cent of the previous time, when the erythema begins to subside.

Find the E_1 dose to calculate the E_2 at the same distance.

SENSITISORS Ultra-violet light consists of two types of rays:

Ultra-violet A rays
Ultra-violet B rays

1. Ultra-violet A rays cause the skin to go brown without burning.
2. Ultra-violet B rays contain the destructive rays which may cause burning, blistering and peeling.

Sensitisors are those substances which make the body react more readily to Ultra-violet light.
There are two types:

A. Those substances which make the body more sensitive to the browning A rays:
The drug Psoralon. With this drug small doses of UVL can be given which will not damage the skin. This drug is given for the treatment of the skin condition Psoriasis.
B. Those substances which make the body more sensitive to the harmful B rays. Examples of these are:

(a) Certain drugs: Insulin, Quinine, Tetracyclines, Sulphonamides.
(b) Some foods may be sensitors in some people: Lobsters, strawberries.
(c) Contact with some plants may cause sensitisation in a few people: parsley, other members of the celery family of plants.

TEST DOSE

A test dose must always be given to ascertain the distance and length of time required to cause a first degree erythema. If a new lamp is used during the course of treatment, a further test dose will be required. The test dose is done on small areas of skin which are normally covered by clothes and which have not been exposed to the elements. For example, suppose that at a distance of one metre away from the lamp, the time will be 5 minutes to produce an E_1 reaction. Three different shapes of about three centimetres are cut out of a sheet of black paper. This is fixed to the area firmly and all other parts are covered. All three shapes are exposed for 4 minutes. One is then covered and the remaining two are exposed for a further minute. The second shape is then covered and the remaining one is left for yet another minute. The lamp is removed. In this way, three exposures of 4, 5 and 6 minutes have been obtained. The client is asked to look 4 hours later and note the reactions most carefully, to discover the first degree erythema.

DISTANCE OF THE LAMP

The nearer the lamp is to the client the stronger the reaction. Always test for any decrease in distance. Never treat nearer than 33 centimetres in beauty therapy.
N.B. Careless use of ultra-violet rays even for only a few minutes can cause permanent

damage to the eyes and skin. It is essential to use the treatments with discretion and to test skin accurately. Too much use is thought to damage the cells of the body, and skin cancer is sometimes attributed to exposure to the sun, although beauty treatments and short exposures are not considered harmful.

TECHNIQUE OF APPLICATION OF ULTRA-VIOLET LIGHT

GENERAL IRRADIATION

1. *Prepare lamp:* switch on and turn face down to the floor.
2. *Prepare client:* shielding all exposed areas, checking safety goggles and supporting client in most comfortable position to allow the rays to strike the skin at right angles. Skin must be clean and dry.
3. *Arrange client and lamp:* client can sit, lie down or stand supported in front of lamp depending on the type of lamp being used. Measure distance required accurately keeping client covered whilst doing so, as the lamp will already be burning. Centralize the lamp to the middle of the body from the burner.
4. *Warn* the client not to move from the position and not to touch the lamp or remove the goggles.
5. *Uncover* client and time carefully, telling her when to turn.
6. *Remove* lamp at end of treatment, either switching it off if not required again, or turning it down as low as possible to face the floor. Ask her to report the effects after 4–6 hours, if any.
7. *Record* client's treatment and effects, also length of burning time of the lamp. The longer it has been used the less effective its irradiation will be.
8. *Overdose* of treatment should be irradiated with infra-red causing a reaction over the whole area. Apply cold cream, and later if there is much itching, calamine lotion. A doctor's advice should be sought with excessive accidental overdoses.

LOCAL IRRADIATION

FACE (as for acne vulgaris)

1. Explain to client that the effect will be a bright erythema and pigmentation, and that it will gradually fade.
2. Prepare client, cleansing face first and expressing blackheads. Remove excess grease with a special ether soap or other acne soap and water.
3. Place client with head supported in sitting position. First treatment of the face should be from the front. The tip of the nose should be protected with cream as it will be nearer to the lamp. The second treatment should be the two sides of the face, exposed separately. Areas not being exposed must be screened with towels.
4. Place lamp in position and then measure the required distance. Time accurately from the moment of uncovering. Cover immediately treatment to one side of the face has been completed and repeat to the other.
5. Special acne cream can be applied after the treatments and at home.

BACK AND CHEST

The whole back or chest can be treated with a second degree erythema dose on alternate treatments when the condition is mild. The procedure as above is followed carefully.

After local irradiation courses are completed, a general tonic course could be given. N.B. Always wash hands before and after all treatments, sterilizing the equipment before further use.

Solaria and sunbeds or couches should be used according to the manufacturers instructions. Goggles should always be worn.

Galvanism

The galvanic current is one which flows in one direction from negative to positive. It is a constant current which does not vary in intensity. This current can be interrupted, however, to produce pulses and when applied to the tissues, in this way it will cause contraction and relaxation of the muscles, similar to the faradic current. The current can be produced from batteries or from the mains supply. Some modern equipment employs both currents and superimposes them for better effects.

GENERAL EFFECTS

1. *Blood vessels:* this current widens the blood vessels and allows more blood to flow, increasing the circulation to the part, causing a hyperaemia.
2. *Waste products* are removed from the tissues and a refreshing effect occurs. Also the increased circulation helps to repair broken-down tissues.
3. *Reduction of oedema* (swelling) is brought about by the fluid being drawn from the positive pole to the negative. This is called the kataphoretic effect.
4. *Ionization:* if a galvanic current is passed through a salt solution, it will split the solution up into two parts. If plates are used for this, the effect will be to draw one part to the other. This effect has proved useful in introducing medicaments (and cosmetics) into the skin.
5. *Destructive effect* occurs when the acids and bases formed at the metal electrodes are sufficiently concentrated.

USES IN BEAUTY THERAPY

1. *Improvement of facial contours* may be obtained from a facial massage with galvanism. Improvement of the circulation and blood flow to the tissues revives tired and exhausted skin and helps to stimulate sagging crêpey tissues. The positive electrode is used over the area for treatment.
2. *Slimming:* sometimes when clients are on a slimming programme the kataphoric effect of the galvanism is used to slim down an area. This reduces the tissue fluids and the part appears thinner and even measures less.
3. *To close the pores* using the positive pole on the area.
4. *Cleansing the skin* by the improved circulation and drawing of impurities to the negative pole can be obtained with galvanism.
5. *Skin softening and skin peeling:* the removal of the keratinous outer skin cells can be aided by using iodine or chlorine ions (the negative pad is used here) and applying the constant current. It is thought, however, that the effect is caused by the current rather than the special cosmetic ion, or gel. Other cosmetic preparations are used utilizing the galvanic current. Scar tissue is softened and treatments can be given in conjunction with plastic surgeons.
6. *Removal of superfluous* hairs, warts, and naevus (non-cancerous) is brought about by the destruction of the tissues due to the acids and bases formed at the two poles. Sometimes this is called 'electrolysis' but most beauty therapists leave warts and naevi for the attention of the doctor.
7. *Tissue fluids* can be drawn to areas using the negative pole, so plumping them out.

PRECAUTIONS TO BE OBSERVED WHEN USING THE GALVANIC CURRENT

1. Inspect and wash the area to be treated.
2. All scratches or spots should be insulated with vaseline.

PLATE 9G   A disincrustation treatment using galvanic ionization

3. Where an increased blood flow only is required, the pads should be of equal size and placed opposite each other.

4. Positive connection Anode.
Negative connection Cathode.
The pad should cover the area to be treated but where cosmetic preparations and ionizations are being introduced into the skin, the active pad must be smaller than the indifferent pad. Roller electrodes are sometimes used on the face for cleansing and opening the pores and also to drive certain products into the skin.

5. The pad should be sixteen lint thicknesses thick, without creases to prevent uneven heating. A metal roller electrode is usually massaged over the face in facial treatments.

6. The pads are soaked thoroughly in a 1 per cent salt solution and should be damp. When using special preparations the active pad should be soaked thoroughly in the 1 per cent solution.

7. A crêpe bandage protected from the pad with rubber covering should be used to hold the pad evenly and firmly in position. Rubber elasticated straps may also be used.

8. Care must be taken to use the correct pole for the chosen effects and the cosmetic preparations, ions, or salts.

9. Precautions against burns must be taken. The electrodes should be smaller than the pads and all wires covered.

10. The current must not exceed 2 milliamperes per $2\frac{1}{2}$ centimetres. It must be increased very slowly.

11. Shocks must be avoided by checking that all controls are at zero before commencement of the treatment or switching on the apparatus. The selector switch must be in the correct position. Always turn the current density up and

down slowly and never remove the electrode from the skin during treatment.

12. Test the skin sensation with a faradic current to make sure that it is normal and also for hot and cold.

13. When treating the face a total of 12 minutes is sufficient time, using both the positive and negative pole effects.

14. Never exceed 20 minutes' treatment with the constant current on other parts of the body.

15. Twice a week for 3 weeks would constitute a course of treatment.

Galvanism is employed in beauty therapy for skin cleansing treatments.

Ionization treatments to the skin using various salts can be most beneficial in improving crêpy skin, and closing pores. Care should be taken when using cosmetic gels for allergic reactions and when the skin is peeling.

Under-Water Massage

A high pressure jet of water or air is used under a hot water bath. The water can contain pine salts or other refreshing fragrances if required. The hose is used to massage the muscles, fat, and skin. It penetrates deeply and moves the tissues strongly against the bones. A good knowledge of anatomy is essential and also of the basic body massage would be helpful. The jets of air or water should always be directed along the limbs, muscles and tissues towards the venous blood and lymphatic flow.

AEROTONE UNDER WATER MASSAGE

The bath is filled and heated to the required temperature. An electric current circulates and bubbles the water in the bath with the client completely immersed except for her head. This thoroughly massages the tissues of the body, stimulating the circulation. Care must be taken to see that the client is sufficiently cooled and relaxed before leaving the salon. Exhaustion can occur if the treatment is prolonged and too vigorous.

Vacuum Suction

DESCRIPTION OF A TYPICAL MACHINE

The cabinet of the vacuum suction machine is made of fibreglass which encloses the motor. On the control panel of the model there is an on and off switch with a pilot light. Also there is a pressure gauge which registers the amount of pressure being exerted by the machine during the treatment at any one time. The intensity of the vacuum is controlled by a regulating switch. A small hole can be found on this panel which is connected to the source of air carried to the suction cup, by means of a plastic tube. The suction cups are screwed into the handle of the tube.

Clear perspex is used for the suction cups which enables the operator to see the action and pressure exerted at all times on the tissues. There are usually at least three to four sizes of cups. Very large cups are used for fatty, well covered areas, medium sized cups for less well protected tissues and small cups for facial use only.

METHOD OF USE

Treatments are always given with oil or a special contact lubricant to ensure that there is freedom and ease of movement across the flesh.

PLATE 9H   Preparation for underwater massage

PLATE 9I   Vacuum suction treatment

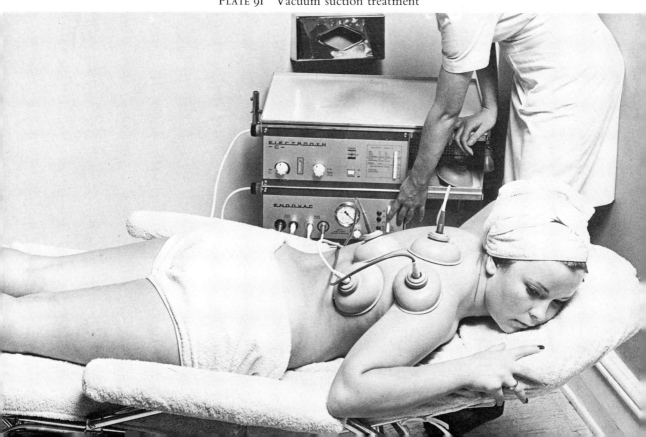

Movements always follow the lymphatic and venous blood flow towards the heart. The suction cup is applied to the areas and moved swiftly with stroking movements for the required treatment time. When the suction needs to be broken, the therapist inserts her finger between the flesh and the rim of the suction cup.

Amount of pressure is indicated by the amount of fatty deposit.

Duration of treatment on any one area must not exceed 20 minutes otherwise bruising may occur.

Facial treatments require upwards movements and should never be given around the delicate eye tissues. It is generally used around the chin area for a maximum of 10 minutes.

Removal of excess oil on completion of the treatment can be with hot towels and spirit. Witch-hazel or rose water can be used on the face.

AREAS TO BE AVOIDED

1. *The kidneys:* strong pressure can cause damage to the kidneys.
2. *The bust:* treatment of the bust is not recommended and should not be given although there are some schools of thought who do recommend this treatment.
3. *The abdomen:* because there is no underlying bone to protect the abdominal organs, treatment using the vacuum suction method should not be given over this area. Again some schools of thought do not regard this as a contra-indicated area, when fatty.

AREA TO BE TREATED

All areas which have sufficient fatty tissue allowing treatment such as legs, back, arms, thighs, and buttocks.

PRECAUTIONS

1. Suction which is too severe can cause bruising so that the pressure must vary according to the area being treated.
2. Extended treatments lead to bruising and fatigue having adverse effects upon the client.
3. Use on areas where there are little fatty deposits will stretch the skin.
4. The suction cup is best kept in motion rather than left stationary on any one spot.
5. During facial treatments care must be taken not to over-stretch the skin.

EFFECTS OF VACUUM SUCTION

1. Skin sensation is increased.
2. Circulation is speeded up and the skin condition is improved.
3. Blood flow to the muscles is increased, so nourishing them and imparting a tonic sensation and relaxing them.
4. Lymph flow is increased and tissue fluids moved along, improving 'orange peel' effect of 'cellulite' conditions.
5. Used to relieve lines and wrinkles on the face, with especially adapted glass applicators.
6. Blackheads can be expressed with the suction effect.
7. Vacuum sprays are used for application of essential oils before heat baths and saunas, also for applications of tonic and astringent waters.

CONTRA-INDICATIONS

1. Varicose veins and bruised areas.
2. Overstretched skin, ageing skin, thin unprotected skin.
3. Bony areas.
4. As for other beauty contra-indications.
   N.B. There are innumerable vacuum suction machines on the market, each with

its own design and specially modified applicators. Terms used include traxation, or lymph massage apparatus and so on. Some apparatus has automatic intermittent suction which enables several cups to be strapped stationary on the parts. Other apparatus incorporates a gentle tapping action and the therapist completes the suction effect by placing her finger or thumb over a hole in the applicator. When using the delicate applicators on the face, the direction of the lymph flow must be especially followed. Headaches may follow due to the rapid increase of blood to the face area, therefore manual strokes away from the face and head should complete the treatment. Preparation of the client follows the usual procedure together with an adequate explanation of the treatment and sensation likely to be experienced to the client.

MASSAGE VIBRATORS

There are three basic types of mechanical vibrators used in electrical massage, and many variations. Their effects are:
1. *Percussion vibration:* a light vibration used mainly on the face or upper back.
2. *Gyratory vibration:* a heavier vibration for use on the body, most resembling all the movements of manual massage.
3. *Audio-sound vibration:* a deep vibration for use in dense thickened and heavy tissues, resembling shaking and vibrations of manual massage. (Modified for use on face.) Care must be taken over the vertebrae, especially at the base of the occiput. Careless use causes nausea and dizziness. All strokes should follow the direction of muscle lengths, and/or lymphatic and venous blood flow.

PERCUSSION VIBRATOR (Pifco)

Several applicators are provided with this light hand vibrator, rubber sponges for the face and ebonite for the body. The repetition of vibrations stimulates the blood flow to the parts being treated and relaxes the tightened tissues, helping the glands to function normally. A cream should be used as a lubricant to avoid pulling or stretching the skin tissues. The client is prepared in the usual way. Gripping the vibrator in the working hand, the beauty therapist follows the same direction of movements as for manual massage. Small rotatory movements may also be given. Even light pressure is used with one hand guiding the vibrator whilst the other massages with it. A maximum of 10 minutes treatment should be given to the face.

USE ON THE FEET AND HANDS

Provides the client with a relaxing treatment which helps to soften hard callouses through stimulation of the skin. Tired and aching feet are relieved. Vibrations stimulate the muscles and muscle fibres.

CONTRA-INDICATIONS

As for general beauty treatments.

VIBRAX 3D (also Massetor Duo)

This heavy duty vibrator is often called the 'beautician's iron'. It has a two speed control, one for slow rhythmic vibrations used in soothing and relaxing treatments and the other for fast stimulating treatments.

AREAS WHICH MUST BE AVOIDED

1. The kidneys.
2. The bust.
3. The abdomen.
4. The face.

All these areas are contra-indicated for treatment to avoid damage of the underlying structures from the strength and weight of the apparatus and its vibrations.

AREAS FOR TREATMENT

1. *Legs:* the gyrator may be safely used on the legs to provide a relaxing or reducing massage. Care must be taken to avoid the shin and the inside of the thigh.
2. *Back:* can be used to relax the back taking care to avoid the kidney area.
3. *Arms:* used particularly on the back of the upper arm which has more fatty deposits.
4. *Thighs and buttocks:* used over the padded fatty deposits on the hips and over the great trochanter on the outside and upper-most part of the thigh.

CONTRA-INDICATIONS

As for all massage and body treatments.

METHOD OF USE

Prepare the client with all necessary clothing removed. Warmth and comfort are essential for all treatments. The Vibrax may be used with a special contact lubricant or with olive oil. It is held firmly with both hands and always used in the direction of venous blood flow back to the heart. Never massage in the opposite direction as this can cause stasis in the veins and may result in dizziness. The area from the back of the knee to the top of the hips is massaged with one long stroke maintaining continuity. Towels should be used to cover all areas not being treated. Slow vibrations may be given from the base of the spine towards the neck region.

Depending on the desired result either slow or fast vibrations are given from the sides of the back in towards the spine but always slowly up the length of the back. A rotatory movement may be used if desired with all strokes; also a dry massage using talcum powder may be preferable.

Gyratory Massage

Manual massage and its value in the treatment of many conditions has been known and appreciated throughout the centuries. Several attempts have been made to emulate the expert touch of the human hand by mechanical means. The gyratory vibrator is one means which provides a real resemblance to the technique employed by the skilled masseuse. Its action on the skin and underlying tissues is that of a true, deep massage and the therapeutic effects are similarly produced in a quicker and more efficient manner which is less tiring to the operator.

The G5 is one such vibratory apparatus. It has several applicators constructed from polyurethane or rubber and of various shapes and sizes. These are selected according to the part to be treated. A special electric motor driving a flexible shaft energizes these applicators. A series of small vibratory circles describes its action. Approximately there are 45 per second. By varying the pressure, the position and the type of applicator head used, so the operator is able to control precisely the depth of penetration on the tissues. During the treatment the client feels these deep vibrations and experiences relaxation both muscular and nervous tension. The overall effect is one of a pleasant sense of well-being. The G5 simulates the pressure manipulations of manual massage, and stimulates the muscles in a tonic manner.

THE APPLICATORS

I. THE ROUND SPONGE APPLICATOR

This is a general purpose applicator to be used with light pressure as an introduction prior to treatment with other applicators. It produces a hyperaemia and induces relaxa-

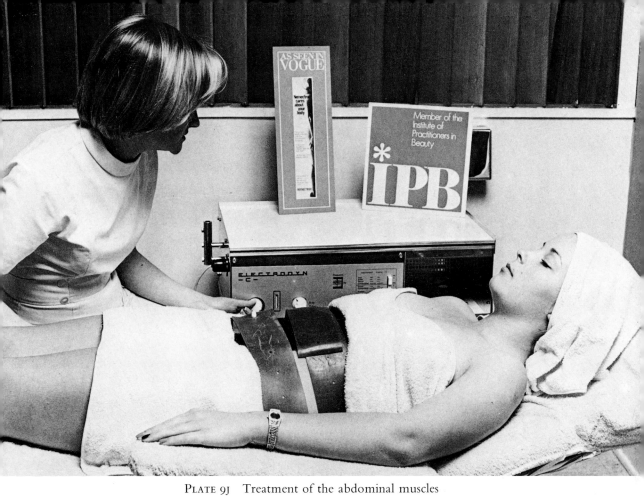

PLATE 9J   Treatment of the abdominal muscles

PLATE 9K   A cleansing treatment using electrical equipment to brush oils into the skin

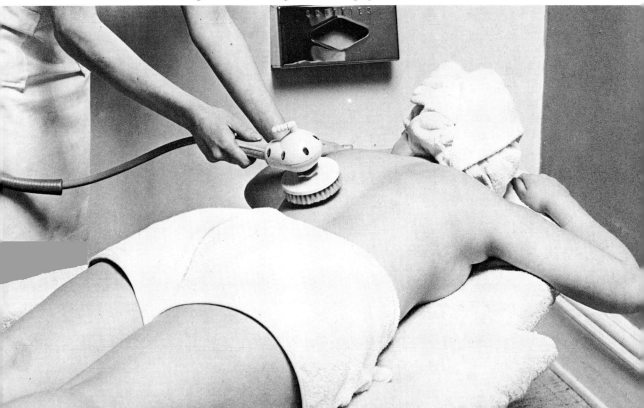

tion of the muscles. It is used with light continuous movements and always in contact with the skin, following the direction of venous flow, as in effleurage.

2. THE CURVED SPONGE APPLICATOR

This is applied to specific areas of the body such as the limbs, shoulders, and ankles. Light pressure in the direction of the lymphatic and venous flow is applied. This can simulate the action of effleurage as in manual massage.

3. THE PIN CUSHION APPLICATOR

This produces a good hyperaemia and is very superficial in its effect. It should not be used on fine thin skin. Rough and pimply skin can be treated and desquamation is aided.

4. THE FOOTBALL APPLICATOR

This is used on heavy tissues and the abdomen (although some schools of thought do not massage this area) for improving the circulation of the muscles of this region. Digestion is also improved. (Heavy application should be avoided.)

5. THE EGG BOX APPLICATOR

This is designed to massage dense fleshy areas of the body such as the thighs and buttocks, with deep pressure.

6. THE HEAVY PRONG APPLICATOR

This is also used for deep application to solid fatty and thick tissue areas, which is well covered.

APPLICATION OF G5

The manual assistance of one hand of the therapist is required for use on the body with the G5. While the manipulation is being made with this hand (left hand) the applicator is held firmly with the other (right hand if the masseuse is right handed). This is done for two reasons:

1. The left hand brings the flesh under the applicator so that it is properly massaged.
2. The left hand maintains the contact and continuity of treatment.

Except for the effleurage applicators, the manipulations are performed in a rotatory manner following the direction of the venous and lymphatic vessels. A good knowledge of the systems of the body and of the basic body massage is essential. The skin must be clean and dry.

CONTRA-INDICATIONS

1. Pregnancy.
2. Swollen areas (oedema).
3. Bruising, new scar tissue.
4. Varicose veins.
5. Medical conditions.
6. Heart complaints.
7. Infectious diseases.
8. Skin conditions.
9. Dizziness.

AREAS CONTRA-INDICATED FOR TREATMENT

1. Face.
2. Abdomen (only treated with extreme precaution).
3. Kidneys.
4. Bust.
5. Bony areas.
6. Unprotected areas (i.e. areas which have little underlying fat).

AREAS COMMONLY TREATED

1. Back.
2. Thighs.

3. Buttocks.
4. Lower leg.
5. Arms, shoulders.
6. Pectoral region using effleurage applicator only (round sponge applicator).

After use the applicators should be washed in tepid water and a mild soap, rinsed thoroughly and left to dry. If the G5 is used frequently it is advisable to have several sets of applicators so that there is always a dry, clean set available. They must never be used whilst still wet.

TECHNIQUE

The G5 machine is always used with powder as a lubricant. Oil or grease must never be used with it.

Commence the treatment by using one of the effleurage applicators, depending upon the area to be treated (shaped effleurage applicator for use on arms and legs only or on the shoulders). Work from the feet up the length of the legs in the direction of the lymph flow. On the arms from the hands to the shoulder and then over the shoulder and upper borders of the trapezius muscle towards the cervical vertebrae. This preliminary treatment induces a condition ideally suitable for a further deep treatment with the other applicators, or for a manual massage.

Continue in the same manner by using one of the heavy duty applicators according to the condition being treated and the desired effect required.

Follow this with the hyperaemia applicator (pin cushion) and then finally apply the effleurage applicator to relax, sooth, and complete the massage.

Remember that too heavy or prolonged treatment can bruise areas especially where there is little fat, or muscle.

TREATMENT

Twice weekly treatments for a maximum of 20 minutes each is sufficient. A course of treatment combined with dieting if for obesity should last for 8 weeks and then a break for 6 weeks before recommencing. The vibratory massage may be followed with a relaxing massage if required and preceded by a steam bath.

Audio-Sound Vibrators

Sound wave vibratory equipment is likened to the deep petrissage of manual massage. It makes use of a series of sound waves which penetrate into the skin and underlying structures. These are produced from solenoids within the apparatus. The vibrations penetrate into the tissues up to two inches. Only a slight prickling sensation is experienced on the surface of the skin, which is accompanied by the buzzing noise of the machine.

Dense heavy tissues can be treated with audio-sound waves. The parts should not be treated for more than 10–15 minutes at a time.

When the face and neck areas are treated with audio-sound a light massage cream can be used and a maximum of 5–6 minutes over the area is sufficient.

Some General Contra-indications for Beauty Therapy

Modifications may be necessary for treatment in these cases:

1. All medical conditions—unless a doctor's consent is obtained—and post-operative conditions.

2. Cases of bruising and varicosed veins.
3. Undiagnosed swellings and lumps.
4. Pregnancy.
5. When clients are taking medicines or drugs.
6. New scar tissue.
7. High temperatures and fevers.
8. Infectious and contagious conditions and diseases of skin and body.
9. Heart diseases, including circulatory diseases of the arteries or veins, and blood pressure.
10. Dizziness, nausea, and headaches.

10. Explain current to client and the noise, if any.
11. Instruct client to speak out as soon as she feels the current and not to endure any discomfort, that is, burning, pressure, skin prickling, pain or muscle contraction which is not normal.
12. Turn current intensity slowly up and down.
13. At termination of treatment, after drying or cleaning areas again, allow client to rest or cool down if desired.
14. Complete record card with details of treatment given and immediate effects (if any experienced).

Preparation Guide for Electrical Treatments

1. Record card of client reviewed and prepared (age, occupation, doctor, medical history, personal measurements, weight, etc.).
2. Choice of electrical treatment must fulfil the purpose for which it is intended.
3. Prepare trolley and couch with equipment required for treatment.
4. Client preparation on couch includes cleansing parts to be treated, supported and covered ready for application.
5. Skin test must be made for hot and cold sensations and that reactions to painful stimulus are normal.
6. Check that clothing and linen are adequately protected by extra towels and rubber sheeting (jaconette) as a safety precaution.
7. Note special precautions necessary and dangers of the machinery being used.
8. Check that all dials are at zero and that the machine is turned off before connecting the client in circuit.
9. Test current before application to client.

Lasers

The use of cosmetic lasers is becoming increasingly popular in Beauty Therapy salons. The word Laser is an abbreviation of Light Amplification by Stimulated Emission of Radiation. A light source is energised by a mains alternating electric current. The light rays or radiations thus produced are then passed through a mixture of gases, usually Helium and Neon, although different lasers use different gases. The molecules of these gases are bombarded by the light rays and begin to vibrate in frequency with them. They in turn produce further radiation which is added to the light already present. These amplified light rays are focussed into an intense beam of visible red light (radiation) which is led via a fibre optics cable to the applicator head. This is then applied to the face. Some lasers are combined with a faradic machine.

EFFECTS AND USES

The red light penetrates the skin and is claimed to have two beneficial effects :-

1. When applied to acupuncture points the superficial facial muscles are tightened and improved in tone.
2. There is a chemical action within the cells of the dermis which causes an improvement in the collagen (white fibres) and elastin (yellow fibres). This is claimed to bring back lost elasticity and "bulk" to the skin.

When both these effects combine, sagging is said to be reduced (tighter muscles) and wrinkles smooth out (improved elasticity).

It is also said to encourage better circulation of the blood to the surface levels of the skin, resulting in better cell metabolism.

It is claimed to be of benefit to people between the age of 30 and 55. Although a majority of cases show a marked improvement after 8 to 12 treatments, each of 20 minutes, it is not necessarily successful on all clients. Present thinking associates lack of success with mental stress in the client, possibly due to a chemical imbalance in the skin.

MEDICAL USES

The Beauty Therapy aspects of "cold laser" treatments are a by-product of research into medical and surgical applications. Two such areas have already proved effective :-
1. Skin ulcers which have proved resistant to other forms of treatment have shown a marked improvement in healing after "cold light" laser treatment.
2. Skin wounds and lacerations have healed more rapidly with less scarring if treated immediately with a "cold light" laser prior to more orthodox treatments being applied.

DANGERS AND CONTRA-INDICATIONS

1. The laser beam should not be allowed to pass directly into the eye as its intensity could seriously damage the retina.
2. In all other aspects the treatment is thought to be harmless and no contra-indications are specified.

Other Types of Lasers

ARGON LASER

The Argon Laser is used to treat some of the more disfiguring birthmarks, such as Port-Wine stains. The Argon Laser produces a blue green light which coagulates the blood vessels under the skin thus leaving the area much lighter in colour.

CARBON DIOXIDE LASER

Carbon Dioxide Lasers are used in the removal of tattoos, warts and skin tags. These powerful beams are capable of penetrating most substances or of producing the lower powered beam which is used cosmetically.

Both the Argon Laser and the Carbon Dioxide Laser are not suitable for use in the Beauty Therapy Salon and are best left to the medical profession.

10. Hazards and Safety Precautions

Wax

HAZARDS

Fire—burns.

SAFETY PRECAUTIONS

1. Keep naked flame away from wax apparatus.
2. Check water levels in baths regularly.
3. Check temperature of wax before use.
4. Extreme care should be taken in porterage of liquid wax.

Ultra-violet Light

HAZARDS

Overdose.
Burns.
Eye exposure.
Conjunctivitis.
Excess ozone—lung tissue damage.

SAFETY PRECAUTIONS

1. Ensure clients and therapist wears goggles.
2. Warn client to wear same clothing for each treatment.
3. Test client's skin reaction before treatment.
4. Warn client of expected reaction.
5. Ensure adequate cooling time of lamps.
6. Ensure accurate dosage and timing.
7. Check reaction to last treatment.
8. Avoid own over-exposure.
9. Ensure adequate ventilation without draughts.
10. Record lamp burning time.
11. Have overhead pulleys serviced regularly for solaria.
12. Check contra indications.

Infra-Red

HAZARDS

Fire—burns.
Electric shock.

SAFETY PRECAUTIONS

1. Area to be treated should be free of clothing and visible to the therapist.
2. Keep inflammable material well away from lamps.
3. Switch off after use and move away.
4. Warn client about overheating.
5. Skin test area to be irradiated for hot and cold skin sensation.
6. Warn client about not touching or moving equipment.
7. Do not place directly over client.

Faradic Equipment Units

HAZARDS

Current sensation shocks.
Shocks.

Rashes.
Exhaustion of muscles.

PRECAUTIONARY MEASURES

1. Check machine controls are at zero before treatment.
2. Increase current during contraction phase very slowly.
3. Check surge control and length of surge before application.
4. Test flow of current through each pair of pads before application.
5. Explain current sensation.
6. Skin test for skin sensation of reaction to pin prick and cotton wool.
7. Keep machine away from water.
8. Do not allow client to touch or operate machine.
9. Time treatment carefully.
10. Use sponge pads in cases of allergies between pad and skin.
11. Check leads and wire connections.

Galvanic Current

HAZARDS

Shock.
Burns.
Rash.

SAFETY PRECAUTIONS

1. Check machine controls are at zero before treatment.
2. Increase and decrease current very, very slowly.
3. Test skin sensation for pin and cotton wool.
4. Wash parts to be treated thoroughly.
5. Check client's skin for breaks or spots.
6. Thoroughly dissolve salt or additives.
7. Ensure pads are of adequate and even thickness and evenly damp.
8. Check firm wiring connections.

9. Test equipment before use on each occasion.
10. Do not allow client to touch machine.
11. Remove all metal in area of treatment.
12. Keep machine and client away from metal pipes, water etc. and any possible earth connections.
13. Use a rubber sheet on the bed.
14. Check skin reaction carefully.

Sauna and Steam Baths

HAZARDS

Scalds.
Burns.
Fainting.
Heat stroke and exhaustion—collapse.
Falls.
Infection fatigue.

PRECAUTIONARY MEASURES

1. Check temperatures carefully of equipment before use.
2. Ensure guard round heating elements is in position.
3. Keep client in view throughout treatment.
4. Do not overheat or expose client for long periods at a time.
5. Instruct client in usage.
6. Ensure adequate rest periods.
7. Examine feet for fungus infections.
8. Use disposable slippers.
9. Shower client before and after treatment.
10. Use dressing gowns and towels once only.
11. Establish a good routine ro remove client from steam or sauna quickly.
12. Take pulse rate, and body temperature before and after (or during) treatment.

Shower

HAZARDS

Falls.

Slipping.
Scalds.

1. Explain use of water control.
2. Secure anti-slip mat.
3. Ensure client's feet are dried before leaving immediate shower area.

Vibration Equipment

HAZARDS

Bruising.
Damage of tissues.
Spread of infection.

PRECAUTIONARY MEASURES

1. Check areas for suitability of treatment.
2. Ensure applicators are firmly attached.
3. Sterilize applicators after each use.

Vacuum Suction

HAZARDS

Damage to tissues.
Spread of infection.

PRECAUTIONARY MEASURES

1. Test pressure of equipment before use.
2. Use sufficient lubrication.
3. Select correct applicator, and size.
4. Ensure pressure is not too great.
5. Break cup seal with finger before removing.
6. Sterilize and clean applicators after each treatment.
7. Check for contra indications thoroughly.

Exercises

HAZARDS

Insufficient space causing danger to persons,

therapist as well as client in the vicinity.
Over-exertion generally, and locally.
Failure of apparatus causing harm.

SAFETY PRECAUTIONS

1. Ensure adequate spacing and free area for exercise performance.
2. Ensure that client is fit enough to exercise specific muscles and generally to perform the required exercise.
3. Supervise constantly.
4. Check all apparatus for signs of failure, wear and tear in ropes, slippery surfaces, weights, and for faulty weight carriers, etc.
5. Check safety of floor surface for slipping.

Electrolysis (Short Wave Method)

HAZARDS

Burns and scarring.

PRECAUTIONARY MEASURES

1. Use lowest current possible that will successfully remove the hair.
2. Only pass current when needle is fully inserted in follicle.
3. Switch off current before removing needle from follicle.
4. Do not work on hairs too near each other.
5. Do not work for too long a period.
6. Instruct client in after-care treatment.

Electrolysis (Galvanic)

HAZARDS

Chemical burn and deep scarring.

PRECAUTIONARY MEASURES

Numbers 1, 4, 5, and 6 as above also:
7. No metal touching client.
8. Wrist electrode must not be dripping wet, but must be evenly damp.